The Tragedy of Labour

MAINSTREAM SERIES

STEPHEN HASELER

The Tragedy of Labour

BASIL BLACKWELL · OXFORD

© Stephen Haseler 1980

First published in 1980 by
Basil Blackwell Publisher
5 Alfred Street
Oxford OX1 4HB
England

British Library Cataloguing in Publication Data

Haseler, Stephen
    The tragedy of labour. – (Mainstream book club).
    1. Labour-Party
    I. Title
    329.9'41   JN1129.L32
ISBN 0-631-11341-X

Printed in Great Britain by
Billing and Sons Ltd
Guildford, London, Oxford, Worcester

Dedicated to the memory
of HUGH GAITSKELL
and the possibility that was Labour

CONTENTS

PREFACE

In this book I am not attempting to construct a contemporary history of the Labour movement. This task, which can already draw upon a rich seam of drama and change, must await the full evolution of events which are now being played out before our eyes. Rather, the aim here is unashamedly political. It is to provide by way of a backdrop an interim assessment, from one who has been intimately involved in the politics of the left for over two decades, of the magnitude of the tragedy that has recently overcome Labour, and then to suggest what can be done about it.

Tragedy is a large word. It excites both pity and fear. In this context it is meant to: pity for the now largely unrepresented working families of Britain whose historic party has deserted them and who live uneasily with the stereotyped roles assigned to them by the tawdry philosophy of pseudo-Marxism that suffuses our activist intellectual left; fear for a future that, for the first time since the advent of the popular franchise, will seemingly produce for the British nation a major political party wholly at variance with national political traditions.

Such an argument, although increasingly acceptable to the wider public, is both highly sensitive and strangely discordant when used as part of Labour's internal debate. Many of Labour's moderates insist in public that no fundamental change is occurring within the party — that the tensions and disputes (and their resolutions) are essentially of the same order as they have always been. Yet in private they are often anxious, confused and alarmed, particularly so since Labour's post-election conference at Brighton in October 1979.

The 1979 Labour conference concentrated the political mind wonderfully. It became clear that Labour's left were set upon nothing less than achieving complete control of all the organs of the party and that the Parliamentary Party (the last bastion of social democracy) was to be cowed into submission by the proposed constitutional changes submitted by the Benn forces. Although the various amendments to the party constitution sought, and largely achieved, by the left were couched in terms of widening the democracy of the party, this was a deception. To hand power from MPs to *either* the National Executive Committee (which in reality is selected by a handful of trade union leaders without consultation with their members) *or* to local groups of unrepresentative activists in the constituencies can hardly be defended on democratic grounds. The left's proposed constitutional changes excluded the bulk of Labour Party members from decision-making and resolutely resisted any say by Labour voters. It was a power-play. Power was to reside in the party apparatus, amongst the dwindling number of extremist activists, and be transmitted from the party to its delegates in Parliament.

Yet, even as all this became increasingly apparent, and the determined left push for complete control was rolling forward, Labour's moderate leaders remained curiously inert and transfixed. They could see a challenge yet they could not respond to it. The reasons are complex. Many of Labour's leading moderates actually believe that the party they joined (a party of fraternity and tolerance that tempered its ideology with the warmth and sense of the traditional working-class Labour club) is still the party they inhabit. Others are social democratic careerists who can simply see no future for themselves except as part of the movement. Hence, Labour folklore and modern career self-interest unite to abhor a schism: the maintenance of the Labour coalition, no matter the nature of its constituent parts or the changing power of its components, is the over-arching strategic aim.

The primary purpose of this short work is to offer a challenge both to this central objective of Labour's Parliamentary leaders and to the analysis upon which it is based. It argues that Labour's present coalition is untenable; that the divide between the Marxist left and the Labour right is ultimately unbridgeable; that Callaghan or Healey or Silkin or Shore had better decide — to use a not imperfect European analogy — whether they are to become Mitterrand or Marchais. They cannot be both. Much better, of course, if they could emulate Helmut Schmidt.

Further it suggests that Britain needs a reordering of its political parties and formations in order to isolate the extreme left that has now captured Labour's apparatus. This calls for a level of political statecraft and imagination that cannot be unattainable even in the midst of our present misfortunes and political uncertainties. Indeed, such an enterprise could become the catalyst, even amidst the despair and cynicism of the age, for a politics that can transcend our national obsession of class and produce a strong, unified, democratic nation capable of surviving in an increasingly dangerous and hostile world.

Chapter 1 attempts to set the present 'socialist generation' which controls Labour in an historical context. It seeks to argue that Labour history, from the birth of the party until the middle-sixties, is a story of resistance to socialism; that in the post-Second World War years the Labour Party, primarily under the influence of Hugh Gaitskell, very nearly became the kind of political force that could have lifted and reconstructed British politics out of its class-based narrowness and complacency, but that this attempt failed; that the seventies have seen a seismic transformation of the politics of Labour as a very extreme form of socialism has taken over its governing councils.

Chapter 2 describes, in some detail, what Labour has become: how it has degenerated into two unattractive factions — one representing a bitter, ungenerous extremism and the other an unelevating careerism.

Chapter 3 describes the failure of political statecraft on the part of Labour's Parliamentary leaders, and the more general failure of Labour's moderates, as they 'responded' to the advance of the left. This part of the book was not written without an awareness of the genuine dilemmas facing moderates and social democrats in times of crisis and instability; nor of the paradox that although Labour right-wingers have become the most discredited of all Britain's politicians they yet inhabit a *tradition* with which the British people feel most comfortable.

Chapter 4 argues that the claim of the modern British socialist class to represent the working people is humbug; that its language and rhetoric about 'the working class' obscures its profoundly undemocratic and unrepresentative nature. It is but a new elite waiting for a collapse to bring it to power.

Chapter 5 is ambitious. It attempts to identify a real, popular constituency within Britain that goes unnoticed by commentators and untapped by politicians. It argues that it is Britain's robust, seemingly unconquerable elitism that both precludes a sensible defence of the liberal democratic state and helps the modern socialist class to edge nearer power. What Britain needs is a deepening of those aspects of its tradition that are democratic. We need more − sensibly led − democracy, not less.

My primary acknowledgements must go to my colleagues in the Social Democratic Alliance, particularly Douglas Eden and Roger Fox, both of whom quite consciously set aside promising political careers in order to publicly campaign against those forces which threaten to extinguish the social democratic traditions and identity of the Labour Party. I am also deeply indebted to those many local Labour Party activists, councillors and trade unionists who in small and unpublicized ways have tried to withstand the pressures to conform to the emerging contours of the new Labour Party. Many have either left politics altogether, joined other parties, fought rather forlorn rearguard actions in their localities, or been expelled. Such isolated acts of courage and principle, particularly when set against less attractive attributes displayed at the apex of power, continue to inspire.

INTRODUCTION

The Importance of Labour

The most significant event of British politics in the twentieth century is the arrival of the Labour movement. Nothing else stands comparison with it. By the late seventies it had assumed a pre-eminence in British national life; and by comparison the institutions of the liberal democratic state – Parliament, the courts, the media — appeared to tremble before it. So too did democratically elected governments. Prime Ministers and Chancellors of the Exchequer, no matter the Parliamentary majority behind them, found it difficult to construct economic, industrial, or indeed social policy without its general acquiescence. Only foreign affairs was left as the preserve of democratic politicians and here they were severely circumscribed by Britain's reduced status and power in the world. Indeed even in the arena of the relations of the British state to foreign nations the Labour movement was beginning to impinge upon this role of statecraft. The heart of the Labour movement (the TUC, the National Executive Committee of the Labour Party, and the advancing left within the Parliamentary Labour Party) was committed to an 'alternative strategy' which had important implications for Britain's membership of the Western trading system, indeed for its future relations with the free world. Even the International Monetary Fund and the European Economic Community find it increasingly difficult to arrange policies with the British government, when they are called on to help, without

1

taking into serious account the likely reaction of the Labour movement.

In a sense the whole history of twentieth-century Britain has been the story of how to react to the rise of Labour, both as a political party and an industrial force. The Liberals failed to enlist it in their cause in the years before 1914. The Conservatives have engaged in seven decades of accommodation to its reality — relying upon their traditional, and usually successful, nostrum that any new class can be tamed by allowing it, carefully and with circumspection, to join the world of politics. Cowling suggests that: 'between 1920 and 1924 the Conservative Party took the long-term decision to make Labour the chief party of opposition.'[1] Even after the defeat of Labour in the General Strike of 1926 the Conservatives reassumed their more traditional policy of accommodation. The Trades Disputes Act of 1927 was a setback for organized labour but not a defeat. Wage-cuts, lockouts, anti-union legislation — all this in the twenties certainly, but nothing that amounted to a successful strategic offensive by the establishment against labour. And whilst the industrial wing of labour was weakened, though by no means counted out, the political wing, the Labour Party, emerged as the main opposition force. The Labour movement, in the post-Second War world, has grown even stronger. Labour has won most of the elections. Organized industrial labour has continued to improve its strategic position within the economy.

The Conservative attitude to this accretion of power has remained much the same as it was in the inter-war period. Anthony Crosland, referring to Tory attitudes to the trade unions in the fifties, was scathing:

The atmosphere in Whitehall is almost deferential, the desire not to give offence positively ostentatious . . . . One Conservative Minister publicly rebukes a firm for declaring redundancy without prior consultation with the unions . . . . And in 1955, 28 years after the Trades Disputes Act, the Conservative government, in the face of considerable public clamour, unites in adamant opposition to proposals for 'outlawing' even unofficial strikes.[2]

Even the Heath government, with its 'hated' Industrial Relations Court, was not attempting surgery. And what little trade union reform it did attempt was met by the most devastating and robust response.

Labour leaders, too, have reacted to the Labour movement with circumspection — as though they did not quite trust or understand the new forces which they nominally controlled. Non-socialist Labour leaders have attempted to steer the movement into constitutional channels, to align it within the boundaries of the liberal, democratic society. Socialists, historically a small minority within the Labour movement, have been wary of its politically conservative nature. Nevertheless, the socialists have clung to it as the only means of advancing their cause. This diligence and patience has recently paid off handsomely.

It cannot be surprising, therefore, that the arrival of Labour should have caused such awe and fear. Lloyd George declared that: 'We cannot take risks with labour. If we did, we should at once create an enemy within our own borders, and one that would be better provided with dangerous weapons than Germany.' Of course, labour was not an 'enemy'. It sprang from Britain itself. Its growth, indeed its pre-eminence, was seemingly natural. Those who wished to resist it, those who appeased it, those who led it, all treated it with a kind of reverence. They had a sense of its very rightness. Britain, after all, was a 'proletarian' nation, arguably the most 'proletarian' of all the nations. Political life had to accommodate to social reality. Just as the 'middle class' had to have its due in 1832, so in the twentieth century should the manual workers and their families. Mass-democracy and the British liberal tradition had, by the volition of their own rules, to admit a new social and political force into the national life.

Indeed, a great British paradox was born. The nation which had given the world the philosophy of liberalism, a pioneering, free-trde, commercial country in which the notion of the individual was ostensibly triumphant, had to coexist with a large, organized, increasingly collectivist, working-class movement. And within this movement, dimly discernible at first, was a nascent socialism that threatened to overturn the liberal world. Labour was always a *potential* threat to the liberal system that had given birth to it.

For a time this embryonic conflict was resolved by powerful social control. Enough of the workers were deferential, though increasingly less so their leaders. As Paul Johnson put it, they were allowed 'a servant's place at the Asquithian feast'.[3] Yet this soon broke down. Authority, in the form of pre-democratic and even pre-capitalist institutions, waned. As the twentieth century progressed religion lost its hold. The Nonconformist Christian tradition, that great motor of 'respectability' for the northern working people, progressively lost its sanction. Also, the Upper English establishment collapsed. Many were killed in the First World War; the Empire, which was their rationale for existence and the source of their legitimacy, was not sustainable; many of them suffered feelings of guilt, a quality nurtured in the public schools. Some of them turned to socialism and held the new proletarian man in awe. The moral authority of the leaders of British society was further undermined by the new democratic age of relentless enquiry and pitiless satire. It was increasingly obvious to workers that there was an emptiness and hypocrisy at the top.

British management, with some notable exceptions, was not so outstandingly successful that it could, by the sheer power of example, persuade workers to work harder; the professions were as riddled with restrictive practices as the trade unions; politicians, both national and local, were not free of the taint of corruption and failure. In short, there was very little any longer worth deferring to.

Yet, the Labour movement, with its members released from deference and possessed of a growing self-confidence, was still not, by the mid-1960s, assuming the proportions of a threat to the liberal, democratic state. Deference may have largely disappeared but labour was reconciled to the nation by the rapid economic growth, mass consumption and 'affluence' of the post-Second World War settlement. Whatever the exact merits of the *embourgeoisement* thesis, about which there is still keen debate, growing affluence was enough to build up a huge political consensus behind social democratic welfare capitalism – the political, social and economic structure pursued and defended by both major parties. Labour was, yet again, reconciled to the state; and stability ensured for a further period. Yet, this new consensus (and the politicians that led it) continued to raise economic expectations. Each general election degenerated into a mock auction. Labour tended to promise unrealistic welfare provision, the Conservatives unsustainable tax-reductions. Britain's economic base was simply unable to respond to the expectations unleashed by party electoral rhetoric. And herein lay the seeds of the present political crisis.

With social deference eroded and the economy unable to satisfy boundless expectations, and a pervasive egalitarianism dominating the political culture, the whole highly organized economic system appears to be fracturing. In the late seventies the threat to the democratic system no longer *appears* to be that posed by a united Labour movement, of the kind that toppled the Heath government in 1974. Rather the picture is one of incipient industrial anarchy, a more generalised threat to all institutions, including the Labour movement itself. Individual groups of workers, paying little heed to past practices, government ministers or trade union bureaucrats, have shown their muscle in a determined attempt to keep up with inflation. Throughout the seventies, and with increasing frequency, each wage-round has seemingly caused greater disruption: lights go out as electricity supplies are turned off, rubbish piles up in the streets, firefighting is abandoned, hospitals closed down, ambulance services curtailed (and even 'emergency cover' removed), newspapers suspended and, apparently most annoying of all, television services interrupted.

The reaction of the political class to this disruption has been confused. Some see Britain's industrial dislocation as best solved by curtailing trade union power and privileges which had been entrenched by legislation. Others on the right see the strikers as part of a 'modern peasants' revolt, against collectivism, big government, Whitehall ministers, trade unionists, industrialists and pompous donkeys'.[4] Others, mostly on the Labour right, think that the best way forward is to strengthen the nascent corporatism of government – trade union leader – employer 'concordats' at national level. The Labour left has supported all strikes and offered 'socialism' as the solution.

The incoherence of the political response to Britain's industrial dislocation of the late seventies – the seeming inability of any political force to get a grip on the situation or to marshal a consensus behind a new settlement – opened up a huge political vacuum in the life of the nation. Power was devolving downward. There was, apparently, little sense of national unity. Also, there was certainly no sense of 'class' unity, as gas workers, coal workers, sewage workers, water workers, electricity workers, dockers, train drivers, other railwaymen all fought against each other for a slice of the cake. The temptation is to believe that such a descent into formlessness will simply continue; that authority will never be able to be restored in what commentators suggest is becoming a post-political age.

I believe this view to be a profound misunderstanding of the consequences of the transformation British life is undergoing. Certainly all institutions have less legitimacy, less of a hold on the imagination and loyalty of 'the people' than previously; and certainly amongst those institutions must be included the Labour movement. But to conclude from this that the vacuum created by the failure of the social democratic consensus will simply go unfilled is both fanciful and unhistorical. The Labour movement remains a centre of power, arguably the primary centre of power. As long as it remains united, and no other power centres are built up, it will always be available to move into the vacuum created by the upheavals of the seventies. This is why the politics of Labour still counts.

It is important, though, to properly understand the nature of Britain's Labour movement. It is a central thesis of this book that the Labour movement is no longer the natural political expression of the working people; that the Labour Party apparatus is no longer representative of those who vote Labour; that trade union leaders, at all levels, distort the *political* aspirations of their members — in short, that the Labour movement has recently undergone a profound political transformation. It has been taken over by a 'socialist' generation that is nearer to national political power than ever before; and not because this 'socialist' generation represents popular aspirations but rather because it has a firm hold on a centre of power in a developing anarchic society in which other power centres and sources of authority are increasingly unsure of themselves.

CHAPTER 1

What Labour Was

The transformation of the politics of Labour is of very recent origin. As late as the early 1960s there could be little debate about Labour's political position, or about the resolution of those who led the party and movement. It was firmly within the broad Western liberal tradition — reformist, Labourist (with a marginal, and largely irrelevant, 'socialist' rhetoric), committed to the constitution, to the mixed economy and to the Western position in the world. By the late 1970s it had become wholly unrecognizable. It had broken with its past. It was as if a new political party had been born.

The full extent of this revolutionary transition can be measured in a number of different ways — by personnel changes, by voting figures for party officerships, by changing relations with other parties at home and abroad: all of this will be discussed later. One particularly instructive method is to assess the general political disposition exhibited by *Labour's Programme, 1976*, the policy document for the medium-term future agreed by the Labour Party in Conference that year. Such policy documents are a sensible guide to underlying trends, more so than party manifestoes which are inevitably tailored for immediate electoral purposes. They are a relatively settled statement of position, more enduring and less transient than individual speeches or policy decisions. Furthermore, by 1976 the newly left-dominated National Executive Committee of the Labour Party, which had drawn up the document, had been in operation for a few years and *Labour's Programme, 1976* was the first result of its thinking.

It is a remarkable document. Ben Pimlott has suggested that: 'The British Labour Party is now the most socialist of the European social democratic parties';[1] yet a careful study of *Labour's Programme, 1976* displays a sweep and intent that is radically different from 'social democracy' at least as it has been understood in the post-war world. In policy, in approach, in language it resembles the kind of political outlook of the more gradualist of the 'Eurocommunist' parties of southern Europe. It is best known for the introduction into Britain's contemporary political language of the word *irreversible*. This term is used in the context of the declared aim 'to bring about an irreversible shift in the balance of power and wealth in favour of working people and their families'.[2] There is no definition of 'working people and their families' in the document but the *irreversible* conception is a glimpse into the political mentality and general theoretical framework which is encountered in 'Eurocommunist' theoreticians. The *irreversibility* concept and problem was raised in an interesting exchange between George Urban and Lombardo Radice (a leading member of the Central Committee of the Italian Communist Party):

Urban: But earlier you said: it would be an impossible hypothesis to suppose that a society which had reached a higher stage of development in the form of socialism would want to go back to a 'lower form of development' — to Helmut Schmidt's Social Democracy, for example. Wouldn't the same apply to Italian society once the 'hegemony' of the proletariat has been established through the offices of your party?

Radice: I'm no prophet; but once the working class has acquired hegemony and led Italian society out of its almost permanent crisis, it would be difficult to envisage anyone wanting a regression from a better state of society to a worse state.[3]

Labour's Programme, 1976 makes no commitment to the mixed economy. This compares with Labour's policy aims as outlined sixteen years previously. In March 1960 the Labour Party policy document, after a major political fight, declared that 'both public and private enterprise have a place in the economy'.[4] In 1957 an official party document could argue that: 'The Labour Party recognizes that, under increasingly professional managements, large firms are as a whole serving the nation well.'[5] It proposed only to nationalize steel and road haulage; and this was the result not of dogma but of residual resentment about the Conservatives' previous denationalization of these industries. By comparison the 1976 programme, even after two decades in which the state sector has continued to mushroom, takes a radically different approach, seeking to expand public ownership virtually to the point where the private sector is effectively emasculated. It seeks to create a 'major public holding company' within the pharmaceutical industry; 'a major new public enterprise stake' within the construction industry; it identifies 32 sectors of the economy 'where public sector enterprise should seek to expand together with those industries where the public sector is the sole, or major customer'.[6] A vital role is assigned to the National Enterprise Board: 'the NEB and other public sector holding companies will need to *control* a successful leading company operating in each of the key sectors in industry and commerce'.[7] The 1976 Labour Conference also passed a resolution 'to proceed with the nationalization of the private banks and insurance companies'.[8]

The all-intrusiveness of the 'planning agreement' proposals outlined in the document is breathtaking. A 'planning agreement is a deal negotiated between a large firm and the Government . . . which sets out what the firm *must* do to help the Government meet certain clearly defined objectives'; 'Planning agreements, we believe, must apply to *all* category 1 companies engaged in manufacturing and immediate priority should be given to concluding them with the top 30 companies by the end of this year and with the top 100 by the end of 1978.'[9] This, in 1979, remained the policy of the party apparatus; the fact that it had not been implemented by the

Labour administration in no way removed it as a central strategic objective of the emerging new Labour Party. Furthermore, the document called for a new Industry Act and argued that: '*We* must take powers . . . to issue, in the national interest, *directives* to companies on a wide range of individual matters.'[10] In 1957 Labour's policy had been to 'recognize that no organization, public or private, can operate effectively if it is subjected to persistent and detailed interventions from above. We have, therefore, no intentions of intervening in the management of any firm which is doing a good job.'[11]

Labour's Programme, 1976 makes no commitment to NATO. In 1960 Labour policy was set out forcefully: 'We must accept the obligations we have undertaken and remain loyal supporters of NATO, in the creation of which . . . the Labour Government played a leading role.'[12] By 1976 the whole axis of the policy had changed. Labour must 'break down the "bloc mentality" '.[13] 'Our proposals involve . . . cuts . . . [of] £1,000 million a year by 1980 on defence.'[14] 'The Labour Party is committed to the ultimate mutual and concurrent dissolution of NATO and The Warsaw Pact.[15] – a view that differs considerably from general Western policy, as such a concurrent dissolution would serve to remove the United States from Europe but not the Soviet Union. The nearest NATO comes to obtaining a recommendation from the document is in the intriguing passage: 'Labour recognizes that it has responsibility to work for these policies particularly *within* the EEC and NATO.'[16] 'These policies' are outlined in a whole page of the document that is replete with support for 'socialist and liberation movements abroad', invocations against 'the exploitative nature of British capitalism' and suchlike other notions. The conception of working *within* NATO and the EEC to achieve 'socialist objectives' is a major feature of the declaratory policy of most of the 'Eurocommunist' parties.[17]

Labour's 1976 programme is essentially neutralist, both in content and in flavour. No mention is made of a threat to Britain's security posed by the Soviet Union. There is a visceral anti-American animus present throughout the foreign policy sections of the programme together with an analysis of global politics and a use of political language that would do credit to the propaganda machines of Eastern Europe. For instance five pages of the document are devoted to rejecting 'US Interventionism' in Latin America whereas not one sentence specifically singles out the Soviet Union for similar − if not worse − malpractices in Eastern Europe. Labour's foreign policy is seemingly constructed as though the Soviet imperium does not exist, as though Chile represents a more powerful and immediate threat to British national interests and liberty. Throughout the document there is constant use of such heavy pseudo-Marxist terminology as 'support for progressive forces'; Labour's aims in the world 'will be achieved *only* in alliance with socialist and *liberation* movements abroad'.[18] Such sentiments are usually the preserve of fringe, ultra-left pamphleteers − although such pamphleteers would be more critical of the human and civil rights abuses in the Soviet Union than is Labour's NEC.

This 1976 policy document of the Labour Party has been amended and refined by subsequent Annual Conference resolutions but in essence remains the key text from which the policy of the Labour Party for the eighties will be derived. It unveils economic, social and industrial mechanisms which, if introduced, would both transform Britain into a bureaucratic socialist society and propel it into a collision course with the Western financial, trading, political and defence systems. The 1976 programme amounts in outline to what is described on the Labour left as an 'alternative strategy' for dealing with Britain's economic crisis. This 'alternative strategy', which had its genesis in the *Tribune* group of Labour MPs and particularly in the writings of Brian Sedgemore and Stuart Holland, is, as it suggests, not a refinement of past Labour government strategies − it is an alternative, a radical (indeed revolutionary) alternative. It is incompatible with the post-war social democratic tradition. As the politics of Labour unfolds into the eighties this incompatability, which has always been denied by Labour's leading politicians, will become increasingly obvious.

Labourism triumphant

To explain the history of the Labour Party and movement as a history of socialism is a typical error, made mainly by those who know little of Labour people and the history of Labour thought. If by 'socialism' is meant the accretion of power by the state, increased public spending and ownership, the arrival of the welfare state and highly managed capitalism, then Labour has certainly helped these developments along. But then so have the Conservatives and Liberals; and it remains an arguable point whether the Conservatives are more responsible than Labour for Britain's present economic profile. In any event there were forces more profound than political parties at work that produced our modern condition. The emergence of mass-democracy, class change, technological developments, industrialism and post-industrialism, the loss of Empire, two World Wars — it is from amongst these great historical events that the primary causes of the British problem should be sought. Labour and Conservative alike have been reacting to them.

If, on the other hand, we mean by socialism the tradition of Marxism, or neo-Marxism, or the various types of crypto-Marxism, then this, assuredly, is what the history of Labour has *not* been about. Not, that is, until very recently. Imported theorizing about class conflict with its incipient totalitarianism and one-party rule is as alien to the British Labour tradition as it is to British liberalism more generally. Also, the more homegrown pre-Bolshevik and pre-Leninist socialist tradition − the 'land to the people', 'common ownership' theories of the utopian socialists − is also without any firm footing within the British Labour tradition. Utopian socialism has certainly had a greater influence upon

Labour than Marxism but it still cannot claim a central place.

In fact, the Labour Party and movement from its inception set its face against socialism of virtually any systematic kind and in any sense that would separate it from other democratic political parties. The story of Labour, from its beginnings in the craft unionism of the nineteenth century right through, as I will argue, to the mid 1960s is essentially the story of Labourism. 'Labourism' is a term coined by socialists who have, historically at least, despaired of the Labour movement. Ralph Miliband uses the term throughout his major work, *Parliamentary Socialism*, as he lambasts the Labour party for being dogmatic 'not about socialism, but about the parliamentary system'.[19] Tom Nairn uses the term to describe Labour's residual and powerful nationalism. He argues that: 'The official apologists of Labourism have always held that there is no contradiction between being a class party and being a national party: the real interests of the class are essentially one with those of the nation'.[20] Tom Forester draws out the distinction between Labourism and socialism in a somewhat elaborate way by suggesting that the Labourist is passive, reflective, empirical, pragmatic, evolutionary, practical and possessed of the 'ethic of responsibility', whereas the socialist is active, educative, ideological, principled, revolutionary and possessed of the 'ethic of ultimate ends'.[21] Much of this may well be the case; but as a description it is altogether too narrow and abstract. The fact is that Labourism was merely an aspect of the more general British liberal tradition dressed up to express the emergence of a new interest in the land, a new sociological outgrowth of industrial Britain. Socialist ideas neither caused this interest, nor explained it, nor particularly aided it; certainly 'socialism', as an explanation of the world or as a framework for action, left both the 'working class' and its authentic leaders utterly cold.

Even today, after decades of socialist propaganda, theorizing, and political activism, and after society, economy and polity have become more collectivist, socialism still has little mass appeal. Hardly ever does one meet, in political canvassing, someone on the doorstep — an actual, real, working-class person — who describes himself as a 'socialist'. 'Labour' is the category to which working people respond. 'We're Labour here' is the typical response; hardly ever 'We're socialist here'. Indeed one is tempted to the bold statement that Labour's advance as a political party is virtually commensurate with the extent to which it has successfully distanced itself from socialism. By and large British working people are not only non-socialist, they are anti-socialist. Labour politicians realize this more than most. At election times, when political power rests with the people, the word 'socialist' is, prudently, hardly ever uttered by a Labour candidate whether from the right or left of the party. Ross McKibbin has argued that: 'There are many socialists in the Labour Party, and possibly an even larger number of anti-socialists, but in practice these were irrelevant categories. Voting Labour implied allegiance to certain working-class traditions and not necessarily to any political ideology.'[22]

If Labour had an ideology or ideological preferences then they were liberal rather than socialist. Most Labourists were Christians and the Labour constituency largely Nonconformist. Labourism was the adaptation of the new class and its movement to the English tradition, with suitable evolving modifications. It represented, it did not depart from, the broad evolution of British national culture and its liberal heritage. The sense in which it did depart from the stricter and purer definitions of the liberal tradition was in its 'class-consciousness' and in trade unionism. But Labourism's class-consciousness was not of a Marxist variety. Alan Beattie suggests that to the leaders of the early Labour Party 'the working class was not a "class" in the marxist sense; it was a group mainly defined in the (negative) terms of its sense of exclusion from communal life and politics'.[23] Labourism's class impetus was in any event as much, if not more, a reaction to the aristocracy as to the 'capitalists'; its class feeling more to do with resentment and anger about poverty, unemployment, low status and English snobbery than with any consciousness of a particular economic relationship to capital or a special political destiny.

The events of 1900 prove the point about the irrelevance of socialism. At the meeting to form the Labour Representation Committee (which in 1906 turned itself into the Labour Party) the vast majority of delegates came from the trade unions and the majority of these unionists were liberals. The Miners' Federation, suspicious of the whole enterprise from the start, stayed away. In fact, the TUC at its previous September conference had only narrowly — by 546,000 to 434,000 votes — passed a motion calling for the conference which set up the LRC. When the conference finally met socialist sects and societies (the Social Democratic Federation, the Independent Labour Party and the Fabian Society) were present but they were swamped by trade union delegates representing 65 unions. The very first Labour Party executive comprised seven trade union members, two ILP members, two SDF members and one Fabian Society member. This was obviously top-heavy with intellectuals and socialists and was soon changed — by 1908 the unions had eleven places, the socialist societies only three with one reserved for trade councils and local Labour parties. The trade unions were to remain in control of the Labour Party apparatus thereafter.

The triumph of Labourism over socialism at this very first conference was secured by the adoption of a motion proposing that there should be 'a distinct Labour group in Parliament, who should have their own whips and agree upon their policy'. The delegates from the socialist Social Democratic Federation wanted this initial conference to declare in favour of 'a distinct party based upon the recognition of the class war and having for its ultimate object the socialization of the means of production, distribution and exchange'. Naturally, this was not acceptable. Labour historians have sometimes argued that this initial conference was a compromise: between reluctant trade unionists frightened of socialism on the one hand and socialists, particularly the ILP, on the other. It was really nothing of the kind. From the very start Keir Hardie had realized that it was to be the socialists who would have to forgo their aims; that if they wanted a separate party for labour with a potential mass appeal then it would have to be on the Labourists' terms – without socialism.

So the early socialists had to make a choice: either they could work within the new Labour Party and yield up, at least temporarily and tactically, their aims to the Labourist-Liberalism of the LRC or they could stand outside and continue to pursue their objectives in a more robust and undiluted manner. Some stayed, some left. The Social Democratic Federation, a quirky English early Marxian organization under the leadership of H. M. Hyndman, withdrew its affiliation to the newly formed Labour Party as early as August 1901. Hyndman considered that the English working class lacked 'class consciousness and class antagonism' and declared himself, in that high-minded and dismissive manner that was to characterize a generation of socialists in the years to come, 'quite astounded at the ignorance and apathy of my countrymen'.[24] The Independent Labour Party struggled on within the LRC and the Labour Party until its withdrawal in 1932. It is an interesting point that even after MacDonald's expulsion and the 'great betrayal' of 1931 the ILP could still consider the Labour Party – shorn of MacDonald – insufficiently socialist. The ILP represented a peculiar mixture of early British Marxism and native liberal radicalism; it was socialist in the sense that it retained a commitment to 'collective and communal ownership of the means of production, distribution and exchange' but Miliband argues that its leaders found it 'much easier to contemplate association with the Liberals than with the Marxists of the Social Democratic Federation'.[25] Indeed, the ILP, more working-class and down to earth than the SDF, was suffused with the religious non-conformity that so captivated early Labour. *The Pendlebury Pioneer* reported an address by its leading figure, Keir Hardie, in 1898, that perfectly captures the flavour of its appeal:

Keir Hardie preached an eloquent sermon from the familiar text, 'Consider the lilies how they grow'. There was a large and appreciative audience. The Speaker . . . declared . . . that . . . all were agreed that if the ethical principles of Christ were adopted today the world would be all the better.[26]

This was not a cynical appeal by Hardie to a potential electorate; the ILP was genuine in its radical non-conformity, mild pacifism and evangelical sermonizing. The debate about the socialist component in the early ILP aside, it has very little in common with the modern British left within the Labour Party, although direct descent is often claimed. Yet, even this ILP, the party of Hardie, Blatchford, Mann and Jowett, found the new Labour Party far too timid and mainstream for its tastes. Although the ILP and the SDF broke away from the Labour Party the other main socialist society, the Fabian Society, remained within the fold. This, together with its more sophisticated intellectualism and a keen sense of political strategy amongst its leaders, accounted for its great influence. Yet the Fabians continued, throughout their long association with Labour, to complain both about the conservative nature of the British working class and the narrowness (as they saw it) of the Labour Party leadership. They were under no illusions about the nature of the party they had affiliated to.

Broadly speaking, the first two decades of the Labour Party's existence confirmed its developing Labourist nature. Organized labour made great strides in the nation; trade union membership, despite legal constraints, rose to over four million, and the Labour Party came out of the second general election of 1910 with 42 parliamentary seats. It was already well on the way to supplanting the Liberals. The reforming, welfare measures of the Liberal governments confirmed in Labourist minds the appropriateness of the parliamentary method for securing change; although the prewar years saw considerable industrial unrest and militancy the

Labour leaders consistently rejected the embrace of revolutionary syndicalism; and, the great test for Labourism, its 'nation before class' instinct surmounted the pacifism of the vocal left around the ILP as it gave support to the war effort. Labour proposed an electoral truce and the TUC an industrial truce for the duration of the war and helped in the recruiting campaign. Arthur Henderson later entered the coalition government. Whatever the merits of the decisions of the man who led the nation into the great catastrophe, Labour was at one both with the working people and with the total national consensus. Opposition to the war from within Labour's ranks was more to do with pacifism, traditional liberal resistance to conscription and mass mobilization, residual articulate working-class resentment of labour being used as gun-fodder than with any notion of international class solidarity in the face of capitalist war. In retrospect the opponents of the war were right (though most of them for the wrong reasons); but Labour was part of the nation, and the nation, not just its leaders, had made up its mind.

With the course of Labourism so firmly set it was somewhat surprising that the party should have adopted a new constitution in 1918 that, formally at least, committed to it 'to the common ownership of the means of production, distribution and exchange', an almost exact replica of the 1893 statement of aims of the ILP. Ever since this discordant event the Labour left have claimed that the party, and hence the people who vote for it, is part of an indigenous socialist tradition of which they are the heirs. The 'common ownership' clause of the constitution, Clause 4, and no other, appears today on the card which every individual member of the Labour Party signs as part of the process of membership. Yet the circumstances surrounding the 1918 constitution belie any intent upon the part of the central managers of the party, the politicians as well as the trade union leaders, to set Labour on a radical new socialist course. Hardly anyone saw 1918 as a great socialist awakening or as the beginning of a political movement dedicated to revolutionary or evolutionary socialist change. What actually happened was that Labour, mainly under the influence of Arthur Henderson, adopted a new constitution as part of a fundamental *organizational* change. Labour ceased to be a loose federation of affiliated organizations run from the centre by trade union bosses and became instead a proper national party organized into local constituencies responsible to a central party apparatus. In fact, before 1918 Labour's lack of a comprehensive local party organization was one of its great weaknesses. In 1914, for instance, it could only boast 158 local Labour organizations, not all of them coterminous with parliamentary constituencies. The ILP, on the other hand, had over 672 local branches.

The 1918 constitution was the product of a deal between the socialists in the ILP and the Labourist bosses of the trade unions in the Labour Party. The ILP had the local branches and Labour wanted to set up a constituency-based party. Clause 4, taken seriously by no one in particular within the Labour Party, was part of the compact.

This constitution, although it landed Labour with Clause 4, was in some senses a reaffirmation of Labourism, as it confirmed Labour's prediliction for parliamentary politics (this was the reason for the need for constituency organizations). Serious Labour historians do not see 1918 as a great watershed in the advance of socialism within the Labour Party. R. H. Tawney wrote in 1932 that: 'In 1918 the Labour party finally declared itself to be a Socialist Party . . . . It supposed and supposes that it thereby became one. It is mistaken. It recorded a wish, that is all: the wish has not been fulfilled.'[27] It is doubtful, amidst the intrigues of 1918, whether even any such wish was recorded, not at least in the minds of the trade unionists. Miliband argues that: 'More and more in the course of the twenties, the ILP found itself compelled to carry on its diverse activities on the wholly justified assumption that the Labour Party's conversion to socialism was as much a thing of the future as it had been before 1918.'[28] It is my contention, however, that before 1918, and for many years after, socialism was not even considered 'a thing of the future'. Labour leaders, by and large, as with the working class that supported them, thought of socialism as a kind of cranky fixation of an intellectual class that was kind enough to write about them in such glowing and important terms.

The 'common ownership' clause of 1918 was, of course, a great 'theoretical' success for the socialists. To commit what was rapidly becoming one of the two great parties of state, albeit in the most formal and legalistic of senses, to socialism was no mean achievement. Even so, it had little effect, of and by itself, either on state policy or on the party. The inter-war years saw significant accretions of state power, but the growth of government intervention took place largely independently of Labour's influence or design. It was the war-time coalition under Lloyd George, and with full Conservative support, that imposed powers for price-fixing, direction of labour, planning of capital investment, the introduction of imperial preference and national mobilization of resources. It was the Baldwin government that passed the Electricity Supply Act in 1926 that created the Central Electricity Board as a public corporation; and a Conservative government set up the BBC. The Conservatives were never particularly ideologically averse to using or increasing state power when necessary, during wartime or during recession or depression. Also, it was under the impact of the Second World War, and the Conservative-dominated coalition, that much of the work that contributed to the planning of social and economic policy under Attlee took place. After all, Beveridge was, in a sense, the product of Churchill. Certainly the Conservatives were lukewarm, to say the least, in their opposition to most of Labour's nationalization measures of 1945-51. Of course, after the war, Labour, of the two parties, was the keener on extending the state sector but its only really 'controversial' measures in these years were the steel and road haulage enactments, and it very nearly, under Herbert Morrison's promptings, abandoned the steel enterprise. In fact, the British economy, had the 1918 clause remained securely in Sidney Webb's imagination only, would probably look very much as it does today. The welfare state, the managed capitalist system, the extensions of public ownership were (certainly up until 1974) part of a total national political consensus; the debates between the parties were over small, peripheral issues and usually and typically mock.

To return to the twenties. Labour certainly did not disport itself as though it was a newly-born socialist party. Its two inter-war administrations, albeit minority ones, were excessively financially orthodox. At the point at which the General Strike looked as though it might get out of control the Labour leadership – in the Parliamentary party but much more significantly in the General Council of the TUC – helped bring the conflict to an end. There was, emphatically, no desire on the part of Labour leaders to use the strike for political purposes, either to get out the Conservative government or to advance towards 'socialism'. By comparison the political agitation of the Wilson opposition in 1973/4, when it lent a degree of political legitimacy to the miners in their struggle with the state, was far more opportunistic and dangerous than the cautious constitutionalism exhibited by the Labourists of 1926.

Also, Labour consistently and rigorously distanced itself from the Communist Party during these years. The British Communist Party was formed in 1920 and sought, at regular intervals, to affiliate to the Labour Party. This, on all occasions, was emphatically rejected. What is more, the Labour Conference introduced 'proscription', whereby no member of the Communist Party could be eligible for membership of the Labour Party. Labour's attitude to the Communist Party was part of a more generalized Labourist reaction against more extreme forms of leftism, a suspicion that became even more acute after the events of 1917 in Russia. If socialism before 1917 had been seen as rather dotty, certainly remote, then the October revolution set it back even further – it assumed the proportions, in many minds, of a politics that was alien and unsavoury. Walter Kendall, in his massive volume *The Revolutionary*

Movement in Britain 1900-21, argues that the importation into Britain of Leninist revolutionary politics (culminating at that time with the establishment of the British Communist Party in 1920) destroyed a previous socialist tradition which, he suggests, was essentially democratic. Indeed, he claims that: 'The revolutionary movement before the transformation took place had been ultra-democratic, opposed to leadership on principle, opposed to the professionalisation of the Labour movement almost as an article of faith.' Whatever the truth of this thesis the whole socialist tradition was compromized by international Communism and the new Moscow regime. It set off interminable debates amongst socialists about the merits of revolutionary politics, about tactics, about the need for a vanguard party, about the very nature of the left. Those socialists who remained within the Labour Party and who rejected Leninism were nevertheless dogged from 1917 onwards by one fundamental problem: even if there was a major distinction to be drawn between authentic English socialism and the revolutionary Russian and continental variety, should British socialists retain an 'opening to the left' strategy? From that time to this the debate about 'left unity' has not been resolved. In the process, though, socialism – as a democratic, homegrown tradition – was challenged. Conservatives and Liberals began to use Communism, and to associate it with Labour, in the internal debate in British politics. The 'Zinoviev Affair' was a particularly effective example of the use to which this new issue could be put. But, more importantly, Labour reacted too. To a very British institution socialism became even more suspect. Kendall argues that 1917 and its reverberations in Britain succeeded in 'isolating the left wing of the Labour movement from the mass party of the working class at the very moment when its presence within the ranks was most important'.[29]

In the thirties Labourism retained its hold. The split of 1931, in which Labour's leader, Ramsay MacDonald, joined the Conservatives and Liberals to form a national government, did not leave the left in control of the Labour Party. In fact the leadership of the party passed into the hands of those who were to form the nucleus of Labour's post-war administration. Bevin remained the dominant figure in the trade union movement on the General Council. Ben Pimlott, in *Labour and the Left in the 1930s*, provides a persuasive case for the isolation of socialism and the triumph of Labourism:

If political effectiveness is the measure, the Labour left in the 1930s scores very poorly indeed . . . led by the brilliant and egotistical figure of Sir Stafford Cripps, taking its cue from an elitist, inward-looking, intellectual coterie, the Labour left . . . were to alienate Labour opinion, and taint its own proposals. Throughout the decade, left-wing leaders showed a disastrous insensivity to the realities of political power and influence *within the Labour movement*.[30]

It seems appropriate that Labour's inter-war experience should end with the expulsion from the party of Stafford Cripps, Aneurin Bevan, George Strauss and Charles Trevelyan because of their support for a 'Popular Front' – an alliance of all 'progressive forces' including the Communist Party. Cripps was expelled by *seventeen votes to one* for refusing to withdraw his 'Popular Front' memorandum and was asked by the executive to 'reaffirm his allegiance to the Labour Party within the meaning of the constitution, programme, principles and policy of the party'. Such action would certainly seem bizarre today (as we shall see in Chapter 2) but in these years Labour drew severe distinctions between itself and revolutionary leftist organizations. This action by the party against Cripps further highlights the hollowness of the party's real belief in Clause 4 of the constitution. If the party was genuinely socialist it would have been difficult to argue that Cripp's actions, which only advocated the co-operation of all socialist forces, was in any sense 'disloyal'. He was expelled on the basis of the Labour party's constitution.

Labour, however, was not a socialist party.

Nor did it become so in the forties and fifties. Attlee, Morrison, Bevin, Gaitskell, Brown, Deakin, Williamson, Watson – little more need be said. The Labour left was an isolated force, mainly consigned to a small group in Parliament (on the back benches) and in the constitutency parties. When Gaitskell became Leader in 1955 the left's isolation was confirmed. Yet it was to get even worse for them: under Gaitskell's tutelage an attempt was made to turn such isolation into political extinction. That Gaitskell was defeated in this daring attempt was not, though, the defeat of Labourism. In fact, Gaitskell's defeat was at the hands of the right-wing trade unionists, and not because they disagreed in principle with Gaitskell but because they simply did not want a row within the party.

The fifties was an empty time for socialism within the Labour party. The left in the Labour Party, devoid of any new ideas about domestic development, concentrated upon foreign and defence policy and were decisively beaten. They lost out on German rearmament and then, most spectacularly, on the issue of unilateral nuclear disarmament. Any weakening in Gaitskell's authority that may have resulted from his unsuccessful attempt to remove Clause 4 was more than restored by his victory on defence in 1961. The net effect of all the new theorizing amongst the social democrats of the fifties, particularly Crosland, Strachey and Jay, is still in dispute. But two propositions about the 'social democracy' of the fifties hold true. First, that for the first time in the history of the party a serious and determined intellectual assault was led upon the basic theoretical framework of Marxism and its application to Britain. Second, it renewed the crucial notion that a party of the left, with a mass working-class base, had as great an interest as a party of the right in defending the West and its traditions. Furthermore, the social democrats of the fifties, notwithstanding their excessive optimism about the possibilities of economic growth and their rather loose view of public spending, did at least construct a consensus — shared in by Labour, Conservatives and Liberals alike — that has lasted to the present day, a consensus which socialists have, until very recently, found it very difficult to break.

Of course the possibilities latent on the right of the Labour party in the fifties were much greater than this.

Labour had one great advantage in the fifties. It was neither Marxist nor Tory. It had the potential for transcending Britain's terrifying psychological and cultural divisions. The Labourism of the early Labour Party, still present in large measure in the fifties, had been an attractive and moving phenomenon, involving the struggle for free trade union rights, for the recognition of the labour interest as part of the political life of the nation, for the dignity of the working people. It represented, particularly through its leaders, a kind of romantic assertion of self-educated working-class Britain — made more impressive and alluring when set in comparison to the debilitated, stuffy, anachronistic and, above all, unsuccessful Tory leadership class *and* set against the narrower, more bitter working-class tradition that was turning to socialism and Marxism.

As late as the 1950s Labour could still inspire. Thousands of young people were drawn into its ranks and many more were voting for it. Some saw it as a movement of reform, for change, for creating a better environment for the class that had brought it into being. Others joined for patriotic motives (unthinkable today), seeing it as a movement for the regeneration of Britain; or wanting, through it, to play their part in improving the country, ending what could already be glimpsed, its economic decline, its increasing shabbiness and third-rateness. Much of the allure of Labour was the potential and possibility that people sensed in the figure of Hugh Gaitskell. The sheer moral force of the man was unusual and, by comparison with contemporary politicians, extraordinary. He had faced down his Party Conference on a major issue of principle involving the defence of the country, when to compromise would have been easy. What is more he seemed to carry within him that transcendent quality so rare in British public life: caricatured as a 'Hampstead intellectual' and embodying many of the routine middle class 'liberal' nostrums, he was nevertheless able to tap considerable working-class support because of his patriotism (exemplified with great fervour in the Common Market debate of 1962 at Brighton) and constitutionalism. The evocation, in the 1962 speech, of 'Vimy Ridge' and 'Gallipoli', of not 'turning our back on a thousand years of history', was strange indeed for a 'revisionist' and shocked some of his more shallow supporters.

Robert Skidelsky has summed up the feelings and motives of a whole generation of non-Marxist young people who saw in the Labour Party of the fifties and early sixties a political home that could satisfy both their patriotism and idealism.[31] He personally was drawn into politics by Gaitskell's leadership and has written: 'To be drawn into politics by the personality of a leader may seem immature. Yet there is sound reason for it. On the quality of leadership depends the possibility of action.'[32] He further suggested that the attributes that he wanted for a Labour Leader were 'bold policies, unflinching courage, eloquent language, compassion, popular appeal'.[33] In the late fifties and early sixties Labour was right and Gaitskell was right. This combination, if Gaitskell had lived, could have tilted the whole axis of British politics. It would certainly have isolated the socialists and may have come near to isolating the Conservatives as well by creating a genuine national democratic movement. Had Hugh Gaitskell become Prime Minister of Britain he might, of course, and under the sheer pressure of events, have gone the way of Harold Wilson. On the other hand, Labour, had it achieved power under Gaitskell, might have created that most elusive of British needs: a party of reform with mass support amongst the working people, but a party steeped in the political traditions of the country (patriotic, democratic) that was nevertheless not encumbered by the cultural and class problems presented to the British people by the Conservatives.

To return to the central theme: Labour in the fifties, right up until a few years into Wilson's Leadership, was only 'socialist' in the sense that it belonged to a 'Socialist International', a grouping of political parties which at that time was somewhere to the right of the modern Conservative Party.

Socialism and elites

Yet, although socialism had no roots in the working people or their developing party its influence remained inordinate amongst elites. And it was through the power and position of these elites that it was kept in being during the decades when Labour, reflecting its voters and supporters, would not embrace it. Samuel Beer has described the ideas, influence and power of what he has termed 'The Socialist Generation' in his book *Modern British Politics*. The genesis of this socialist generation arose from amongst the critics of Victorian society. Sceptical about the merits of industrialism, compassionate for the poor, it romanticized the golden age of the more stable, ordered and 'humane' world of feudal England. Edward Carpenter, in a savage attack upon the values of Victorian capitalist society, harked back to a time

when the rich man had duties attending his wealth. The lord or baron was a petty king and had kingly responsibilities as well as power . . . . But the modern rush of steam engines, and the creation of an enormous class of wealthy folk living on stocks, have completely subverted the old order. It has let loose on society a horde of wolves![34]

Together with this upper English nostalgia went a more systematic, 'scientific', criticism of Victorian economy in the form of the epoch-making Marxist tradition. Between this backward-looking, pessimistic nostalgia and the forward-looking, optimistic, revolutionary communism was a whole host of ideas, responses, impulses, declamations that added up to the English socialist awakening. It formed a massive reaction to and a total rejection of the Victorian age. In one way or another all the early English radical organizations fell under the sway of this socialist awakening: the Christian Socialist movement, the Social Democratic Federation, the Socialist League, the Fabian Society, the Independent Labour Party, the British Socialist Party, the Communist Party, the Socialist Labour Party, the National Guilds League and many others. The Labour and Liberal Parties were the only parties of significance on the left that remained relatively immune.

This socialist awakening was part of a massive disenchantment with the condition of industrial Britain on the part, mainly, of upper, upper-middle and middle-class intellectuals. The social origins of the most powerful thinkers of the socialist awakening are interesting. Marx himself was no worker. Engels was a capitalist. Christian Socialists such as F. D. Maurice, Charles Kingsley and J. M. Ludlow had little relationship with industrial England. Maurice was a clergyman, Kingsley a novelist clergyman, Ludlow a barrister. Frederick Harrison, an early anti-capitalist, was also a barrister, Edward Carpenter a cleric. H. M. Hyndman (the Leader of the SDF) was a City of London businessman. H. H. Champion (SDF secretary) was an army officer. Belfort Bax was a journalist. William Morris (the founder of the Socialist League) was an entrepreneur. The Fabians have been described by Henry Pelling as a 'middle-class group who preferred drawing-room discussion to street-corner agitation'.[35] Edward Pease came from a well-off Quaker family. George Bernard Shaw was a journalist originally; his father described him as 'a gentleman without a gentleman's means . . . and so only a penniless snob'.[36] Beatrice Webb, perhaps the most intelligent and influential of all the Fabians, came from a prosperous Victorian family. She was the recipient of considerable inherited wealth from her capitalist father. In rebelling, she said of him: 'The central article of his political faith was a direct denial of democracy.'[37] Sidney

Webb came from the 'genteel fringe of the lower middle class'.[38] His father was an accountant. H. G. Wells was from a poor family, son of a lady's maid but his father did become a shopkeeper. Sydney Oliver came from a well-off Anglican family in Colchester – another son of the Anglican clergy. R. B. Haldane came from a 'good' Scots family and became a barrister. Norman and Jeanne Mackenzie's account of Fabian life is intriguing:

The ascetic high-mindedness of this group of Fabians was complemented by the bohemian style of Hubert and Edith Bland, whose home in south London became a meeting place for Fabians whose socialism was an expression of aesthetic revolt against the ugliness and moral conventions of Victorian society. At one pole, in Hampstead, there was an academic study circle; at the other, in Lee, there were parties, charades, musical evenings, enthusiasm for the arts and craft movement, and advanced ideas in the theatre.[39]

It cannot be surprising that 'socialism' came to be associated in the Edwardian mind with progressive, unorthodox, bohemian ideas – a kind of early twentieth-century counterculture. It would not go down well in Labour areas.

Others of those who associated with the Fabian Society and the SDF, and in leading positions, also came from nonmanual backgrounds. Edward Aveling was the son of a congregational minister; Annie Besant was raised by 'a benevolent but rigorously Evangelical spinster who made it her vocation to bring up impoverished girls of good family'.[40] The evangelicalism is seemingly ever-present. There is something to the thesis that the socialist generation was an offshoot of a more general extreme disaffected liberalism and evangelicalism that pervaded the English public schools during the Victorian era. In some of the early socialists there is present much of the moralism, romantic idealism and guilt of that generation.

Nor were the leading lights of inter-war socialism – Brailsford, Strachey, Tawney, Cripps, Laski, G. D. H. and

Margaret Cole – particularly tangential to industrial · England.

By and large most of the socialist thinkers and activists who form the corpus of the socialist generation have come from privileged backgrounds, often religious, and appear in some way or another to be engaged in some great rebellion against their background, their parents, the system, their country, their wealth or whatever. Bertrand Russell once asked Lytton Strachey, the historian, 'Why are you a Socialist? Did you hate your father, your childhood or your public school?'. Strachey is reported as replying: 'A bit of all three'.[41] George Orwell could write that: 'Except for a handful of 'self-made men' and Labour politicians, those who control our destinies are the products of about a dozen public schools and two universities.'[42] It is somewhat fitting that modern political leaders of the socialist generation, such as Michael Foot, Anthony Wedgwood-Benn and a good number of the members of the board of the *New Left Review*, should also be public school boys from privileged backgrounds.

Of course, amongst early English socialist thinkers and organizers there were some genuine, self-educated workers — Joseph Lane of the Socialist League, Tom Mann and F. W. Jowett of the ILP, and, above all, Keir Hardie. These, however, were exceptional men, as were the thousands of self-educated working-class socialists from South Wales, the North of England and Scotland. Aneurin Bevan comes in this tradition. Yet none of these were thinkers of the first rank, and most of their ideas were copies of the more eminent, privileged socialists. Whilst the socialist generation was constructing socialist thought, most intelligent working men were getting on with the job of building up the Labour movement – mainly in the trade unions – in isolation from socialist intellectualism.

The point of this sociological detour is not to attempt to devalue socialist ideas simply by virtue of their social origins; rather it is to make the point that the British socialist experience has largely been intellectual, not popular. This differs radically from the politics of continental Europe where various brands of socialism and communism have deep roots in some of the industrial areas. In Britain there have always been 'two nations' on the left – the socialist intelligentsia and the working people. They rarely met. Furthermore, the elite nature of the socialist generation can help to explain its inordinate influence, not only upon British political life but, through it, upon countless elite groups throughout the West and the Third World. Although the socialist generation could make little headway within the Labourist Labour movement it did make great strides where, arguably, it counted much more – at the centre, in London. Beatrice Webb felt 'assured that with the London School of Economics as the teaching body, the Fabian Society as the propagandist organization, the London County Council as an object lesson in electoral success, no young man or woman who is anxious to study or work in public affairs can fail to come under our influence'.[43] And many of them did so, with access to the publishing houses, universities, schools and the developing medium of television.

The question remains: with Labourism triumphant, socialism contained and communism anathema why did socialism survive within the Labour movement? – survive, what is more, to make such a strong and all-powerful comeback, in various distorted forms, by the late seventies?

The answer, I believe, lies in the imperative of tactics and the importance of rhetoric in internal Labour politics. First, tactics. As an intellectual construct (in all its various forms) socialism (as we have seen) retained and enhanced its power amongst elites and intellectuals, and the number of 'intellectuals' has grown within the Labour movement as society has developed. Also, 'socialism' had assumed the proportions of a quasi-utopian cure-all for poverty amongst a small though activist manual worker class who were attracted into the early Labour Party. These socialist intellectuals and workers were always present within the Labour movement, in the meetings, committees and corridors of local and regional party power. They were a powerful, though minority, faction. This faction, if Labour was to remain united (and its Labourist leaders always wanted it so to be), had to be appeased – at least to some extent. So the assertion of 'socialist belief' on the part of Labour leaders became a tactic for keeping the party united – often used in order to secure some non-socialist objective. Bevin, Gaitskell, Attlee and MacDonald all used the term at Labour meetings. So does Callaghan, sparingly. If Labour leaders could argue at meetings in halls packed with committed party activists that they too were 'socialists', then unnecessary aggravation could be avoided. How often was it heard from a Labour leader (Parliamentary, local government, trade union) whose every instinct was anti-socialist: 'I too am a socialist, you know', or '*My* kind of socialism means' (there would then follow a description of the world that had no socialist content whatsoever), or 'the left does not have a monopoly of socialist conviction' or some such contrivance. It became a safety mechanism against being called a secret Tory. Certainly Labour leaders were genuinely anti-Tory but only, like their voters, in a social and cultural sense.

Secondly, the importance of rhetoric in politics should not be undervalued. Every new interest group and its emerging set of leaders appears to need a governing philosophy, a theoretical position, that can distinguish them from their opponents. The Conservatives were the party of church and nation, the Liberals were the party of classical liberalism. After the leaders of labour discovered that the Liberals would not really tolerate a lasting association with the trade unions they turned to the only other seemingly viable philosophic package on offer. There was no intent to implement it or indeed to try and believe in it. Beer argues that: 'The adoption of socialism as an ideology was functional to this choice of political independence. If the party was to pursue power independently, it needed a set of beliefs and values distinguishing it from other parties.'[44] Yet, because of its constant evocation and its omnipresence at the level of rhetoric, 'socialism' came, over the years, to mean something rather more compelling. It assumed the proportions of a catch-all phrase for 'putting right' all that was wrong. It was by way of a plea for a better life. To be against it in the Labour movement was to be against a better life. Consequently no one was against it.

One further point should be added. 'Socialism' elevated the working class to a special role or, at the very least, constantly pitted itself on the side of the 'workers'. To the Labourists in the Labour movement this was irresistible. Labourists were naturally 'in favour' of the working class, the 'people from whence they came' — as Ray Gunter put it on leaving government office. For Labour's leaders and supporters 'socialism' rarely meant more than this assertion of the rights of the labour interest within the nation.

That is, until today.

CHAPTER 2

What Labour Is

A Labour Party member recently remarked, in one of those despairing moments when over-rich hyperbolical language takes over, that the modern Labour Party had become 'half corrupt, half communist'. Yet, over-rich hyperbole notwithstanding, there is a grain of tragic truth in this assessment. Two converging calamities have recently overtaken the politics of Labour. One is the degeneration of the Labourist tradition into careerism, the transmutation of the centre-right of the party from a political force with political values into a bureaucratic force with bureaucratic values, an officialdom uninterested in achievement, action, regeneration — in short into a political machine, an attempt at a kind of national 'Tammany Hall'. The other, far more dangerous, development is the arrival of the Labour left at a commanding position within the Labour movement apparatus outside Parliament. This Labour left owes little to early English socialism or indeed to Marxism. It has vulgarized both these traditions in its quest for power.

The bureaucratization of the Labour right has essentially disarmed it in its struggle with the left. Devoid of vision, philosophy or hope, mentally trapped within the comforting walls of the 'movement', it can do no other than yield up to the advancing left what remains of the organized labour interest within the land. Some keen spirits will break out, and

35

such a dash for freedom may well realign the centre-left and isolate the Labour left for a decade or two, perhaps even for much longer.

Labour may then assume the proportions of the French Communist Party: isolated electorally, ideologically rigid, pro-Eastern in foreign policy but retaining its power in society through its influence in strategically placed trade unions. In fact, by the late seventies Labour had arguably become such a party – only Britain's electoral system (which gave Labour an inordinate number of seats for its paltry 36 per cent of the vote) disguised its isolation. Labour, with a dwindling proletarian base, was no more than a trade union elite bureaucracy increasingly interpenetrated by various varieties of Marxist and communist sects.

The Labour bureaucracy

The Labour bureaucracy should be seen in total. Too often it is only perceived in its constituent parts, like the trade union leaderships or the Parliamentary Labour Party or local government Labour groups. In reality the Labour machine is an interconnected, relatively highly organized set of elites and senior people who meet regularly, are organized hierarchically and have their own system of punishments and rewards.

It is difficult to estimate exactly how many people are involved in the key decisions which the various top organizations of the Labour machine take. One complicating factor is that the same people often fill different positions: for instance, a Labour Member of Parliament as well as fulfilling the function of an elected representative and taking a senior position in the parliamentary machine can also be a member of the executive of a regional council of the Labour Party, a member of the National Executive of the Labour Party and a trade union official as well. Similarly a trade union general secretary can, as well as taking decisions in his own union, serve on the General Council of the TUC and its subcommittees and also ensure that his 'deputy' votes the right way on the NEC of the Labour Party. When Labour is in government Cabinet Ministers, governed by Cabinet collective responsibility, can also be members of the NEC; in this position they can act for some hours of the day as Cabinet Ministers and for others as party officials – often pursuing contradictory policies.

Even amidst all this complication the locus of power within the Labour movement essentially resides within the separate trade union executives. In reality it is these people who determine how the votes are cast both at the Trades Union Congress and at the Labour Party Conference – and most of the key decisions, sooner or later, flow from these votes. There can be no more than a few hundred people involved in these crucial decisions.

There are, in theory, over ten million votes cast at Trades Union Congresses every year and over six million at Labour Party Annual Conferences. These votes are cast in 'block' form. This means that a trade union delegation (often no more than twenty or so) can decide upon a course of action by a small majority (say eleven to nine) and then in the TUC or the Labour Conference they cast their 'block' vote (sometimes over a million) in that direction. Consequently a small number of trade union officials actually determine the outcome of ballots which seemingly represent millions of people.

Yet the circle is probably tighter than this even. On political matters, when trade union delegations come to decide how they vote at the Labour Conference, say on a motion about Namibia or defence, then the leaders of the delegations (usually general secretaries or Presidents of unions) have inordinate influence. The leaders of these delegations, simply because so many decisions need to be taken quickly, often bargain with leaders of other delegations or with the Prime Minister and Leader of the Party, and vote accordingly. Often in Labour conferences it comes down to who is actually holding 'the card' (representing thousands of votes) which goes into the ballot-box. There have been some celebrated occasions when the person holding 'the card' (in reality there are tickets for and against each motion) voted contrary to the views of the delegation, if expressed. This was a charge often made against Bill Carron, the right-wing President of the Engineering Union in the late fifties and early sixties. It was elevated into a standard jibe – 'Carron's law'. Hugh Scanlon (now Lord Scanlon), the left-wing President of the Engineers during the Wilson-Callaghan years, was also charged with placing the mammoth Engineering block vote in the wrong column following the 're-selection of MPs' debate at the Labour conference of 1978.

A closer examination of the mechanics of the Labour Party Conference will reveal the full extent of the power of these small groups. Just under 60 trade unions are affiliated to the Labour Party and between them in 1977 they cast 5,800,000 votes out of 6,500,000, the rest coming from constituency parties and affiliated socialist societies and the co-operative affliates.[1] Consequently the trade union delegates to the Conference essentially control it. This means control of policy and the determination of the complexion of the National Executive Committee. Yet it only takes just a small handful of the largest unions to garner a majority of the votes. Together about ten trade unions (which means ten trade union delegations) can absolutely ensure a majority vote. The illusion of mass democracy is created by the ponderous announcement of millions for and against; the reality is fixing and bargaining amongst a few dozen people.

The National Executive Committee is an essential cog in the Labour machine. Its composition is determined in much the same way as policy is determined – by a small group of trade union bosses. It has 29 members. Of these 18 are elected either directly or indirectly by the 'block' votes of the trade union delegations. Again, a small number of trade unionists therefore decide who shall and who shall not run the party executive. For an executive member to incur the displeasure of a senior trade union bureaucrat who can influence the wielding of thousands of votes for the trade union or women's section of the NEC is a serious matter.

The NEC not only determines policy in between Annual Conferences but also draws up policy documents. It sets the political tone for the whole party apparatus. It is also involved in the candidate selection process and can thereby help determine the future complexion of the Parliamentary Labour Party. It endorses all Labour candidates for Parliament and for the European Parliament, it has to approve of any attempt to unseat an existing MP, and it has powers to abolish and reform local constituency parties. It is not a body for an individual Member of Parliament to fall foul of. This NEC role in candidate selection or ousting is an indirect but crucial link between the trade unionists who 'elect' the NEC and the Labour Member of Parliament. It is far more important than the 'trade union sponsoring system' as a mechanism of party control over MPs. Take the case of Reg Prentice, who was ousted as Labour candidate for Newham North-East during the Wilson administration of 1974-6. Prentice was also a 'sponsored' candidate of the Transport Workers' Union and incurred their displeasure because of his outspoken public attacks upon the excesses of trade union power. Yet the withdrawal of his 'sponsorship' would not have lost him his constituency support and candidature. This de-selection of a candidate is decided by the constituency party and the NEC together. Once a constituency has decided to 'de-select' then it is up to the NEC to approve the decision. In previous years the NEC would not tolerate local activists overthrowing a sitting MP because of views held. In Prentice's case it did. So the NEC is the mechanism whereby power and sentiment within one wing of the Labour machine (the party apparatus controlled by the trade unions) percolates through to another (the parliamentary party). It is an important interconnection.

This indirect link between the trade union leaderships and the Parliamentary Labour Party is supplemented by other links. In most constituency parties, particularly those with

Labour MPs, local trade unions are affiliated organizations and wield votes at candidate selection and de-selection meetings. Trade union representatives on local constituency parties often, though not always, reflect the political views of their trade union bureaucracy. In any event this local affiliation mechanism can allow a major trade union to reach into any constituency in the country and, with diligent work and careful co-ordination, to have a considerable influence upon local politics and through that upon candidates and Members of Parliament. Trade union 'sponsorship', although not crucial in de-selection, can be important in the actual selection mechanism in the first place. For instance, when a constituency is looking for a candidate the fact that one of the nominees is 'sponsored' means that the constituency party will, if it selects this 'sponsored' person, have many of its election expenses paid by the union. This is a powerful inducement. Furthermore, there is increasing pressure exerted on 'sponsored' MPs by trade union leaders. They cannot exactly tell an MP how to vote – this runs counter to parliamentary privilege – but they can make their views known to the MP. He, or she, can be called to meetings by the 'sponsoring' trade union and 'union policy' will be 'explained'.

In fact, around the figure of the increasingly beleaguered and powerless Labour MP we can see at work all the interconnecting strands of the octupus-like Labour machine. The Labour Member of Parliament has to balance a number of, often conflicting, considerations and bend to a number of, often conflicting, pressures – that is, if he or she wishes to survive. First, there is the local constituency party. Second, there is the National Executive Committee. Third, there is the Parliamentary leadership, and the whips. Very rarely can a Labour Member of Parliament, even if so inclined, put the interests of his constituents ahead of the pressures and needs of the Labour machine. Any direct relationship between the MP and constituents, populist talk notwithstanding, is dangerous for career prospects. The wretched Labour MP is locked into a bureaucratic system which precludes him, except within the limits laid down by that system, from real politics – from articulating, promoting or leading popular opinion and interest. What is more, the sanctions of the machine are not only passive, denying promotion. They are active: a member of the bureaucracy who steps too far out of line, outside the carefully prescribed limits of action, can be expelled from the bureaucracy.

About the only really *political* freedom which a Member of Parliament has left is the decision he can make to join one of the two acceptable Parliamentary Labour Party factions – the Manifesto group for the centre-right MP or the Tribune group for the centre-left MP. Even this can cause great trouble back in the constituency, and this accounts for the significant number of 'secret' members of the Manifesto group (that is, Labour MPs who will generally support Manifesto group policies, even attend meetings, but who wish to keep their support private). Such an act – the decision to publicly associate with a parliamentary faction, particularly the Manifesto group – is a real political commitment of a kind, and represents about the only contemporary act of heroism that is left in Labour politics.

At the 1979 Labour Party Conference the noose of the party machine was more firmly tightened round the neck of the Labour MP. A constitutional amendment was passed by the party machine which made a re-selection procedure *mandatory* upon local party constituencies. This new procedure means that during the period of every Parliament every single Labour MP will *automatically* be vulnerable to being ousted as Labour candidate by his or her local party caucus. On the face of it this new procedure can be presented as an honest and simple extension of democracy; and the argument 'Why should an MP be protected from the judgement of the party workers every few years?' appears difficult to refute. In reality, though, the democratic argument for 're-selection' does not hold up. First, most of the polling evidence suggests that the average Labour MP more accurately reflects the views of

Labour voters than do the local Labour caucuses. Second, the Labour caucuses rarely properly represent the views of the Labour membership. The proponents of automatic re-selection of MPs, although in favour of MP 'accountability', are only in favour of 'accountability to the caucus', not to the membership as a whole or to the Labour voters. Consequently they set their faces like flint against the 'primary system', which would involve Labour voters in determining their candidates. The Labour left, who advocate re-selection, are in essence only inspired by the 'democracy of the committed' — the ideologues, the activists, those with the time and inclination to sit through endless hours of party business and *agit-prop*.

Even so, the Labour right has been seriously out-manoeuvred on the democracy issue. Every time the left have urged an extension of democracy, Labour leaders have simply and limply affirmed the 'independence of the PLP' or some such other rather unappealing contrivance. Instead the right should have 'taken on' the left on its own ground; it should have said that it was indeed concerned with democratic control but that democracy meant more than the caucus — it meant involving the working people as a whole. The Labour right should have been in the forefront of new thinking about primaries and referenda. In fact, the only right-wing group which has consistently urged such new thinking is the Social Democratic Alliance. When moderate MPs who fall foul of their local caucuses start arguing, for the first time, about primaries it sounds a shade inauthentic.

The Labour bureaucracy at lower levels is subject to the same kinds of restraint as Members of Parliament. Local and regional councillors are no more independent than their superiors in the hierarchy. A tight, implicit, disciplinary system exists from top to bottom of the Labour movement. Promotion from the lowest rung through the middle to the top has very little to do with popular appeal or with special flair or merit. Party orthodoxy, or faction orthodoxy, is the key. The particular skills that are rewarded in this environment are: hard, routine work for the party machine, an aptitude for acceptable stultified sloganeering, loyal service within a party faction of a not too adventurous kind, an ability to master procedure and detail. Of course, parties have always had a large bureaucratic element who put loyalty to the party organization above any other consideration, and who do not see politics in terms of the clash of ideas or interests; furthermore the British electoral system, devoid of primaries and other mechanisms which could loosen party control, does not encourage such independence. The point here, however, is that the bureaucratic element in 'politics' and the bureaucratic mentality have increased alongside the increasing bureaucratization of society. This may, in part, account for the all-pervasive dullness of modern party politicians and particularly for the 'greyness' and anonymity of many of Labour's senior political leaders. Bureaucracies produce placemen and 'hacks'.

The Labour machine reaches beyond the Labour Party. Loyal service to the machine can bring rewards other than those of promotion through the ranks of the party and movement bureaucracy itself. At local level party members can be nominated to a host of civic organizations, from the management boards of schools to the bench. At regional level the party apparatus nominates acceptable persons to water authorities, regional planning councils, arts authorities and the like. Many of these posts carry financial remuneration. At national level the top bureaucracy of the movement makes nominations to a variety of public positions and authorities; and the Labour bureaucracy, when it has control of the state, tends to increase the number of authorities to which appointments can be made. The possibility of securing such appointments, particularly the prestigious peerages and other honours, often ensures that an MP, coming to the end of his career and entertaining thoughts of rebellion, can be kept loyal. Previous ideological commitments against the second chamber are seemingly easily abandoned — as several left wing peers have demonstrated.

Then there is the whole 'Quango' network. These are the

'quasi-autonomous non-governmental organizations' which have proliferated as state power has grown, though attempts are being made to check this. The possibility of a 'Quango' appointment is a massive inducement to loyalty. The number of trade union bosses who have accepted positions in these quasi-governmental organizations is illuminating. In 1977 39 members of the TUC General Council held as many as 180 state-appointed positions between them. As well as the 'Quangos' there is the insidious growth of 'fringe bodies'. Paul Johnson has referred to these institutions as 'this sinister doppelganger of the Whitehall bureaucracy'[2] and has coined the term 'Fribs' to describe them in shorthand. It has been estimated that these bodies − the Manpower Services Commission, the Employment Services Agency, the Training Services Agency and the like − are spending well over half a billion pounds a year.[3] In 1975 171 chairmen of 'Fribs' were appointed by Labour ministers. In 1979 17 ministers had in their gift 18,000 paid and 25,000 unpaid appointments. Johnson has described this power and patronage as 'beyond the dreams of Whig avarice'.[4] The blending of party bureaucracy with state power and appointment has always been a troublesome concept; but the recent growth of 'Quangos' and 'Fribs', when added to the more traditional, and by comparison innocent, honours system gives to party bureaucracy a massive accretion of power which can help to induce loyalty and obedience in its members still further. And these inducements are available to a new group of leaders should they be able to control the party and then the state. This all-pervasive system of patronage at the top of political life can be used to squeeze pockets of ideological resistance both out of the party and eventually out of the state and society.

As with all bureaucratic organisms the Labour movement has become expansionist, privileged and corrupt. First, expansionism. The Labour machine seeks *lebensraum*. In order to make itself more secure as an organization within society the party and movement seeks, almost unconsciously, to provide itself with more and more weapons with which to reinforce its existence. And it is usually to the state that it turns to secure these further instruments. We have already seen how the patronage over Quangos and Fribs helps. Also, the Labour NEC has supported the notion of state funding for political parties. This conception, if ever passed into legislation, will secure for the Labour bureaucracy access to public funds in a more direct and obvious way than it can command at the moment. Also, the trade union bureaucracies have sought, and achieved through legislation, specific legal provisions which entrench *existing* trade union leaderships in power over working people. Closed-shop legislation is sought by the trade union bureaucracy on the grounds that without it an unfair advantage would lie with the employer as against the employee. Yet, what in effect it does is to make it impossible for workers who are dissatisfied with their union bureaucracies to form new unions which might more properly represent them in negotiations. An employee is essentially tied to his *existing* union as his job depends upon his continuing membership. Any attempt by workers to break-out and set up *new* unions is virtually impossible — and this kind of activity would, naturally, threaten the very existence of the present trade union bureaucracies. Earlier campaigns for trade union rights were motivated by the desire to remove legal obstacles to trade union organization. Although this remains the loudly proclaimed purpose of those who continue to talk of 'trade union rights' the reality is a different motivation: the need to entrench the power of *existing* unions over their members.

As well as using state power to entrench and expand its position the Labour machine can now call in aid the power and influence of a new class in society, one that it has helped to create in the first place. This 'new class' must ultimately defend and protect the Labour machine because its very existence is dependent upon it. Irving Kristol, in the context of surveying the changing sociological landscape of the

United States, has coined this term 'new class' to describe what he sees as an emerging and domineering new group which, amongst other things, is set against the American capitalist and business system and culture. He suggests that this new class 'consists of a goodly proportion of those college-educated people whose skills and vocations proliferate in a post-industrial society'.[5] Kristol lists the components of this new class as scientists, teachers, educational administrators, journalists and others in the communications industry, psychologists, social workers, those lawyers and doctors who make their careers in the expanding public sector, city planners, the staffs of the larger foundations, and the upper levels of the government bureaucracy.

In Britain too we can see the emerging contours of a similar new class. Indeed, as Britain (arguably) has entered the post-industrial age earlier than the United States, and has a larger public sector, our new class should, at least theoretically, be more maturely embedded in our national life than is the case on the other side of the Atlantic. Certainly we share with the United States and most other democratic mass capitalist societies a large educated public-sector class whose members in varying degrees disdain 'bourgeois' values, are largely disenchanted with the system and culture, and in being so separate themselves from the working people who, broadly, still adhere to them. Also, as Britain's business community is less productive, less secure, and accorded less status than the American our own 'new class' is more self-confident, seemingly better armed with more persuasive arguments, and possessed of a greater sense of future conquest. Furthermore, the American new class is less radically set against the system than the British. In the United States the new class is essentially 'liberal'. Its values and underlying assumptions are quintessentially American – it is not really against the system but rather against the excesses of the system (corruption, intimidatingly large corporate power, rampant commercialism), particularly when they are perceived to lead to aggregations of power which threaten individualism, political freedom and civil liberties. In Britain, by contrast, our new class is more collectivist in its assumptions, less liberal at the level of fundamentals. Amongst our teachers, educational administrators, social workers, city planners and government bureaucrats there is a socialist stratum which is virtually absent amongst their equivalents in the United States. This stratum is not necessarily self-consciously socialist, nor would some of its members describe themselves as such – although an increasing number now do so. Yet, particularly at the younger level of the new class, discontents are increasingly expressed in socialist terms and by socialist-sloganized thinking.

This new public-sector class does more than simply share the rhetoric of socialism with the Labour machine. It shares an interest. Throughout this educated public-sector class there are no doubt many thousands who neither vote Labour nor share socialist assumptions. Yet as the Labour machine is increasingly perceived as the major political protector of the public sector then, ineluctably, it will be seen as the guarantor of their own employment and status. Status is not a great concern for most of the working people who are employed in, or dependent upon, the state sector; but here too the Labour machine may come to be seen as a guarantor of livelihood. Calculations are difficult to make but, if dependants are included, then probably more than half of the entire population of the country is now dependent, in one way or another, upon state expenditure. Of course there are many millions of working people in, or dependent upon, the state sector who remain suspicious of all-pervasive state power or who see that too large a state will be unproductive for the country as a whole. But there are no doubt many in the Labour machine who see these residual instincts amongst the public fading away, forming a kind of historic memory of an old economic system which will be expunged as society becomes more bureaucratized and bureaucracy becomes both more acceptable and more necessary. The Labour machine, and the socialists within it, could shortly be in a position where it alone can guarantee the educated public sector (the new class) the status it desires and the working people the jobs they need.

Of course both the Labour machine and the new class continue to justify high public expenditure in terms of welfare and compassion; and a large state sector is promulgated in terms of redressing the balance within society as between the rich and the not-so-rich. But a large public sector is also in the interests of the new class which leads and administers it. Hence, there emerges a convenient convergence between the legitimate needs of welfare on the one hand and the necessary power base for the new class and the Labour machine on the other. To construct a society in which a sizeable public sector need not spawn an overweening state governing class is not an unattainable goal. With high technology, slim-line administrative machinery can now easily administer a not unsubstantial public sector.

The Labour machine also has powerful supporters in the private sector. Centres of corporate power in the private sector are extremely sensitive to trends and opinions within the Labour machine — whether it is in or out of power. Private businessmen also support the machine, some out of traditional left convictions, but some to gain power and influence and status. The host of businessmen and financiers who associated themselves, in varying ways, with the Labour Party during the Premiership and Leadership of Harold Wilson, and were in receipt of various honours, is legendary. Yet few senior figures in the Labour machine, left or right, have seen fit to systematically denounce this incestuous relationship between private corporate interests and the Labour bureaucracy.

Most of the media remain privately owned and they are, broadly, hostile to the Labour machine. But the Labour machine, particularly when in office, can minimize hostility by a powerful armoury of weapons. Publishers and editors can be wooed and cajoled. Government advertising can be selectively handled. Sources of information can be cut off. Individual journalists can be favoured or punished by the state machine upon which they depend for information. Politicians and trade union leaders no longer seem to be able to take press criticisms in their stride. Many top figures are constantly writing to, or phoning, publishers and editors to complain about criticisms made of them. This is a source of pressure which although normally resisted can leave its mark over the years in more deferential and circumspect reporting and comment.

Even when the Labour machine is not in office it can induce support within the media. A notoriously pliant group of journalists, with some very impressive exceptions, are the industrial correspondents who cover trade union affairs. Keen, quite naturally, to maintain their trade union sources, they tend to give minimal offence to top trade union bosses. Consequently many of the abuses by union officialdom of their members' subscriptions (expense account extravagances, special mortgage repayments, indefensible trips abroad, unnecessary perks, over-plush head offices) rarely get reported and the standard, popular, impression that it is only 'management' that is excessive in its corporate life-style maintains its force. The point here is not to evoke puritan rage at quite normal human activity; rather it is to display the hypocrisy of many trade union leaders in their constant and persistent claim to be on the side of the 'poor', the 'under-privileged' and the 'workers'. Throughout the top corridors of trade union power there is a rich seam of hypocrisy to expose, if ever investigatory journalism should come to Britain.

Therefore there exists a number of powerful elites and individuals who both feed off the Labour machine and in return lend it support. There is a nexus of interest between the Labour machine, large parts of the new class in the public sector, journalists and businessmen that has little to do with shared political conviction but a lot to do with subtle, unspoken, unformulated agreements about power, status and wealth. No doubt there is conviction too; but this motive for supporting the Labour machine by those not directly involved in it must be less widespread than at any time in the Labour movement's history.

Of course the Labour machine is itself changed by the elites which support it or join it. It is not as if there remains intact an autonomous Labour political and industrial machine, manned only by trade union leaders and Labour parliamentarians, which operates completely independently. The Labour machine is not hermetically sealed off from the rest of the nation, it is not untouched by social change. For instance, the new class, particularly many of its most articulate and active members, have already become part of the Labour machine, mainly at lower and middle levels. As we shall see later (in Chapter 4) the Labour Party at local level is declining and its traditional members are being supplanted by 'new class' types. As the new class moves in on the Labour machine at local level Labour becomes further detached from its roots amongst the manual workers and their families.

Bureaucratic politics entrenches privilege. Special advantages and benefits are secured by those who run a bureaucracy. In the most extreme bureaucratic society, possibly the Soviet Union, formal privileges exist – such as special stores set aside for party members. Entry into this particular party state bureaucracy is not determined by heredity or merit or wealth or valour but rather by *political* tests. In Britain, as in most other Western countries, a multiplicity of routes to privilege exist – heredity (still), intellectual accomplishment, wealth, educational background (particularly certain schools and universities), political background, trade union connections and so on. But as Britain becomes more bureaucratized, and the incestuous relationship between party and state builds up, then the purely *political* route to privilege expands and forces out the other routes. By political route here, though, I mean *party-political*. The Labour movement has traditionally been a mechanism for the leaders of working people to advance themselves, and in a society in which other avenues of advance were blocked the Labour Party enabled many talented people to play their full part in the nation's affairs. The problem now though is that the Labour machine, partly through its own volition, partly as a result of the sheer momentum of bureaucratic hegemony, may soon be in the position where it is the *sole* route to power and influence, the sole source of privilege.

Furthermore, there seems to be little objection on the part of the leaders of Labour to the 'life-styles' of the 'establishment' which many of them have criticized for most of their political life, garnering many votes as a result. Apart from the good living that attaches simply to the political state offices they hold, it is not unusual for a Labour Cabinet Minister to own two or more rather grand homes. Senior Labour figures often leave surprisingly large sums in their wills; and they often educate their children at expensive private schools. The point here is not the hypocrisy involved, although hypocrisy is not the most alluring of attributes (even today). Nor is the point the need for frugality on the part of politicians, although a degree of frugality is helpful in ensuring respect for public life and public officials. Rather, it is that many Labour leaders exhibit a decided taste for those ways of living that defined 'ruling classes' in the past. There can be little objection, therefore, to class life or a class system *as such*: the objection can only be to a class system based upon a multiplicity of sources, upon wealth or merit or heredity. A *political* derivation is not opposed.

The Labour machine, as (and because) it becomes less interested in ideas, more bureaucratic and more enmeshed with state power at national and local level, is not untainted by corruption. Labour's historic association with nonconformity gave it a puritan and responsible outlook on life, particularly public life. Yet this tradition is withering. In areas of the country where Labour control of local authorities goes unchallenged for decades on end, where there is effectively 'one-party rule' and an assumption that such 'one-party rule' will continue, the temptation is ever present to abuse public office for personal gain. Following the disclosures surrounding the Poulson inquiry and the subsequent conviction of senior Labour figures in the North-East, radical commentators, usually Trotskyites, tended, unfairly, to associate corruption in public life with 'right-wing' Labour councils; and this theme was developed in the intra-party propaganda battle. Yet it is unconvincing to suggest that corruption has any particular ideological or factional basis to it. It appears, rather, to be the product of unchallenged Labour rule and in the North-East it is simply an historical accident that the Labour right has been in control. Furthermore, corruption – and the possibilities for corruption – is always a feature of single-party dominance; and is widespread in the single-party socialist nations, the 'people's democracies' which so many on the extreme left look to for inspiration.

By far the worst consequence of the bureaucratization of Labour is its effect upon the Labour right. Whatever the modern Labour right is or is not it is not totalitarian by inclination, nor even incipiently so. A Labour movement, even one increasingly enmeshed with the state, that is run by Labourist placemen is certainly not attractive; but neither is it lethal. Democratic politics and political and civil liberties are not threatened by an officialdom that is simply content to enjoy the fruits of office that the Labour movement might put in its way, that possesses some kind of native restraint in the use of power, and essentially wants to work *for ever* within a pluralistic political and economic system and a two-party framework – owing some kind of dual loyalty (both to the Labour interest and to some notion of a wider national interest) in the political world. The tragedy of the Labour right is not that they pose a threat to freedoms but that they have, apparently, turned into empty cynics.

It is the dynamics within the Labour bureaucracy that

poses the threat. The scene over the next few years is set for a two-stage development: first, the progressive takeover of the Labour machine by the left and the extreme left; and secondly, a further aggregation of power by that machine as it seeks to establish its hegemony over British society and to expunge other centres of political power.

The problem is the transitory nature of the Labour right within the Labour machine. Labour's centre-right politicians are transitory because they possess no defences against the advancing left. Unlike the left they are unable to inspire loyalty and support from articulate, politically active groups. John Lloyd has recently asked of social democracy: 'How strong an edifice was it, how good was it at mobilising cadres in its defence if ever attacked?'[6] The answer is: 'not very'. The heirs of Labourism, the 'Tammany Hall' right, whether in the unions or in the Parliamentary Labour Party are no longer politicians in the traditional sense of the term. They are without traditional political gifts and skills. They cannot use language either to inspire or simply to communicate effectively. They display only a minimal understanding of, or interest in, history. They are unable thereby to draw upon the past, even their own Labour history, in order to explain the present or exhort properly for the future. The world of political ideas, ethical enquiry and reflection, is alien to them. So is the world of political action; they will not and cannot take risks. Hence, the bone-cracking dullness of their speeches, their inability to talk about anything other than economics (rather in the manner of a chairman of a board of directors), their incapacity to tap deep feelings within the community, to command authority, awe or respect. Labour's modern bureaucracy can throw up, from within its higher or middle ranks, no political thinkers of the calibre of Crosland or Strachey, no polemicists like Crossman or the earlier Foot, no 'characters' like George Brown, no romantic figures like Aneurin Bevan, certainly no 'saints' like Fenner Brockway. The colour has drained out of the politics of Labour. Eloquence has declined in measure with the decline in commitment. All is dull and grey and bureaucratic.

This narrowing process incapacitates the Labour machine man in his dealings with a troubled and changing world. It is hardly the most suitable preparation for either recognizing change, evaluating it, promoting it or resisting it. The modern social democrat bureaucrat appears to see his function as administering 'what is'. But, as 'what is' is constantly changing, the Labour bureaucrat becomes but a cork on the water, moved about by tides over which he has no control.

This emptiness is compounded by a monumental complacency, the most insidious characteristic of the worldlywise social democrat who runs contemporary Britain. The modern social democrat attempts to turn his powerlessness into a virtue. For instance, Dr David Owen, whilst Foreign Secretary, actually went as far as to *proselytize* on the merits of compromise. In a sermon at St Andrew's Church in Plymouth in the spring of 1978 he devoted a whole address to a ringing declaration of pride in the various compromises he had had to make in conducting the foreign policy of the government. He stated that: 'I do not underrate the value at times of the use of expedience or expediency', and he warned of the 'dangers of dogma, rigidity, enforced order and regimentation'. All acceptable nostrums. Yet he went on to declare that: 'Compromise, far from being the enemy of morality, is its friend.' The problem with this formulation is not that it chides those who are never willing to compromise – only impossible zealots could take that position. Rather, Owen, by elevating compromise almost into a virtue in itself, sends a terrifying message to his opponents (of whom there are many, both in the Labour Party and in the world). That message, put starkly, is that they can always win if they only push hard enough. Since Owen has announced, *in advance* of any political clash, that compromise is morality's friend, his enemies can but take comfort in the ease with which he will abandon his position. Dr Owen, in this sense, is virtually inviting defeat because he has prepared the moral grounds for such a defeat ahead of time by sanctifying compromise as morality. In other words, he will be able to live with himself as he compromises his, and other people's, position away. In fact, to elevate compromise to a moral precept is probably not to hold to any position at all. Only the style of operations counts; and the style is compromise. The importance of this address in Plymouth lies in the glimpse that it gives us into the social democratic mind as it existed in the late seventies: there is, no longer, anything worth fighting for; political wisdom resides in a politically and morally neutral statecraft. Yet those who adopt this 'philosophy' are not doing it for themselves, as private persons. That would be another matter. They are representing nations or political traditions within parties or whatever. This abdication is being made *on behalf of others* whose lives are affected by decisions taken by politicians.

Such an approach to politics often provokes charges of cowardice. This accusation was made most forcefully by Alexander Solzhenitsyn in his 1978 Commencement Day address at Harvard University. In a passage that was obviously aimed at the totality of the Western intellectual and political class − but would seemingly apply quite aptly to the Western foreign policy establishment of the late seventies − he argued that the lack of 'civil courage' was the most important feature of the character of modern leadership. Yet I believe that this charge, certainly widely supported, misses the mark. Lack of courage is obviously a feature of political life; but this has probably always been the case. What we have today in the West is, arguably, something quite new − the replacement of traditional cowardice by bureaucratic emptiness, by the lack of all convictions, values, standards, morality, commitment (either to groups of people or abstract ideas). One cannot be a coward if one holds nothing to be true.

Such an attitude to compromise, as exhibited by Dr Owen, might help explain why the Labour left had advanced so far within the Labour machine. All that they had to do was to keep pushing at a door held open for them by the moderates. The Labour left would compromise too; but always on ground further to the left than their previous compromise.

The dynamics of the politics of Labour are such that the remnants of the social democratic generation, atrophied into bureaucracy, will inevitably give way within the Labour movement to a more ideological, and more dangerous, political class that comes out of a wholly different political tradition. Towards the end of the 1970s the scene was set for the emergence of the communist generation as controlling partners in the Labour movement – and for the push towards the communist society.

The communist generation

> Do you think that we can become overnight the pacifists, unilateralists and fellow travellers that other people are?
>
> Hugh Gaitskell,
> Leader of the Labour Party,
> 1960 Annual Conference

By the late 1970s it was no longer unfashionable or considered eccentric to suggest that the Labour party apparatus outside Parliament had undergone a profound change, had been taken over by what was often loosely referred to as 'the left'. Although this process of change had obviously been proceeding apace throughout the seventies the standard view at the mid-point of the decade was similar to that propounded by Alan Watkins in an article in the *New Statesman* in October 1974, entitled 'The myth of the left wing takeover'. The title speaks for itself but the general thesis was that hardly any significant change had occurred in the power balance of the party since 1945, or indeed in politics generally. Lord George-Brown, as early as 1972, had given *his* view:

We have been taken over . . . by a collection of people who call themselves activists . . . they are for the most part people who do not believe in our social democratic outlook . . . . In each case the constituency party consists of a half-dozen of the 'extremists' who have moved in. And these fellows have now captured control of the Labour movement at every level.[7]

But such notions, even from those who knew the Labour movement inside out, were generally dismissed as exaggerated and over-blown.

Such complacency was not to be rewarded by events. As the seventies rolled on it became more and more obvious that something fairly dramatic had indeed happened to the Labour Party. Most of the top social democrats had fled, *Labour's Programme, 1976* had been published, Michael Foot had come within a whisker of Downing Street, Andrew Bevan had been ensconced in Transport House as National Youth Officer, moderate MPs had been ousted from their candidatures, party-to-party relations had been established between Labour and Eastern-bloc Communist parties, more moderates were removed from the NEC every year, the TUC had adopted an 'alternative strategy' for dealing with Britain's economic problems which was remarkably similar to that of the Tribune group. Certainly *something* had been happening in the Labour Party and movement. But then a new consensus of London-based opinion settled down, this time rather more uneasily: certainly Labour had changed somewhat, the 'left' had made advances but they posed no serious threat to the democratic system. Previously, trends within the Labour Party had been misread; now the nature of the Labour left was being misread.

A very important day in the history of the politics of Labour was 15 December 1976. On that day the full dimension of Labour's transformation became apparent. The issue was a seemingly insignificant one, although it was attended by some considerable press publicity – the National Executive Committee of the Labour Party met to decide whether to confirm the appointment of Andrew Bevan as National Youth Officer of the party. The scene was set for a major clash between the then Prime Minister, James Callaghan, and his Cabinet subordinate, Anthony Wedgwood-Benn. Callaghan, who normally tried to avoid open clashes with the NEC, had personally intervened in the issue of Bevan's appointment; he publicly, as Prime Minister and Leader of the party, asked the NEC not to appoint Bevan. But Wedgwood-Benn decided to make this appointment a major issue of principle. He decided to lead the forces on the NEC who were not prepared to accept the Prime Minister's intervention, and he did so, as a Cabinet Minister, in the most dramatic and public way. In effect he challenged Callaghan by issuing a statement to his Executive colleagues which was published in full in the *Guardian* two days before the crucial meeting. It was a long, detailed, and powerfully argued statement which supported Andrew Bevan's appointment, repudiated the Prime Minister's attitude, and did so on the issue of the relevance of Marxism as a 'legitimate stream of thought' within the Labour Party. Both Callaghan and Benn attended the meeting, which amounted to a serious showdown between what forces the traditional social democrats and Labourists could muster and the newly entrenched forces of left Labour. Benn won, Callaghan lost. Andrew Bevan was appointed.

In a sense the left were fighting on their weakest ground. It was not an argument about policy; it was an argument about theory, about the role and relevance of Marxism to a party which had hitherto not been associated in the public mind with anything more than the mildest form of social democracy. It was a sign of the power and confidence of the left that they decided to take Callaghan on, and to beat him, on this issue.

Benn's own theoretical position is confused. He made his name over the issue of heredity when he resigned his peerage in the fifties and stood for Parliament; he was then for many years a centrist in party terms, supporting amongst other things Britain's application to join the Common Market; in the first and second Wilson governments he was mainly concerned with issues of technology; he then began developing a political position based upon ideas outlined in a Fabian tract of 1970 entitled *The new politics: a socialist reconnaissance*, which flirted with notions of participatory politics. In this pamphlet Benn called for the emergence of a 'new citizen' who would be familiar with 'alternative analyses of events – capitalist, Marxist, socialist, Freudian, Christian, Maoist and Buddhist'.[8] None of this, however, is quite the point. Benn had been emerging as the leader, together with Michael Foot, of left Labour, and his challenge to Callaghan over the Andrew Bevan appointment, together with his subsequent challenges, was a sign of his willingness to put himself at the head of the now dominant left faction in the NEC and to take a general political line that was to their liking. Benn himself is not a Marxist but many of his left supporters both in Parliament and on the NEC are; and the governing faction on the NEC demanded the Andrew Bevan appointment. Benn acceded.

Bevan is a supporter of the 'Militant' tendency within the Labour Party Young Socialists. This is a group within the Labour Party organized around the paper *Militant*, which describes itself as the 'Marxist Paper for Labour and Youth'. Its ideological position is somewhat confused and confusing but it embraces a general predeliction for Marxism and Leninism. Andrew Bevan himself is an avowed Marxist, but he is also rather more. He supports the Leninist and Trotskyite tradition as well. This in itself is uninteresting. Labour has usually carried within its younger ranks those who feel an attraction for all kinds of socialist theory and these philosophies are usually held not as part of a general, educated, view of the world but rather as a rebellion against the Labour establishment. However, Bevan was to be appointed National Youth Officer and his views became a great issue of moment within the party, the basis of the trial of strength between left and right.

Thus there was established within the Labour Party, within

its very headquarters, a legitimate and legitimized Marxist, Leninist, Trotskyist 'stream' of thinking. This kind of politics went much further than the application of various kinds of Marxist analysis and theory to British society and development. The left had always flirted with aspects of the more general Marxist analysis. The SDF had been at the original 1900 conference which set up the party but had withdrawn soon after. Herbert Morrison himself was given to extolling a 'revolutionary Marxist line' in his early days in the Labour movement, although it should be added that this was well before the 1917 revolution when Marxism took on a wholly different connotation. Michael Foot recounts, in his biography of Aneurin Bevan, a dinner he attended with Bevan in Soho in 1952. In this rather unproletarian environment Bevan, according to Foot, 'drank a toast to the great man's memory and there was no sign then — or at any other time, for that matter, in my knowledge of him — that Bevan wished to disown his debt to Marxism, so long, of course, as the doctrine was undogmatically interpreted'.[9] This may indeed have been Bevan's view but it was not one that he chose to repeat in public. Nor did any of his colleagues who led the Labour left. Nor do those who lead the Labour left today tend to broadcast such views. This, no doubt, is for sensible, practical political reasons to do with the continuing British distaste for Marxism.

The Andrew Bevan appointment, however, involved much more than the relevance of Marxism to the Labour Party. By endorsing Bevan the NEC reached beyond Marxism to endorse, implicitly at any rate, Leninism and Trotskyism as well. Benn, in his statement published in the *Guardian*, quoted approvingly from Bevan himself who declared at the time of the great party row:

We describe ourselves as Marxists, we proudly describe ourselves as Marxists, and what we mean by that [is that] we stand on the traditions of Marx and Engels, Lenin and Trotsky, but not treating their ideas as dogma, you know, but as a method and a way of explaining events, of putting forward a programme that can really show the way forward for the Labour Party.[10]

The 'we' Andrew Bevan was referring to was the 'Militant' tendency within the Labour Party Young Socialists. This group, along with Bevan, was continually supported and endorsed by Labour's NEC.

Andrew Bevan and the Labour Party Young Socialists believe in a kind of romanticized Bolshevism as a model for Britain. The Labour Party Young Socialists, with NEC approval and access to Labour Party funds, published a pamphlet on the occasion of the 60th anniversary of the Bolshevik revolution. It argued that the Bolshevik revolution represented for socialists 'the greatest event in human history', it scorned the Mensheviks for seeing it as 'their duty to play second fiddle to the liberal capitalist and peasant parties', it rejected Stalinist terror and bureaucracy (this created a 'deformed workers' state' in the Soviet Union), but it set its present political position firmly within the Leninist and Trotskyite tradition.[11] Indeed the LPYS view of the Soviet Union is somewhat more sceptical than those of senior figures on the NEC, such as Mr Alex Kitson. The precise application the principles of Bolshevism are supposed to have to modern Britain are spelt out with charming clarity. The LPYS propose the nationalization of the 220 largest firms, banks and insurance companies 'with compensation paid only on the basis of need', a national plan of production drawn up by the trade unions and the Labour Party, the abolition of the House of Lords, the abolition of the monarchy, the nationalization of the press industry under workers' control and management, and control 'by the Labour movement of the radio and TV'.[12]

In a sense the decision to appoint Andrew Bevan, and the public defeat which it involved for Callaghan, was much more than a victory by the Labour left, albeit on a crucial point of theology, over the right. It effectively sent out a message of support to all the young Trotskyites working in the constituencies: the NEC not only 'tolerated' their views but was sympathetic to them and was willing to fight for them. As far as the future development of the party was concerned it certainly appeared that the NEC shared more in common with the young Trotskyites than they did with the then Prime Minister. This could have been suspected before December 1976. The NEC had supported local extremist groups against Reg Prentice in the battle of Newham North-East; and it had shelved a report by its own regional organizer, Reg Underhill, about infiltration into the Labour Party by various revolutionary socialist groups. This report, presented to the NEC in October 1975,[12] documented in detail the various 'entryist' activities of Trotskyite organizations. No action was taken. The Bevan decision, probably because Callaghan made an issue out of it, settled the question of the NEC's political and strategic position beyond doubt.

The National Executive Committee is where real power within the Labour Party apparatus resides; and it is where a second, largely non-Trotskyite, strand of Labour Marxism-Leninism is to be found in surprising breadth and depth. The governing faction on the NEC is decidedly older than the youthful Trotskyites in the constituencies. They are much more realistic too. Their predispositions are, largely, for structured, serious leftism; 'the workers' to them, are not particularly romantic figures or linked by supranational bonds to some international class communion. The profound socialist transformation that NEC socialism seeks will come about solely through the power of the Labour movement and through trade union power, by disciplined and carefully planned strategy. In short, the governing faction within the NEC is more practical, more political and more likely to be successful than the young Trotskyites.

Unlike the young Trotskyites none of them are newcomers to Labour politics. The controlling group, or groups, on the NEC have been active in Labour politics for most of their political lives – as trade unionists, local councillors or MPs. This governing faction is partly composed of the seasoned political fighters of the left – right conflicts of the fifties and early sixties. Then they were in a decided minority. For many years left Labour figures like Frank Allaun, Lena Jeger and Ian Mikardo had fought a lonely battle, an isolated rearguard action against the Gaitskellite majority. But by the mid-seventies this 'left' caucus had dramatically expanded; by the late seventies it was in full control, so much so that at the 1978 Annual Conference Ian Mikardo could be removed from the NEC at the same time as its complexion was getting even more left-wing. Over the years Allaun and Mikardo were to be joined by Norman Atkinson (as Party Treasurer), Eric Heffer, Joan Maynard, Judith Hart, Renée Short, Joan Lestor, Joan Richardson, Alex Kitson, Emlyn Williams, Nick Bradley, Neil Kinnock, Denis Skinner and Les Huckfield – many of whom replaced defeated moderates like Denis Healey, John Cartwright and Jack Ashley. The left also had an accretion of support from a new generation of trade unionists who succeeded the Labourist figures who so dominated the executive in the fifties. If one adds to this left component on the NEC those figures such as Anthony Wedgewood-Benn and Michael Foot, who when Cabinet responsibilities allowed them usually sided with the hard left, then the Labour right on the NEC looks small, pitiful and isolated. On issue after issue as the seventies developed this left faction carried the day against both Wilson and Callaghan.

To give an accurate political designation to the governing majority on Labour's NEC is somewhat hazardous. They are not 'all of a piece' either politically or philosophically. As with all parties and factions the Labour left is a coalition. Yet a goodly number of NEC left-wingers would describe themselves as Marxists. Irrespective, though, of their philosophical predelictions – and in high politics precise ideological affinities are usually obscure and obscured, undisclosed, implicit or incoherent – the governing majority on Labour's

NEC (in its actions, statements and policies) is difficult to distinguish from the Marxist-Leninist 'Eurocommunist' parties of southern Europe. Making a rough and ready comparison, Labour's NEC probably falls somewhere between the Italian Communist party to its right and the French Communist party to its left.

Eric Heffer, who by today's NEC standards is a 'moderate', has suggested that 'a new regenerated European democratic socialist movement could emerge' out of increased exchanges between the Labour Party and the Communist parties of southern Europe. Indeed, he argued that 'the future of a civilized Europe may well depend on it'.[14] So standard is this kind of statement from a Labour leader that commentators no longer find it particularly discordant. Nor, indeed, is it. Even though Labour remains formally in the 'Socialist International' − the grouping of social democratic parties of the world − it invites as 'observers' to its conferences representatives of the 'Eurocommunist' parties; in 1977 Santiago Carrillo (leader of the Spanish Communists) and Giorgio Napolitano (economics spokesman of the Italian Communists) turned up. The issue today is whether the Labour NEC, if it were to achieve power, would represent more of a break with the existing economic and political system in Britain than would the 'Eurocommunist' parties in their countries. Certainly Labour (as we shall see later in the chapter) is far less critical of the Soviet Union than are most of the 'Eurocommunist' parties.

Of course at the level of official doctrine the European Communist parties are *avowedly* Marxist-Leninist. Labour is not. However, this may not reflect the aggregate of views of the majority of the left on the NEC; but rather the unpopular nature of this philosophic term amongst the general British public, the immense political difficulties of securing any fundamental change in official, constitutional, party terminology, and a general, rather British, reluctance to be very rigorous about ideas. In any event, 'Socialism', the official doctrine of the Labour party, is, in the present

political climate of Western Europe, virtually interchange-
able with the more liberal interpretations of
Marxism/Leninism. Yet, even at the level of party doctrine
some of the 'Eurocommunist' parties (particularly the
Spanish and Italian) appear more 'revisionist' than the
Labour left. The Italians and Spanish, probably in part for
public consumption, seem to be giving continual thought to
up-dating and refining their doctrines, to reaching some kind
of *modus vivendi* between the revolutionary tradition and the
liberal, democratic society of which they are also a part. By
contrast the Labour left seem altogether more conservative,
intransigent, traditional and narrow-minded, more devoted
than their European counterparts to encrusted slogans that
pass for theory.

On policy matters of a domestic and economic nature the
Labour left poses a far greater threat to the mixed economy
than does the Italian Communist party – at least in the short
run. The Italians, no doubt as part of their tactical search for
a political coalition with the Christian Democrats (the idea of
the 'historic compromise'), have even gone so far as to
promise some denationalisations in their programme. This
kind of proposal is, in Britain, usually associated with the
classical liberal wing of the Conservative party.
Denationalisation of *anything at all* is anathema to the
Labour left and unacceptable to the Labour 'moderates'.
Also, the Italians regularly refer to the public sector as 'over-
blown' and public expenditure as 'high enough'. There is also
a general inclination on their part of criticize the excesses and
inefficiency of bureaucracy. The Labour left, on the other
hand, seem unable to depart from traditional impulses to
seek greater and greater expansion of the public sector,
usually in the most statist and bureaucratic manner.
Naturally, the Italian Communists may simply be engaging in
some electoral trimming which the Labour left have no need
of – Labour's 'moderates' serve as *their* 'human face' to the
electors; yet it must remain of some intriguing significance
that a major Communist party can appear to be less of a

threat to the private/public balance in the economy than an avowedly democratic socialist one.

The one area where Labour continues to distinguish itself from the Communist parties of southern Europe is in the matter of internal party organization. All of the 'Eurocommunist' parties operate the Leninist organizational model of 'democratic centralism'. Essentially, this system ensures that party decisions are made at the very top of the apparatus and thence transmitted downwards. Certainly there is room for considerable discussion amongst party members but not for organized, factional challenges. Once the decision is taken at the top – in the politburo or central committee – then all members are expected to support the decision in public. Discipline and expulsions are also a regular feature of this practice. Labour, under the control of the left, does not operate in this way. In fact the organizational principle adopted by the Labour left is that of an 'open party' and they continually counterpoise this approach with the 'bans', 'proscriptions', 'expulsions' (of Trotskyites and fellow travellers) that took place when Labour was under the control of the right. Of course the practice of an 'open party' has benefited left control because the only people who would remotely consider joining the Labour party these days are either non-political types who still think of the Labour party as some kind of left-of-centre alternative to the Conservatives or zealots of the extreme left. In fact, under this 'open party' regime the basic trend has been a large exodus, at all levels, of social democrats – either back into private life or to the Liberals and Conservatives. Labour, of course, does not need to implement 'democratic centralism' anyway; most of its decisions are taken at the 'centre' already (by small groups of trade unionists at its Annual Conference) and the declining membership of the party, a result of its increasing socialist character, means that it is hardly likely to experience a large intake of non-socialist workers who will upset the power balance.

With the exception, then, of its organizational practice the

Labour Party, under left control, has assumed many of the dimensions and characteristics of a fully-fledged 'Eurocommunist' party. Although *Labour's Programme 1976* and the Tribune Group's 'alternative strategy' might seem to some 'Eurocommunist' leaders far too extreme and *dirigiste* many 'Eurocommunist' leaders see Labour NEC socialism as a positive development. From the European Communist parties' perspectives Labour's NEC, for so long considered a bastion of social democracy, now appears to be merging into the European-wide communist tradition. In a recent interview with me in Rome Giorgio Napolitano talked of a 'convergence' between the Labour NEC and the Italian Communist party.[15] Labour, although not linked by blood to European Communists, seems to have become an adopted 'sister' party. It certainly has more to say to its adopted sisters than to its erstwhile sibling, the West German SPD.

It was utterly predictable that as Labour's NEC moved to the left the Communist Party of Great Britain should seek a closer relationship with the Labour Party. The British Communist Party (CPGB) has a membership of just under 30,000; it can make no headway electorally but has an impressive industrial apparatus that plays a key role in many trade unions. Its main strategic objective, having failed at the ballot-box, is to work closely with the Labour Party. As we saw in Chapter 1, Labour throughout its history consistently rejected all forms of association with the Communist Party, whether by rejecting outright affiliation or 'Popular Frontism'. The Labour Party also used to 'proscribe' Communist-front organizations, thereby making people who joined them ineligible for membership of the Labour Party. That, however, was how things used to be − under the Leaderships of Attlee and Gaitskell. The notion was that Labour, which sprang from a totally different political tradition from the CPGB's, should not only distance itself from the Communists but should also be seen to do so. Hence, during the forties, fifties and sixties Labour figures were discouraged from speaking at Communist Party meetings or writing for CPGB newspapers and journals. Apart from the point that such action would lend legitimacy to the Communist Party, Labour was conscious of the indivisibility of its anti-totalitarianism: Conservatives would rightly be denounced by the left if they lent support to fascist groups, so Labour should not employ double standards.

Labour's traditional 'arms-length' policy towards the Communist Party was abandoned during the seventies. Communist Party front organizations were no longer 'proscribed'; leading Labour figures (including the Deputy Prime Minister, Michael Foot) appeared at rallies of the Communist Party newspaper, the *Morning Star*, or as guest columnists for that paper. The number of top Labour politicians and trade unionists who have associated themselves with the CPGB in this way is so large that a list would be tedious.[16] What however is surprising, and insidious, is the number of 'moderates' in the Labour party who have also begun to break with precedent and associate themselves publicly with the Communist party. David Basnett, General Secretary of the moderate General and Municipal Workers' Union, has written for the *Morning Star*; Phillip Whitehead, MP, a member of the Manifesto group, has spoken at a Communist Party-sponsored meeting in his constituency; and, most surprising of all, John Gilbert, MP, a minister in the Defence Ministry during the seventies, has written twice for the Communist Party journal *Labour Monthly*.[17] Such actions under Attlee and Gaitskell would have been unthinkable. They would have sacked or publicly rebuked any of their supporters who, however inadvertently, lent their names (and their Labour credentials) to Communist organizations. Attlee was particularly resolute about the Communist problem in a democratic society. In a statement to the House of Commons as Prime Minister he said:

The Government has . . . reached the conclusion that the only prudent course to adopt is to ensure that no one who is known to be a member of the Communist Party, or to be associated with it in such a way as to raise legitimate doubts about his or her reliability, is employed in connection with work the nature of which is vital to the security of the state.[18]

Gaitskell was similarly tough-minded on the Communist issue. Throughout his Leadership of the party (much to the annoyance of some of the sensitive souls around him, but the great pleasure of the trade union bosses who had to fight the CPGB on a daily basis) he was consistently raising the issue of Communist penetration of his movement.

Sidney Bidwell, MP, chairman of the Tribune group (1976 – 7), went so far as to declare recently: 'I find my differences with the Communist party nowadays . . . negligible.' He went on to suggest that the way should be cleared for the Communist party to 'seek re-affiliation to the Labour Party itself'.[19]

So total had the break with the tradition of non-recognition and contact between the Labour Party and the Communist Party become and so intertwined were many of their causes and official contacts that it seemed thematic for the Communist Party, in the spring of 1978, to launch an appeal aimed at creating a joint political alliance between it and Labour. In an open letter to all Labour MPs, the NEC and the Co-operative movement, the CPGB leaders argued that the time had come for the 'Labour movement' to come together and agree upon a common policy. The CPGB had obviously been preparing the ground for such an approach for some time. It had withstood a factional desertion from its ranks from a group led by its Surrey Branch, who claimed that it was far too moderate and that it was diluting traditional orthodoxy in an attempt to 'follow behind the Labour Party'. It had produced a revamped policy document, *The British Road to Socialism*, which was most notable for its 'broad left' objective. For instance, the CPGB document recognized that 'the left within the Labour Party . . . has often succeeded in winning the annual conference for a left position on important questions. Its influence in the Labour party executive has also increased.'[20] This masterly understatement was then followed by some advice upon how to proceed: 'Its [the Labout left's] growth is of great significance and could be assisted by more activity by ward and constituency Labour parties, with the fullest participation of trade union delegates.' The none too veiled meaning here was obvious: that CP members who were trade unionists should become increasingly active in determining Labour Party policy by their activities at union level.

Through their trade unions Communist Party members can affect both the trade union 'block' votes cast at Labour Party conferences and the way local union delegations vote at constituency Labour Party meetings.

The Communist Party then spelt out fully the priorities for change within the Labour Party, priorities that are also felt keenly within the Labour left: 'But more than this is needed to bring about real changes, particularly in strengthening democracy within the Labour Party, in the selection of MPs and in their relationship to the local parties, and in the election of the party leader.' At the Labour Party Conference of 1978 a proposal to change the method of electing the Leader of the party (to give the conference more say and take the decision out of the hands of Labour MPs) achieved over two million votes. Furthermore, a proposal to subject Labour MPs to a rigorous re-selection procedure every Parliament was only narrowly beaten. These left causes have a habit of winning out in the end. It is not difficult to imagine a future Labour Party, some time in the eighties, which would con- duct itself very much on the lines set out in the Communist Party policy document: the Party Leader to be elected by the Annual Conference (which means the 'block' votes of the trade unions) and Labour Members of Parliament becoming mere ciphers for unrepresentative groups of local activists. 'Party control' over the legislature would be complete. James Callaghan could easily be the last Labour Prime Minister to have been elected by Labour MPs.

In short, Communist Party analysis and strategy, as it appeared in the late seventies, was as follows: there was little to distinguish the Labour left from the Communist party (Bidwell's thesis was accepted); they were both working for, essentially, the same ends; the Labour left had made considerable headway in recent years and CPGB strategy must be to build up on that base; without formally dissolving their own separate party organization the CPGB would so construct its policy and affairs as to make itself increasingly acceptable to the Labour left; it saw the main political batle of the coming years not in terms of its own party advance but in the context of the growth in the power of the left within Labour. There was only one power centre in the entire Labour movement that was outside the control of the left; and that was the Parliamentary Labour Party, where the moderates possessed a narrow majority (just under 40 out of over 300, the majority achieved by Callaghan over Foot in the Premiership race in 1976). However, the Labour MPs could be 'softened up' by continuous pressure at grass-roots level, the kind that had already ousted Reg Prentice in Newham North-East, Frank Tomney in Hammersmith North, Ernest Perry in Battersea North, Eddie Griffiths in Sheffield Brightside and Dick Taverne in Lincoln. The British Communist Party – small, disciplined, strategically sophisticated – had simply put into words what was already the central objective of the governing left faction on Labour's executive.

Yet, when the British Communist Party made its appeal for a joint political alliance with Labour it was rejected. Ron Hayward, Labour's general secretary, reportedly told the Communist Party boss Gordon Maclellan that: 'The Labour Party has no desire to have any discussions or contact whatsoever with your party.'[21] This response, seen in the light of the Labour Party's readiness to have 'discussions and contacts' with a host of East European Communist parties (including the Communist party of the Soviet Union itself) and of all the *contacts* between Labour figures and

Communist Party organizations, was somewhat comic and incongruous. One possible explanation was that the Communist Party was premature in its approach; it made it on the eve of a general election in Britain, and any positive response from Labour would have adversely affected its image. There was obviously no *principled* objection to such an alliance from the governing faction on the NEC. The decision was tactical, and wise.

Labour's growing convergence with the British Communist Party towards the end of the seventies was rather neatly captured in the changing political posture of Jimmy Reid, one of the Communist Party's top leaders. Reid had been a Communisty Party member all his adult political life, and rose into its senior ranks. He made a national name for himself during the 'Upper Clyde' sit-in the early seventies — indeed became something of a 'folk hero' in the Glasgow area. Yet, popular though he was, he stood for Parliament as a Communist in 1974 and was badly beaten. By 1979 he had been adopted as a Labour candidate.

By the end of the seventies the Communist Party could take great comfort from the fact that Labour's traditional hostility to it had been laid firmly to rest. The Tribune group of Labour MPs had produced an 'alternative strategy' (including import controls, defence cuts, compulsory planning agreements and the like) that was not very far removed from the central economic strategy of the CPGB. The TUC, at its 1978 Congress, had also adopted this 'alternative strategy' — its main economic policy motion had been moved and seconded by members of the Communist Party, and passed.

By the end of the fateful seventies Labour had produced a leadership class who, although in no way linked organizationally to the Communist Party, had developed a brand of socialism and a general political disposition which was in a much more fundamental sense 'communist'. The term 'communism' is often falsely associated with Communist parties. A distinction, however, should be made.

'Communism' is a body of ideas deriving from Marxism and, arguably, going further back than that. Communist parties take as their model the Leninist adaptation of 'communism' in 1917; most Western European Communist parties were founded in 1920 on the basis of this model. Labour, as we have seen, has so far eschewed the Leninist model of party development, particularly 'democratic centralism'; but in most other senses it is beginning to appear indistinguishable from the modern, up-dated, 'liberal' communism of the West European variety.

Labour's leaders in the party hierarchy no longer look for inspiration to social democracy. Nor are their guiding principles drawn from the early English utopian, Christian, Owenite tradition − that went out with Aneurin Bevan, Greenwood, Brockway and the early Foot. What is left? Put starkly, a British variant of the West European communist tradition. Tactical differences aside, many of which are the products of differing national situations, the 'Euro-communist' parties and the Labour left can be fairly be classified as occupying a European political position that is wholly at variance with that of Schmidt, Wilson, Callaghan and traditional social democracy. All the settlements of the seventies − the enthronement of Marxism and Leninism through the Andrew Bevan affair, the developing theoretical engagement with the 'Eurocommunists', the increasing contacts with the CPGB, the changed attitude to the Soviet Union − underscore this point.

How can it be that an incipient totalitarian class can sit astride the power centres of a major party in a nation whose traditions (intellectual, political, cultural) are so profoundly liberal? Part of the answer lies in a seeming paradox at the heart of which is Britain's inordinate popular resistance to communism. Communist parties are systematically rejected at the polls by the British people. Consequently Britain has produced no mass Communist party which could serve as the focal point of a clear and present danger. In contrast to the southern European nations, communism is not a public issue here. Nor, unlike West Germany, have we a totalitarian past which could serve to make us conscious of its potential, ever-present, threat. Britain had developed (perhaps it was the nation's great achievement) a strong social democratic Labour movement. Yet there was a price to pay for such seeming and endless stability and moderation. Not only did it spread a false notion of the supreme invincibility of decency and tolerance; but it also led to a sublime unconsciousness, a complacency which became endemic in the character of British elites, of the undercurrent of totalitarianism present in our political life. Conservatives were particularly oblivious to it. Labour leaders were always nearer to the problem than their Conservative opponents; and there used to be a tendency amongst Conservative establishment politicians to consider Labour right leaders as far too anxious, with their 'proscriptions' and 'expulsions', about the extreme left threat. When Gaitskell and Brown (both Privy Councillors) approached the Conservative government in the early sixties for permission to see the security service files on extreme left-wing members of their own party they were reportedly denied access to them. [22]

Nor was Britain disturbed, as was the United States in the post-Second World War years, with an internal anti-Communist convulsion. The British *Zeitgeist* was not troubled by the 'loss of China', and Britain was spared absurd McCarthyism. Certainly Britain had its share of spectacular spy scandals; but Maclean, Burgess, Philby and others were considered to be isolated traitors. In the United States, by contrast, the Hiss trial was not an *ad hoc* event. It was suffused with mammoth internal political consequences involving the belief amongst 'New Dealers' that their whole generation was on trial. In Britain political life was less frenetic; and Conservatives were more scrupulous than some of their Republican cousins — for instance, there was no attempt to use the spy scandals of the fifties for internal political purposes against the Labour party. Harold Macmillan, in his autobiography, refers throughout his text to 'left-wingers and fellow-travellers' or 'Communists and fellow-travellers'[23] when dealing with the Labour left. But, during his Premiership and those of other Conservatives, there was no attempt to make Labour's fellow-travellers into a major issue — indeed it would have been difficult so to do whilst Labour had its left under such tight control.

Britain therefore escaped, during the fifties, an unwarranted obsession with communists and communism. Yet the result was to further enhance complacency.

But perhaps the most conducive phenomenon of all for the communist and Marxist generation was the respectability within the Labour movement and amongst elites of the term 'socialist'. The old Labour left, with their romantic illusions about creating a democratic, socialist commonwealth (gentle, free, Christian, communal) were obviously no threat to the free society, not least of all because they were utterly hopeless at the level of political action. Yet their rhetoric of 'socialism' permeated the Labour movement. Marxists and communists naturally saw these old Labour left socialists as their Trojan Horse. The old Labour left socialist was against 'capitalism', so was the communist; the old Labour left was for 'peace' and for cutting defence expenditure and for unilateral nuclear disarmament; and although they retained severe misgivings about the nature of the Soviet state, these were never enough to outweigh their fundamental anti-Americanism.

Furthermore the old Labour left were fatally attracted to 'no enemies to the left' strategies. The harder leftist could reasonably assume that should these utopian socialists come to power within the party the 'bans and proscriptions' would be lifted; and if they should come to power in the *state* then the old Labour left would allow the communists into power. For these reasons the Marxist-Leninist generation have seen the utopian socialist as amiable, theoretically befuddled, organizationally weak, politically incoherent, but exceedingly important, allies. Of course recent Labour history is *not* the story of the advance of the old Labour left to power within the party. Michael Foot is an isolated case. Rather it is the progress of a coalition of Leftist-utopians, Marxists, Marxist-Leninists — with the axis within this coalition ever more tilted towards the hard-liners, but with the hard-liners adopting the gentle and attractive rhetoric of the old socialist romanticism.

Labour, Britain and the Soviet Union

It can be argued, indeed is (though not by me), that Labour's transformation in the seventies, although troublesome, is containable. After all, it might be suggested, Marxism is a powerful and increasingly respectable intellectual position, particularly so in the light of the failures of social democracy; it is hardly surprising that young people should turn to Trotskyism or that older, more orthodox, Marxists should see the 'Eurocommunists' as natural allies or an 'alternative strategy' as some kind of way out of an intractable economic crisis. In the end, so the argument might run, all this upsurge of revolutionary thinking will but merge into a compromise with Britain's democratic traditions. Revolutions, and revolutionary movements, have been tamed before; they can be tamed again. There is little to worry about.

Yet none of these complacent responses and analyses get to grips with one of the more ominous consequences of Labour's ideological transformation. As Labour becomes ever more suffused with Marxist rhetoric and impulses it also, and not surprisingly (for cause and effect are at work here), adopts a more pliant posture towards the Soviet Union. Indeed, during the seventies Labour's NEC, backed by many of the trade union oligarchies that sustain it, has gone even further: Labour's pro-Soviet faction has succeeded in pushing the whole party in a direction which even the dictates and momentum of détente cannot explain. Labour (as we shall see) shares with the French Communist Party the dubious 'honour' of being the most pro-Soviet of all the major political parties in the large industrial nations of the West.

It remains an astounding and seemingly wilful feature of Britain's intellectual climate that Labour's gathering pro-Sovietism is rarely analysed, let alone condemned. The British intellectual and establishment right seems unaware of the dimensions of pro-Soviet feelings in Labour's ranks; or if they are aware they appear to feel that raising the issue would be somewhat distasteful and offensive, something best left to the occasional outburst of a vulgar, popular newspaper. The British left, of course, are divided on the question. Some actively support the Soviet Union; those who do not (ranging from the moderates in the PLP to some anti-Soviet Trotskyites) are usually embarrassed into silence by the sheer audacity of the fellow-travelling wing within Labour's NEC.

There appears to be a gentleman's agreement (stretching across the political frontiers) that too harsh an investigation into pro-Soviet sympathies within the Labour movement would unleash some kind of 'McCarthyite ugliness'. This was one of the reasons why the Labour left refused to pursue the political establishment over the 'Blunt affair' – the revelation that a Soviet agent, highly placed and connected, had been given immunity from prosecution whilst traitors of lower social standing had been sent to prison. Any authentic left-of-centre, popular party, radical and democratic in its instincts – but free from communist influence – could properly and confidently censure the 'establishment' over their handling of the Blunts of this world. Labour cannot: it has too much to lose by directing popular attention to Soviet and communist influence within Britain. As Hugh Trevor-Roper has written, at the time of the Blunt exposure: 'It is the function of MI5 to keep an eye on suspect contacts, and who can say exactly where, in the amorphous Labour Party, the eastern frontiers are now drawn?.'[24]

Labour's Eastern camp – those who draw the frontiers far to the east of the Elbe – has not yet had a discernable influence upon the party's specific foreign policy proposals. Even the late 70's had seen no ringing declarations about withdrawal from NATO (although a phased withdrawal has been advocated by Robin Cook, Labour MP for Edinburgh Central, and a leading Tribune defence spokesman);[25] there was no *overt* commitment to unilateral nuclear disarmament; no clear suggestions that Britain should assume some kind of neutral position in the world as a leading member of the 'Third World' — although the totality of the approach outlined in *Labour's Programme, 1976* came close to it. The Labour left's foreign policy was twofold. First, to work for peace through a more fully developed and deepened détente. Second, and as part of this objective, to cut defence expenditure severely and unilaterally. Any overt declaration of intent about Britain's place within the Western alliance would have opened up the Labour Party to charges from the Conservatives that it was neutralist, unpatriotic or worse; and the Labour right too, although generally supine, could have caused problems.

Labour's gathering pro-Sovietism takes several forms. For instance, the Labour left increasingly assumes the role of spokesman for Soviet interests whenever they appear to come into conflict with those of China. A party which was seemingly moving to the left, increasingly imbued with various hues of Marxism, would, on the face of it, not want to take firm positions as between the two communist superpowers. There would tend to be an ambiguity in attitudes towards the various communist regimes, siding one moment with the one, the other moment with the other. Yet as the seventies developed this kind of evenhandedness was not much in evidence. Rather, it was always Moscow that was supported — and apparently in a determinedly selective manner.

Leading Labour left-wingers revealed their thinking during the 'Neil Cameron affair' in May of 1978. Sir Neil Cameron, Marshal of the RAF and Chief of the Defence Staff, stated during a visit to tank troops in China that: 'Our two countries are coming more and more together. This must be good because we both have an enemy at our door whose capital is Moscow.[26] Norman Atkinson, MP (the Treasurer of the

Labour Party) and Frank Allaun, MP (then Vice-Chairman of the Labour Party and to become its Chairman for 1978/9) called for Sir Neil's resignation, claiming that his remarks 'would worsen international relations and damage the prospects for détente'. [27] In 1979 leading Labour left-wingers, including Energy Secretary Anthony Wedgwood-Benn and Frank Allaun (now Chairman of the party), were also prominent in the campaign to oppose the sale of British Harrier aircraft fighters to China.

In fact there are some striking similarities between the Labour Party's attitudes to the Soviet Union and those of the 'Eurocommunist' parties. They both side with the Soviet Union against China; they both tend to support Soviet-backed Third World 'national liberation struggles'; they both support only certain kinds of East European dissidents — for instance the Charter 77 group in Czechoslovakia and Roy Medvedev in the Soviet Union, but not those Soviet Jews who wish to emigrate to Israel or the Solzhenitsyn and Bukovsky faction of dissidents. Neither the Labour left nor the 'Eurocommunists' develop any systematic criticism of the Soviet regime. No link is made between communism and repression. Even Santiago Carrillo, leader of the Spanish Communist party, has gone further than any senior left Labour figure in distancing himself from Soviet oppression and human rights violations. The British TUC, in the middle and late seventies, was ostentatious in its refusal to condemn Soviet repression. Douglas Eden has written about the reception given by the TUC to an Amnesty International report pressing the case for Russian workers who were persecuted for trying to set up free trade unions: 'The General Council disposed of Amnesty's report by seeking the views of the Soviet TUC. The Soviet reply finally came six months later "that a group composed of complainants claiming to be a trade union could not pretend to pursue trade union objectives . . ." It was pointed out at the General Council, according to its annual report, that the Soviet comments "were directed to the substance of the matter".

Maintaining and developing friendly relations with the Soviet TUC were more important and should not be put at risk.'[28] For some years the TUC simply refused, although constantly urged by the Electricians' Union, led by Frank Chapple, to denounce Soviet repression. For instance, when the TUC was asked to protest against the treatment of Soviet dissident Yuri Orlov it was pointed out at the General Council that the Orlov case 'raised no trade union issue'.[29]

Even more alarmingly, Mr Alex Kitson, representing the British *Labour* Party at the 60th anniversary of the Bolshevik revolution in Moscow in 1977, said:

I think that the Labour Party Executive now have started to establish contacts with many parties throughout the world . . . I think that it is very very important that we do develop our relationships with the Communist Party of the Soviet Union . . . I would say that this is a good thing that for the first time the British Labour Party has agreed to send a representative to the Soviet Union to join in the celebrations of the 60th anniversary. [and] On behalf of British trade unionists . . . we are still trying to achieve the kind of thing that workers in the Soviet Union have achieved. [and, in reference to the Soviet Union] They have done more in 50 years than we have done in 200 years.[30]

It is difficult to imagine even one of the 'Eurocommunist' leaders talking in these terms. Kitson was representing the Labour Party NEC. Such was the transformation of Labour.

In fact Kitson's visit to the Soviet Union was but part of a wider initiative taken by the newly left-dominated Labour NEC: Labour broke completely with all precedent and opened up party-to-party relations with Eastern bloc Communist parties. This historic opening to the East on the part of Britain's Labour Party went unnoticed for some time, largely because the Western media find international labour affairs both boring and uninteresting.

In 1974, under the chairmanship of Ian Mikardo, and with the blessing of the NEC, Labour's International Committee took the first steps along their new path. On 25 November

1974 Mikardo himself went (according to Labour's Annual Conference report of the following year) as a delegate to the Romanian Communist Party Congress in Bucharest. In 1975 Alex Kitson and Jennie Little (Labour's International Secretary), both representing the British Labour Party, visited East Germany for 'talks with trade unionists and *party* officials'.[31] In the same year Labour's general secretary, Ron Hayward, also went to East Germany 'for talks with *party* and government leaders'.[32]

These new party-to-party contacts are no pedantic point. Labour has traditionally made a clear and precise distinction between state-to-state relations and party-to-party relations. State-to-state relations are natural, even between adversaries, in order that diplomatic relations may be carried on. What is more, Labour would regularly send delegations to countries of which they disapproved, *but* not on a party-to-party basis. This kind of relationship confers on a communist regime a wholly different kind of blessing – an ideological acceptability by a 'social democratic' party in the West. Prime Minister Callaghan spelt out this difference at the Labour Party Conference of 1976: 'We proceed on the assumption that the Soviet Union is earnest in its wish to improve relations between states – I emphasize the word 'states' – even though, as their own statements have told us, the ideological struggle will continue between parties.'[33] He then went on to declare: 'Let there be no doubt about their intentions on that.'[34] Yet, as these very words were being spoken by the Party Leader his own Executive was continuing with its new strategy; indeed the Executive had invited to the very conference that Callaghan was addressing 'observers' from most of the Eastern bloc Communist parties and regimes. In the early sixties the only official foreign party 'observers' sitting in the international gallery at Labour Party conferences would be those representing parties in the Socialist International. By 1978, it was calculated that virtually every Communist party in Western and Eastern Europe (with the exception of the Portuguese and a few others) had 'observers' present in that same gallery. In fact, Callaghan was utterly isolated within his own party on this issue. His defiant words were those of someone who had already lost the battle.

Indeed not only did these party-to-party relations develop and deepen but the atmosphere suffusing these visits and exchanges became increasingly cordial. Of particular note was the visit of Ron Hayward to East Germany. He went further than simply visiting the East German dictatorship party as part of a fact-finding mission; he praised it, and its boss Eric Honecker.[35]

A high point in this new international venture occurred on 28 October 1976. The Labour Party, at its own invitation, received a delegation in Britain from the Communist Party of the Soviet Union itself. This delegation was led by Boris Ponomarev, Secretary of the General Committee of the Soviet Communist Party and the man in Kremlin responsible for the co-ordination of the world's non-governing *Communist* parties. Also on the delegation was Viktor Afanasyev, the editor-in-chief of *Pravda*. There was some doubt about the actual nature of the delegation – it was thinly disguised as a delegation from the Institute of World Economy and International Relations of the Soviet Academy of Sciences – but this was cleared up at the airport upon Ponomarev's arrival. He was met by Ian Mikardo on behalf of the Labour Party, and made it clear that the delegation represented the Communist Party of the Soviet Union. The Soviet news agency TASS issued a revealing and intriguing statement on the visit: 'He [Ponomarev] said that the main purpose of the visit was to hold serious discussions about the need for joint efforts between the Soviet Communist Party and the Labour Party.'[36] What kind of 'joint efforts' had Ponomarev in mind? Labour had never before engaged in any 'joint efforts' with the CPSU.

It was apparent that on this issue Callaghan's writ did not run through his party apparatus. General Secretary Brezhnev was obviously aware of this when he referred to better relations between the Communist Party of the Soviet Union and the British Labour Party in his address to the 25th Congress of the Soviet Party in 1976. He said that the Soviet *party* had extended ties with progressive socialist parties – revolutionary-democratic – and Left socialist . . . . Our contacts with the socialist and social democratic parties of a number of countries, including . . . Britain . . . have noticeably expanded . . . . We shall continue to work in the same direction.'[37] The Soviet party had pulled off something of a coup by Ponomarev's visit.

The deepening of relations between the Labour Party and the Soviet party should be seen within the context of a parallel set of increased contacts and relations between the British trade unions and Eastern bloc Communist regimes. Bevin, Deakin, Carron, even Cousins, would not tolerate relations between the British trade union movement and Communist 'trade unions'. Their argument was simple, and unimpeachable: as no such entities as free trade unions exist in Communist societies, and as these so-called 'trade unions' are ruthlessly controlled by the party and state, then to meet with Eastern bloc 'trade unionists' is a monstrous fiction. What could possibly be sensibly discussed between party bosses whose regimes obliterated free trade unions and trade unionists in the West? Certainly not free collective bargaining. Furthermore, by meeting Eastern bloc 'trade unions' and dignifying them as the authentic representatives of working people the Western trade union leaders were legitimizing regimes which broke every principle of worker representation. This arm's-length attitude to Communist 'trade unions' remains the dominant one within the American trade union organization (the AFL-C10), and the Americans have been highly critical of recent TUC actions. British union leaders have been instrumental in attempting to bring together Western and Eastern 'trade union centres' in a series of meetings in Geneva. The TUC has invited to Britain a whole host of spuriously entitled 'trade union' delegations. The most sensational TUC invitation was issued to the former head of the KGB, Alexandr Shelepin, who visited Britain for talks with British union leaders in 1975.

Many trade union officials, at all levels within the British trade union movement, are now invited to go on delegations to the Eastern bloc. Many simply go for the joy of travelling; others to genuinely enquire into conditions of work; others to improve East-West contacts, although visiting trade unionists are rarely allowed to see any aspect of industrial life not approved by the party that supervises such visits. Others, however, are quite obviously politically inspired. Into this latter category fits Jack Jones, general secretary of the giant Transport and General Workers Union from the late sixties until 1978. Jack Jones was the senior British trade union leader for virtually a decade, and according to opinion polls he was considered by the British public to be the most powerful man in Britain, more powerful than the Prime Minister himself. Jack Jones was the architect of Britain's social contract and the guiding light behind the trade union agreement to wage restraint. Indeed, Jones's influence in securing wage restraint in the summer of 1975, and helping to sustain it thereafter, was an important factor in keeping the Wilson government afloat.

In many respects Jones is an attractive man – frugal, decent, serious and compassionate. And he represents, in a larger-than-life sense, the politics of a generation of trade unionists in the Labour movement. He was deeply marked by his experiences in the Spanish civil war. However, unlike many of his contemporaries who fought in that war on the Republican side (Orwell particularly), he has never seen fit to repudiate the role of the Spanish Communist Party during those fateful years. He seemingly retained during his career as a trade union leader the belief that working people (whom he obviously cares deeply about – in a genuine way not usually exhibited by modern trade union bureaucrats) had much to gain from even the most extreme forms of socialism. Indeed, during his latter days as a top trade union leader he revealed some interesting insights into his thinking. On a visit to the

Soviet Union in 1976 he made some quite extraordinary comments on political and industrial life in that country that went well beyond politeness to a host. In a country in which trade unions, in any real sense, do not exist — are but an arm of state and party, are often peopled by intelligence officers, cannot engage in collective bargaining — he vouchsafed the following remarks at a Moscow press conference: 'The Russian trade union movement was facing up to the responsibility of ensuring human values at the place of work and in the environment'; and Russian 'trade unions' were doing 'an exceptionally good job'.[38] On the same visit Jones went on to visit Russified and Soviet-controlled Latvia and stated that 'people were well contented' and, incredibly, 'running their own affairs very effectively'.[39]

How can the Labour left's attitude to the Soviet Union be explained? What is the reason for Labour's 'Russia Complex'?[40] And, how can the British left more generally be so ambiguous about one of the most reprehensible regimes in the history of human kind — one that according to some accounts has been responsible for the deaths (in internal repression alone) of over 66 million people?[41]

One reason, perhaps the most crucial, is the changed balance of world power or, what the Soviets themselves call the changed 'correlation of world forces'. Labour's top leadership, including many trade union figures, are power politicians. The Soviet Union is now, without question, the most powerful European military power and, with the traditional American commitment to defend Western Europe still intact but less secure, arguably the strongest politically too. In this shifting international power scene the attitude of the Soviet leadership to parties and factions within West European societies becomes a matter of moment. To be considered 'friendly' to the Soviet Union — an anti-'anti-Soviet' — must be beginning to shape up in some minds as a sound opportunistic posture. If Western Europe is to be 'Finlandized' then pro-Sovietism makes (sordid) sense.

Of course, such political opportunism or defeatism in the West must be balanced against the changing *intellectual* climate. There is no longer any respectable support in the West for the Soviet system. The intellectual climate of the twenties and thirties that conditioned a goodly portion of the Western intelligentsia has now evaporated; hardly anyone (apart that is, from the older fellow-travellers) has anything pleasant to say about the Soviet system. Most young Marxists in the West would, if pressed, be critical of the Soviet regime. The children of the uprising of 1968 in Paris have turned on the Soviet regime with a vengeance. Bernard-Henri Lévy describes it as 'reactionary', Glucksmann calls it 'fascist'. The full range of Western *liberal* opinion is also now under few illusions about the nature of life in the Soviet Union. *Le Nouvel Observateur*, the *New York Review of Books*, the *Guardian*, the *New Statesman*, liberals, social democrats, democratic socialists (even the Swedish Social Democratic Party) now all agree: the Soviet Union is no longer the 'paradise' that it used to be depicted as in the thirties, nor is it marginally reprehensible: it is a Gulag. Even the American liberals of the Vietnam era concur. This disaffection even spreads as far as some of the 'Eurocommunists'. In sum, the debate is now no longer about the nature of Soviet society under the Soviet regime; it is now about whether or not the Soviet Union is expansionist, and about how best to deal with it. Orwell, Koestler, Hook — all are now acceptable and respected, at least on the Soviet question. In Britain there is no longer a lively debate about Orwell's veracity; now it is about whether this new-found sage was a man of the 'right' or the 'left', about who can claim him. On top of all this the broad mass of working people, as always, remain hostile to the Soviet Union and 'communism' more generally. For once, and on this issue, the intellectuals and the people are as one.

Even Marxism itself is increasingly discredited. It has never had much popular support, but intellectuals as well are now turning against it. Lesek Kolakowski has argued that

'Marxism neither interprets the world nor changes it: it is merely a repertoire of slogans serving to organize various interests.'[42] And even the interests which it 'serves to organize' – presumably the Communist parties of the East – are peopled by *apparatchiks* who neither understand it nor believe in it. In the West some intellectuals are even reopening the question of a link between Marxism and totalitarian repression. One of the French 'new philosopher' school has declared: 'There is no worm in the fruit, no sin was added later, for the worm is the fruit and the sin is Marx.'[43] This kind of thinking represents a central challenge to the standard new left argument that all the ills of Communism stem from Stalin. For years the British 'new left' have used Stalin, quite ruthlessly and disingenuously, to get them off the hook: Stalin's crimes were the worm that could be plucked from the otherwise edible diet of Marx, Lenin and Trotsky. Now all of this is under challenge – but typically in the more daring and stimulating new left intellectual circles in Paris; it has not yet reached 'new left' coteries in London, Nottingham and Sheffield. The British Labour Party, as it listens more insistently to the insular and unimaginative British 'new left', is buying itself into the past.

Yet, even as intellectual opinion shifts ever more decisively against both the Soviet Union *and* Marxism the 'correlation of world forces' (particularly the military balance) still shifts in favour of the Soviet Union. There is a terrifying race developing between this shifting 'correlation' on the one hand and hardening anti-Soviet instincts and opinions (not only in the West but throughout the Soviet bloc too) on the other.

Labour's 'Russia complex' can partly be explained by the insularity of the British Labour Party and the British left more generally. Labour has simply remained unaffected by the changing intellectual climate in the West. There remains a mammoth, immovable fixation on the part of the British left with the 1917 Bolshevik revolution. The intellectual inheritance of the inter-war years – decades dominated by the frighteningly influential upper English Oxbridge red elite – still cloud contemporary judgements of the Soviet state.

The 1917 revolution was a singular event for British socialists. For many left-wing intellectuals it heralded not only the dawn of socialism in Russia but also a worldwide revolution. Maurice Orbach, MP, has stated that: 'When the revolution came in 1917 it was like the coming of a new Messiah. It was the great event of the century . . .'[44] This was the standard view of a host of influential figures on the British left who throughout the twenties and thirties remained more or less faithful to the ideals of October; certainly, despite particular criticisms, the fledgling Soviet state represented hope in a cruel and unjust world, and needed to be defended against its enemies in the West.

Intellectuals, journalists and scientists, most of them not in the Labour Party or on its fringes, supported the new Soviet regime. Such notables as Philip Toynbee, D. N. Pritt, Eric Hobsbawn, Christopher Hill, J. B. S. Haldane, J. D. Bernal, P. M. S. Blackett, Stephen Spender, W. H. Auden, Christopher Isherwood, Maurice Dobb, H. N. Brailsford, G. D. H. Cole and Harold Laski helped determine a climate of opinion at the superior end of English intellectual life that was to last well into the late forties.

We now know that the prevalent pro-Soviet feelings of the time led some of the inter-war intellectuals into treason. Andrew Boyle, in his lucid and extensively researched work *The Climate of Treason*, discloses that Cambridge in the thirties was a recruiting-ground for Soviety spy-masters. Unlike those who simply flirted with Marxism and the Soviet Union, Burgess, Maclean, Philby and Blunt dedicated their lives to the Soviet interest. These 'lords of human kind' – supercilious, incestuous, often homosexual – represented all that can go wrong when intelligence and privilege are unrelieved by character.

Leading Fabians were also caught up in the pro-Soviet momentum of the times. Norman and Jeanne Mackenzie in

The First Fabians report on the visit to Russia or Sidney and Beatrice Webb in 1932:

Dismissing the reports of famine in the country-side and of forced labour and deportations as inevitable shortcomings in a backward country, they were fascinated by the discovery that the formal structure of Soviet society corresponded so closely to their own notions of a socialist state in which the individual was subordinated to the collective, public morals were ascetically puritanical, and private profit was replaced by planning for social purposes . . . and in the strict discipline of the Communist Party they saw the 'new religious order' which Beatrice had so often insisted must assume the task of making a new civilisation.[45]

Upon their return from the Soviet Union the Webbs produced *Soviet Communism*, a massive work that amounted to an apologia for the Moscow regime – a regime that had *already* embarked upon an internal repression of considerable magnitude. Beatrice Webb summed it all up in that peculiar upper English way: 'Old people often fall in love in extraordinary and ridiculous ways – with their chauffers [sic], for instance: we feel it more dignified to have fallen in love with Soviet communism.'[46] George Bernard Shaw had his flirtation with the new regime, declaring upon his return from Russia in 1931 that the Stalin regime was but 'applied Fabianism'.[47]

John Strachey, probably the most penetrating political mind of all amongst the English left intelligentsia in the inter-war years, also fell into a pro-Soviet position. In *The Coming Struggle for Power*, published in November 1931, he set forth a rigorous Marxist thesis during which he argued that '160 million men and women have already . . . leapt out of the kingdom of necessity towards the kingdom of freedom – Russia.'[48] Strachey, of course, was later to break completely with this past; yet so all-powerful was the resistance on the British left to criticism of the Soviet Union that even Strachey could accept the Soviet rationale for its invasion of Poland in 1939 along with the Nazi-Soviet pact.[49]

So powerful a grip upon left-wing intellectual life did the Fabians, the Stracheys, the Oxbridge Communists manage to exert, so complete was their 'hegemony' that the left-wing press and publishing world (including the Left Book Club) could find no room for systematic denunciations of the Soviet regime. Not that many were forthcoming from those who had the time or money to write. George Orwell was the only serious left opponent of the pro-Soviet school. He was a lone voice. Orwell, who turned both on the regime and, with more ferocity still, upon its British apologists (following his experiences in the Spanish Civil War) was often ostracized — and his offerings on the Soviet system suppressed. Kingsley Martin refused an Orwell piece critical of the Communists in Spain;[50] *Animal Farm* was turned down by a succession of publishers; even a mildly critical review by Orwell of Harold Laski's treatise *Faith, Reason and Civilisation* was rejected by the *Manchester Evening News* (although this may have had more to do with the war effort, the need to please the Soviets, than with any ideological predisposition). Orwell, exasperated, complained that: 'any hostile criticism of the present Russian regime is liable to be taken as propaganda *against socialism*'.[51] This kind of reasoning echoes down through the years — it is still one held by many British leftists within the Labour Party, although it is now couched in rather more careful terms: anti-Sovietism is *today* against 'peace'.

Not only was the left-wing press hostile to attacks upon the Soviet regime: so, too, was much of the official establishment. The Ministry of Information intervened with a publisher, who was all set to publish *Animal Farm*, with the following letter:

If the fable were addressed generally to dictators and dictatorships at large then publication would be all right, but the fable does follow, as I see now, so completely the progress of the Russian Soviets and their two dictators, that it can only apply to Russia, to the exclusion of other dictatorships. Another thing: it would be less offensive if the predominant caste in the fable were not pigs. I think the choice of pigs as the ruling caste will no doubt give offence to many people, and particularly to anyone who is a bit touchy, as undoubtedly the Russians are.

This letter was written in 1943 and such censorship in wartime is understandable though not particularly elevating. However, such a mentality — 'do not give offence', 'people are a bit touchy' — exhibited about a powerful ally in wartime can so easily be adopted about a powerful adversary in peacetime.

How can the pro-Soviet feelings of the inter-war left intelligentsia best be explained? Part of the answer must lie in the increasing desperation of the times. Capitalism appeared to be on its last legs: the political establishment offered no answer to the crisis in the system which had produced such high levels of unemployment, such poverty and misery. Intellectuals were impatient for change. Labour's leaders — both in Parliament and in the TUC — were considered insufficiently intelligent and imaginative. Snowden's financial orthodoxy was repellent. Labour's rejection of Mosley's radical economic solutions increased disillusionment. Labour's two inter-war minority governments were simply not up to the task at hand, and disaffection with Labour drove intellectuals leftwards towards Marxism and Communism and into an increasingly sanguine view of the revolutionary Soviet state.

And then there was the 'great betrayal'. MacDonald's decision to head a national coalition, and his subsequent massive endorsement by the electorate in 1931, caused a further disenchantment. On the one hand the MacDonald victory proved to the socialist generation that the British working class was 'hopelessly' wedded to the system. On the other the remaining Labour Party, decimated at the polls, was seen as too small and ineffective to create a socialist society; and the intelligentsia suspected anyway, and rightly, that many of its leaders were still insufficiently revolutionary. This led to a total rejection of 'Labourism' and, in exasperation, provided further fuel for the radical allure of the Soviet state.

And then came the horror of European fascism. The emergence of the dictators in Italy and Germany tended to prove the Marxist notion that 'capitalism in crisis' turns to fascism to protect it. The German social democrats were blamed for Hitler's rise − for having caused it or for having no strategy to deal with it. The Soviet Union came to be seen as the last hope − as a real bastion of power standing in the way of a Fascist European imperium. The Western democracies were seen as too feeble to deal with this menace; and Soviet support for the republicans in Spain further underscored the image of the Soviet Union as the last refuge against a Fascist future. The Soviet invasion of Finland and the Nazi − Soviet Pact unsettled the gathering thesis; but once the Soviet Union was in the general war, as an ally, then all was well again.

Yet these explanations of the pro-Sovietism of the times are over-generous. An intellectual rejection of capitalism and a fear of fascism were only part of the story. There were more profound, and insidious, explanations. Many of the leading intellectual doyens of the pro-Soviet movement were not ethereal book-trained Marxists honestly and patriotically searching for a way out of the traumas of the twenties and thirties, diligently endeavouring to save Britain from Fascism, gullibly attracted to the new paradise in Russia. Many of the leaders of the inter-war socialist generation made pilgrimages to Moscow where they were fêted. Most of them were bright enough to know what they were seeing, and what they were not being shown. Stories of internal Soviet repression were beginning to surface quite some time before Fascism was a serious European problem. Orwell was right when he said that: 'all people who are morally sound have known since 1931 that the Russian regime stinks.'[53]

The treason, the Communism, and some of the extreme forms of socialism that flourished in the inter-war years were but part of the classical formula: the disaffection and alienation of the socially privileged intellectual. After all the socialist generation were the best and the brightest. They represented the cream of British political and economic thinking; and they had few intellectual peers from amongst the Tory right or the social democratic centre. Combined with a high and rich intellectuality the inter-war socialists were possessed of a certain social cachet. Almost without exception the leading lights of intellectual socialism were the products of the English public school; or if not they were very much to the manner born with adopted accents, mannerisms and all the other cultural paraphernalia. This socialist generation, and the mass of its followers and successors who today comprise its progeny, were given in their education all the skills needed to impress in English social life. They were socially intimidating; their throwaway lines were devastating. They combined intellectual excellence with what Herbert Spencer, as early as 1861, had described as the vices of the English educational system − its diligence 'in teaching whatever adds to refinement, polish, éclat'. In short, they were born to rule, but they were not ruling.

And yet, in that strange upper English socialist way they were contemptuous of their own public schools. Snobs themselves, they detested snobbery. They considered the standard Tory or Liberal product of the public schools stupid and shallow, indeed rather vulgar; and Labour clubs at Oxbridge were detested. The nation they inhabited was rotten philistine, unexciting. They hated their class, their country and probably themselves. In any event the 'capitalist system', so stubbornly adhered to by their fellow-countrymen, was doomed to failure.

So they turned to the workers, but in the most theoretical way. The upper English socialist generation could not find a home there either. About the British working class they were by turn exhilarated by the possibilities and exasperated by the fact. They, as with the remnants of this socialist class today, were utterly at sea when they ever − which was rare − met a worker or a workers' leader. A nice cameo of this grave social problem occurred at a Fabian summer school in Keswick. Bruce Glasier reported in his diary that Keir Hardie led the rousing singing of a number of traditional Scots songs in the presence of Sidney and Beatrice Webb. They, in Glasier's words, 'sat through it all as if witnessing for sociological purposes an Indian orgy'.[54] Beatrice Webb was to call the leaders of the TUC 'pigs'.

Contemptuous of upper-class Tory and Liberal types (whom they often associated with the contemptuous 'hearties' they had known at public schools), ill at ease with the workers, the socialist intellectual was unrooted: without loyalty to or identity with any aspect of national life. Such 'alienation', more profound than anything felt by the working people, quite naturally led many of them to turn for comfort and inspiration to the revolutionary nation that had been born in 1917.

Furthermore, the ordered, planned 'socialism' of the Soviet state was a far more conducive environment for ruling-class socialists than the random, inefficient, increasingly democratic society of capitalist Britain.

The Labour movement remained virtually immune from the 'Russia complex' of the socialist intellectuals. Labour voters, activists and supporters, the Britain that worked, the Britain of the clubs and pubs, remained largely unaffected by the workers' Paradise. The heart of organized political and industrial labour, which in those days represented their members, took a very different view of the events in Russia. Broadly speaking, Labour was sceptical from the start. The Soviet state that was the product of the Bolshevik Revolution was never, until very recently, to have many friends at the heart of the organs of labour. The trade union executives and Labour's Parliamentary leaders could not summon up the enthusiasm for the revolution felt by the intellectuals.

Of course, in the very early years of the Revolution there was some support forthcoming from organized industrial and political labour. This was particularly so whilst the

Mensheviks were in power and the issue of Russia's with-drawal from the war was on the agenda. There was also some sympathy for the new Bolshevik regime whilst British troops were intervening in the Russian upheaval. The Labour movement was genuinely split over the political initiative taken by the three executives of the Triple Alliance on 16 April 1919. They called upon the Parliamentary Committee of the TUC to call a conference to secure the withdrawal of British troops from Russia, but there were also other political demands involved, particularly the withdrawal of the con-scription Bill then before Parliament.

Labour's primary concern appeared to be to prevent war, and the slaughter of workers, rather than to adopt any committed ideological posture towards the new Soviet regime. The massive loss of life in the Great War was dominating most minds and the Labour movement was anxious not to spill further British blood. When war broke out between Poland and the Soviet Union in 1920 senior Labour figures were worried about Britain getting involved in this dispute. There was some generalized, inchoate, sympathy for the Soviet regime − not for Communism, but for what was considered to be a 'workers' government' that had dis-placed the hated Tsars. It was in this atmosphere that the *Jolly George* incident occurred. Dockers refused to load a ship that was suspected of carrying munitions to the Poles. Bevin backed up the dockers. He declared, in language which hardly displayed any ideological sympathy with the Soviet system: 'Whatever may be the merits or demerits of the theory of government of Russia, that is a matter for Russia, and we have no right to determine their form of government, any more than we would tolerate Russia determining our form of government.'[55] When Bevin argued that: 'I think we have a right to refuse to have our labour prostituted to carry on wars of this character' it was a case of Bevin's labour machismo, used in aid of peace, rather than any sign of a political sympathy.[56]

Later, as the Red Army approached Warsaw there was

more fear of war. The trade union leaders as well as the leaders of the PLP were united – but not in favour of the Soviets, rather against war. The famous *Daily Herald* headline 'Not a Man, Not a Gun, Not a Sou' was the spirit of the time. No longer was labour going to be forced into conflict against its will, as many believed it had been during the Great War. This was the emotional engine that sped Labour's opposition to Poland in its conflict with the Soviets; it had little to do with overt or covert pro-Sovietism. The TUC's joint committee with Soviet 'trade unionists' was wound up in 1927.

It would be false though to depict Labour leaders as actively and determinedly hostile to the new Soviet regime at this early stage in its development. The attitude of non-intellectual Labour was rather ambiguous, suffused by ignorance, simple and false romanticism, yearnings for peace and visceral anti-Toryism. The Tsars were generally viewed as oppressors and 'a bad thing'. Kerensky seemed a vast improvement. There was no particularly adept or sophisticated understanding of the radically new nature of the October regime. And as the Tories wanted the new Soviet regime finished off then it couldn't be *all* bad.

Yet at the same time, even in the early years of Bolshevism, there was no great feeling that a workers' revolution had been secured that had any relevance for Britain. Even as early as 1917 Arthur Henderson, back from a visit on behalf of the coalition government, was convinced that a negotiated peace was the best mechanism for avoiding a Bolshevik takeover. And in the same year, an interesting conference was called in Leeds, at the Coliseum, that showed something about the nature of the interest in the events in Russia amongst the British Left. The official Labour Party and the TUC showed little interest. The conference was organized by a small unofficial group calling itself the United Social Council. Amongst the delegates, and taking a leading part in the proceedings, were intellectuals like Bertrand Russell and Sylvia Pankhurst, pacifist-inclined (at that time) left-wingers like Ramsay MacDonald, unrepresentative British Communists like Willie Gallacher. Bullock reports that this meeting 'was a preview of the British Left between the wars, anarchical, Utopian, already fascinated by and profoundly ignorant of Russian experience'. He also records that: 'Neither of the two delegates from the Dockers' Union, Ben Tillett and Ernest Bevin, felt at home in this assembly.'[57]

Slavish pro-Sovietism at the political level was the preserve of small left political factions — the British Socialist Party, the Socialist Labour Party, the Workers' Socialist Federation and from 1920 the Communist Party of Great Britain. There was also an organization called the Socialist League which worked, largely under the influence of Harold Laski and Stafford Cripps, within the Labour Party. The Socialist League was the archetypal middle-class Marxist sect. As Jones suggests: 'They closely identified their brand of Socialism with the cause of the USSR.'[58] It made little headway in the Labour Party.

The real test of Labour's attitude toward the new Bolshevik State, however, was revealed by its response to the overtures made to it throughout the inter-war years by the Moscow-controlled CPGB. The constant Communist Party strategic aim was the establishment of a united front, or even better, actual affiliation to the Labour Party. A series of attempts at affiliation were regularly rejected by the Labour Party by large majorities. In 1925, for instance, the majority against affiliation was fourteen to one; and, in the same year, the Conference passed a constitutional provision proscribing all dealings with it. This was an early manifestation of the 'bans and proscriptions' edict, an object of left-wing wrath from that time until 1973 when the 'proscribed list' was abolished.

From the early twenties right up until the mid-seventies the National Executive went out of its way to distance itself not only from the CPGB but also from any hint that its democratic socialism has any ideological affinity with the Communism of the Soviet State. Even in the most favourable atmosphere for the pro-Soviet faction within the British left, the aftermath of the Spanish Civil War and the growing threat from Fascism, the NEC set its face like flint against association with pro-Sovietism or Communism. The United Front Campaign 'against Fascism, Reaction and War' − the most alluring possible nostrums for socialists in the Labour Party − led to a major act of retaliation by the National Executive. The Socialist League, which led this campaign, and was itself led by Cripps, Bevan and Strauss, was expelled from the party on 25 January 1937. What reservoirs of pro-Sovietism remained after that time were isolated. The fellow-travellers on Labour's back benches after the war, most notably Konni Zilliacus, were men ostracized and without a particle of influence.

The reasons behind Labour's refusal to agree to affiliation, to countenance United Frontism or put itself in the position of a Soviet apologist, were an amalgam of pragmatic self-preservation and genuine ideological hostility. The Zinoviev Scare of 1924 left its mark; but even before 1924 Labour's central leadership − Henderson particularly − had come to the conclusion that the Soviet regime was as different from their own brand of politics as chalk from cheese. There was another, more profound, factor at work. British Labour was patriotic. It was a movement born of this country, as much a part of the nation as any other political movement; it was as authentic a British interest as the Tory Party or the Liberal tradition; it was national, and both the Soviet Union and communism were foreign and alien. It was not simply a question of securing its electoral flank against Tory charges of being an agent of foreign influence, it was that Labour was no such thing. Whatever sympathies it might express about the Revolution of 1917, February or October, were to do with internal domestic battles, not with loyalties held outside these shores. In other words, Labour's historic anti-Sovietism (and anti-communism) was genuine.

Yet, although the socialist intellectuals lost a major battle in the twenties and thirties as Labour stayed true to its working-class origins and its concomitant patriotism, the allure of 1917 was not to die. Sickly and debilitated though the 'Russia Complex' might have been during the years of the 'Cold War' and the revisionist Labour Leadership of the fifties, it was kept alive somehow. It must have been very difficult. Ernest Bevin bestrode the stage of the post-war Labour Government and set his imprint upon twenty years of Labour anti-Sovietism. Cabinet documents released in 1979 tell of the visceral nature of his anti-Communism: 'The cardinal error is ever to let the Communists into a government in the vain hope that they will play the game according to Westminster rules'; of the Czech tragedy of 1948 he said: 'The whole episode illustrates once again that all Communists are unprincipled thugs, wolves in sheep's clothing, and that they will do anything at Moscow's bidding.'[59] Even Aneurin Bevan, representing the bulk of the Labour left, wrote a foreword to a short book entitled *The Curtain Falls* in which he roundly condemned Soviet behaviour in the post-war period. He wrote: 'The Communist does not look upon the Socialist in common cause. He looks upon him as a dupe, a temporary convenience, as something to be thrust aside ruthlessly when he has served his purpose.'[60] Here Bevan was referring to the 'social democrats' of Eastern Europe whose parties had, in the immediate post-war period, been infiltrated by Communists or been in coalitions with Communists, only later to find themselves in prison.

In these 'dark days' for the Soviet cause in the West left-wing sympathies for the Soviet Union went underground, into very low profile. They remained the preserve of a small group of Communist party *apparatchiks* in King Street, a small group of fellow-travelling MPs on the Labour benches (including Zilliacus, William Warbey and Tom Driberg), some unreconstructed Stalinist intellectuals and some hardened veterans of the republican cause in the Spanish Civil War located in the lower echelons of the trade union movement. Yet, such perseverance was to eventually pay off handsomely. Only fifteen years after Aneurin Bevan's death

Labour's NEC began its initiative to establish relations between it and the Eastern bloc Communist parties.

In the late sixties two 'external' developments gave an added impetus to the Soviet cause within the politics of Labour. First, many on the Labour left saw British 'capitalism' as entering an acute phase of crisis. Growing antipathy on the part of the British left to the *In Place of Strife* proposals, followed by the Heath government's Industrial Relations Act and incomes policies, had an inevitable spillover affect in heightening opposition, on the part of the articulate, activist Left, to the 'capitalist system'. In this atmosphere there inevitably developed a less critical attitude throughout the Labour movement to 'socialist' regimes abroad. Traditional socialist escapism re-emerged: with 'capitalism in crisis' 'socialist systems' − apparently not suffering from the 'contradictions of capitalism' with its high levels of inflation and unemployment − assumed, by contrast, an alluring prospect. Trotskyites who, on a theoretical level and in normal times, would be critical of the Soviet regime tended to suspend their anti-Sovietism as the crisis built up in Britain. Furthermore, active Trotskyites began to see any 'anti-Soviet propaganda' (from the 'Tory press' or whatever) as a subtle means of 'brainwashing' the 'working class' who otherwise would increasingly turn against their own system. Hence a coalition built up between more traditional Soviet sympathizers and young Trotskyites.

Secondly, there was a wholly fortuitous international political development which happened to coincide with this domestic British evolution. The Nixon administration in the United States began its retreat from Vietnam and initiated the doctrine of détente with the Soviet Union. The 'opening to China', although conceived as a tentative anti-Soviet move in the international chess game, added further momentum to this process. Both the policy of détente and the 'opening to China', no matter what their validity at the level of international politics, had a devastating affect upon the anti-

Communist and anti-Soviet position in the British Labour movement – and in other social democratic parties as well. As the whole Western foreign policy establishment embraced a new international strategy for dealing with Soviet power then, inevitably, the anti-Communist elements within the Labour movement were seriously undercut – intellectually, politically, psychologically. There was simply less poignancy and moment left in the denunciation of pro-Sovietism in the Labour movement when the pro-Soviet faction could defend their actions and overtures to the East as being in accord with those of Nixon and détente. Better relations between Labour and the Communist parties in the East could be defended by fellow-travellers as part of the 'search for peace'. The counter-arguments (that the Helsinki agreements which attempted to enact better relations between Communist and non-Communist *states*, did not preclude a continuing ideological battle between *parties*) became far too subtle.

In fact, not only détente but the whole 'convergence' school of thinking emerging in the West in the seventies has helped, no doubt unwittingly, to undermine the anti-Communist factions within the strategically important Labour and social democratic movements of Western Europe.

Labour anti-Communists have also had to contend with that continuing strand of European conservative thinking that has always found the anti-Communist liberal tradition somewhat distasteful. Its liberalism is considered shallow; its strategic thinking inadequate; its anti-Sovietism but a form of special pleading for minorities (Latvians, Lithuanians, Jews, Armenians, dissidents). Statecraft, this kind of European conservative argues, is a more serious enterprise than this. It is about relations between states, not primarily about values or minorities. The Soviet Union, so the argument runs, is essentially a 'conservative' power and some suggest that it can be made even more conservative by cutting down anti-Soviet propaganda at home and increasing trade between East and West: 'A fat Communist or Russian is better than a hungry one.' Hence the maturing of the détente policy.

Maurice Cowling has written about liberal anti-Communism in an interesting and thought-provoking essay published in 1978. He argues that:

It is not, however, Marxism that it should be the object of British policy to resist. What it should be the object of British policy to resist is any threat to the independence and integrity of the United Kingdom, and in relation to this, EEC, NATO and the Commonwealth are merely instruments with no permanent claim on loyalty or attention. The only permanent claims are those which arise from the national interest defined in terms of sovereignty, historic continuity and national identity, and beyond these no other focus of loyalty is either necessary or desirable. [61]

This amounts, although the total argument is more subtle than a short quotation can describe, to a classic but flawed conservative attitude. There are two problems with this view. First it, implicitly at least, assumes that there can never be an internal threat; that anything that exists within a country, 'Marxism' say, must in some sense be acceptable. Secondly it assumes, again implicitly, that the adherance to a particular doctrine, again say 'Marxism', that is held strongly by a corpus of opinion within a country can have no, or few, implications for that country's foreign policy or its 'national interest defined in terms of sovereignty, historic continuity ...'. Also, the trouble with this traditional kind of conservatism (although not with Cowling who knows the Labour movement well, indeed has written books about it) is that it tends both to devalue the importance of the Labour movement and to discount the affect upon British state foreign policy which changing currents within it can produce. Furthermore, when Enoch Powell [62] advocates an alliance between Britain and the USSR then, apart from any other considerations, the pro-Soviet group within the Labour Party, fully aware of Powell's appeal to Labour voters, is thereby strengthened.

Traditional Conservatives are, no doubt, increasingly anxious about a foreign policy based upon human rights and freedoms, and the seeming failure of President Carter's endeavours in this area will only strengthen this anxiety. Yet President Carter *inherited* a very bleak strategic position which, incidentally, was handed over to him by more traditional *realpolitik* conservatives. What is more a nation, in conducting its foreign policy, cannot stand outside its own traditions, and in Britain's case (no less than in America's) this must mean, in part, a defence of its history and culture of freedom.

Finally: there is some sense in which the Western elites have gone sour on the notion of freedom; and the temptation must exist to do some kind of deal with the Soviet leadership, and with the internal socialists. But, if this should happen, it will be done over the heads of the peoples and consequently will not last. The inherited public instinct for the free society is too great.

Cowling, earlier in the same essay, suggests that: ' . . . the Labour Party is not Bolshevism . . . at its worst it is East German socialism.' The Labour Party, as it enters the eighties, is certainly not Bolshevik − it is far too chaotic and riddled with all kinds of left factions for that. Nor is it 'East German socialism'. Yet the mere fact that a serious student of Labour can deem it necessary to issue such an analytical edict, no matter how broad-brush, is surely a sign of ominously changing times; and is a further measure of the transformation of Labour.

CHAPTER 3

Why Did It Happen
(So Quickly)?

The transformation of the politics of Labour may have been inevitable. After all, Britain in recent decades has gone through a trauma of change. The loss of Empire; a severely reduced position in world politics; a weakened role even in Europe and an unhappy relationship with the EEC; the collapse in authority of traditional institutions; a growing distaste for the two-party system and for its politicians; threats to the unity of the nation itself; even the growth of terrorism on the mainland. The list is endless. Concurrent with these political upheavals, and (no doubt) a part-cause of some of them, has gone an economy that cannot fulfil expectations, that persists with high levels of unemployment and inflation. It would indeed have been surprising if this catalogue of disasters had not produced political consequences for at least one of Britain's major parties.

As well as these 'shocks to the system' we must add in some of the profound social changes of the last few decades: the growth of 'the new class' in the public sector, and the expansion of that public sector, particularly local government; the weakening of the resolve of the private-sector middle class and the questioning of traditional middle-class values; an industrial managerial class increasingly dependent upon government; a more aggressive and less deferential 'affluent worker' class; increasing social divisions between the declining North and the less declining South — and so on. On top of all this British politics has had to cope with a changing intellectual climate: primarily the burgeoning, during the sixties, of vulgarized Marxist thinking and rhetoric and a seeming loss of confidence by non-Marxist intellectuals as they increasingly questioned the validity of the social democratic, Keynsian consensus. Labour was bound to be pushed leftward by these changes.

Yet, at the same time, we should weigh, as balancing factors, powerful sources of continuity: a continuing, though residual, respect for some institutions (particularly the Monarchy); a continuing absolute high standard of living; a continuing social conservatism amongst the broad mass of the people; a surprising resilience of liberal ideals and values amongst opinion-formers; a persistent rejection by the electorate (not least by Labour voters) of various forms of political extremism.

In sum, Britain has not changed as completely as Labour has. In this sense Labour's transformation appears somewhat strangely precipitate. Why has Labour's metamorphosis been both so swift and so complete? And why has so profound a political change not produced (as at the time of writing) an organic split in the Labour movement on the continental model?

The answer, I believe, lies exclusively in the high politics of the Labour movement and party; and, in particular, in the tragic flaws in the central strategic management of Labour by its two most recent Leaders, Harold Wilson and James Callaghan. The Leader of the Labour Party, particularly when Prime Minister, has immense potential power – not necessarily over the country but certainly over the direction of the politics of Labour. A Labour Prime Minister has any number of levers that he can pull: the power of patronage over both his MPs and trade union leaders; instant access to the media to make a political case; the natural popular support accruing to a moderate Labour Prime Minister when confronted by challenges from his left wing; the ability to raise abundant funds for political purposes from individuals, from the City and from some trade unions. Neither Wilson nor Callaghan, during their tenures at Downing Street, chose to use any of these powers against the advancing left within their own party. They were content simply to administer the affairs of the nation whilst the complexion of their own party changed under their very noses. In this sense they will be responsible for the nature of the Labour Party that will confront the British people in the eighties.

Neither Wilson nor Callaghan are socialists, in the sense that they seek the 'transformation of society' that is the objective of the Labour left. They are both party politicians who have made their careers in the Labour Party, and to the extent that they think politically they no doubt prefer the party as it was to that which it has become. Yet they were both confronted with profound political changes in the party they led and their reactions to these changes, although there are differences of nuance between them, were broadly the same. The advancing left was to be resisted where possible, contained if possible; but at all costs, the party was to remain united. And, within the framework of this unity no major offensive against the left in the party apparatus was to be launched and no attempt was to be made to secure, for the future, a corpus of organizational or intellectual work which could grow over the years and present the left with a permanent challenge to its ascendancy. In short, Wilson and Callaghan were very much on the defensive with no clear view of the future.

And this strategic posture of the Labour leadership in Parliament was wholly acceptable to the Labour left in the party apparatus. Their central aim, too, was to keep the movement united so that, eventually, they could assume leadership of it whole and intact. The Parliamentary Party must be prevented from splitting off, as must the trade unions. Another 1931 was to be avoided at all costs. Michael Foot, who came under much pressure from the ultra-left in the middle and late seventies, revealed his thinking when he stated that all his actions were dominated by the need to 'prevent such a catastrophe happening again'.[1] Eric Heffer, in a most perceptive article in *Political Quarterly* in 1975, prophesied that the Labour Party would not split:

Two conditions are necessary for there to be a split in the Party. First, a split would occur if the trade unions abandoned the Party and disaffiliated and secondly, if the entire Programme of 1973 were not only abandoned by the Government but repudiated by the Conference. These conditions are not likely to be fulfilled and because of this a split of a fundamental kind leading to an organizational division is not likely to take place.[2]

Furthermore, he predicted that: 'It is possible that if the Party moved even further to the Left, then some at present in the Party would seek other political pastures . . . . However, as far as I can see they are a minority — and have no real support.'[3] Left leaders could boast about the future being theirs. Neil Kinnock, MP, argued in 1977 that the 'older generation' in the Labour Party were 'timid' because of the time in which they grew up and that the younger generation will carry out 'Left Socialism'. Eric Heffer could proclaim: 'The future is with us.'[4] Such confidence was based upon the sure knowledge that Labour's Parliamentary leadership would refuse either to break up the party or launch *a serious offensive from within the party* against the Left.

And the Labour left played their hand with consummate skill. No left policy was pushed to the point where the Labour leaders had no alternative but to resign or break up the party. The left trade union leaders accepted wage restraint in 1975; the IMF crisis in 1976 was not used to attempt to impose the left's 'alternative strategy'; entry into the Common Market was accepted (in the belief that the issue could be raised again later); Benn did not resign from the Wilson and Callaghan Cabinets even though he disagreed with their central economic strategy. The Labour left, in Parliament, and in the NEC, was willing to wait, to allow Wilson and Callaghan to enjoy the fruits of office, whilst improving their position within the Labour Party apparatus.

Eric Heffer, in his *Political Quarterly* article, saw the weakness in the Labour leaders: if they refused to bust up the party they had no hand. Both Wilson and Callaghan had essentially 'been read'. They were safe 'party men', 'fourth republic' politicians only.

Wilson

First, Wilson: it is of value to understand that Wilson's assumption of the Leadership in 1963, following Gaitskell's early death, was an incongruity. At the time that Wilson took over, every major organ of the Labour Party was under right control – certainly the Parliamentary Party but also the Annual Conference and the National Executive. The party organization was so controlled because the social democrats and Labourites also controlled the major centres of trade union power. In party faction terms, then, the profile of power within the Labour Party was much as it had been when Gaitskell assumed the Leadership in 1956. Yet by a strange twist of fate it was a left-of-centre 'socialist' who was to inherit a party in which the left of centre was in a decided minority.

The reasons for this outcome were essentially personal. Put simply, George Brown was unacceptable to enough people on the right of the Party for Wilson to be preferable. Callaghan, who would have been a formidable contender to Wilson on the second ballot, could not amass enough support to get past the first hurdle. Callaghan was to have to wait another fifteen years for Labour's top job and he assumed it in far less favourable conditions than would have been the case in 1963. In any event, because of Brown's perceived unacceptability (a judgement many of those on the right who voted for Wilson came to regret) and because of the vagaries of the balloting system (which excluded Callaghan after the first ballot) the election resulted in the appointment of Harold Wilson, a quirky yet momentous event in Labour Party history.

Many of those on the Labour right (including dedicated Gaitskellites) voted for Wilson because they believed he could lead them to victory in the coming general election, and that his political principles were sufficiently flexible to allow him to mount a moderate, social democratic campaign. He was obviously competent and, attractive in debate, was a worthy opponent for Harold Macmillan. When the Conservatives chose Lord Home as Prime Minister Wilson skilfully took advantage of the new situation: he derided the new Tory choice as a symptom of a Conservative reversion to the reactionary right and moved – much to the delight of the Gaitskellites who had voted for him – to the supposed centre ground. Yet as Prime Minister Wilson was to disappoint Labour's right wing. As with most politicians he bore the scars of past factional battles and saw them in personal terms rather than as a contest of ideas. His 'friends' were on the centre left. His supporters during the great party schisms of the early sixties (when he opposed Gaitskell for Leader in 1960) were to be rewarded. Hence in his first government of 1964 some unlikely figures (unlikely that is by Gaitskellite standards) saw political office. Anthony Greenwood, Richard Crossman, Frank Cousins and Barbara Castle, all of them on the left of the Party and unlikely to be preferred by Gaitskell, became Cabinet Ministers or ministers of Cabinet rank. In fact it is instructive to compare Gaitskell's last Shadow Cabinet with Wilson's first Cabinet. A minor, though crucial, shift is discernible in the disposition of the factions. At the end of 1963 only one member of the Shadow Cabinet could be described as not being on the right – and that was Harold Wilson himself. It is not inconceivable that had Hugh Gaitskell become Premier in 1964 instead of Wilson, his Cabinet in party faction terms would have resembled that of his Shadow Cabinet at the time of his death. There is no reason to believe that Cousins, Greenwood, Crossman or Castle would have been offered Cabinet positions.

Naturally Wilson had to appease the still powerful right within his Parliamentary Party by surrounding himself in the Cabinet with Gaitskell's supporters – George Brown, Patrick Gordon Walker, Michael Stewart, Denis Healey and Ray Gunter. Yet the addition of some key left-wingers, those who would not have been elected to the Shadow Cabinet by the PLP, to top governmental positions was both a signal to his corpus of support in the party – the centre and left – that he was had not forgotten them and a sign of further things to come.

These personnel changes, apparently obscure and unimportant in themselves, were, however, a part of a radically different approach to Labour leadership. As well as rewarding old friends of old battles Wilson was embarking upon a radically new method of party leadership. He was opening up the party to the left, previously excluded, and softening up the leaderless and demoralised right.

Wilson's opening to the left was to continue during the course of his various governments. Under his Premiership Anthony Wedgwood-Benn was promoted to Cabinet level and then later Michael Foot, Peter Shore, Eric Varley and John Silkin. Below them were a host of other left-wingers who would most likely have been excluded by Gaitskell, who had many supporters of his own who would have been promoted. Wilson, for instance, denied office to some very able 'Gaitskellites' such as Brian Walden, John MacIntosh and David Marquand, who languised on the back benches whilst MPs of lesser ability but better left-wing credentials were included in Wilson governments.

Wilson's opening to the left happened to coincide with two crucial events in contemporary British political history for which he was not particularly responsible; but these events nevertheless enabled Wilson to carry his 'opening to the Left' even further and at the same time to make such an opening more acceptable. The first was the changed complexion of the trade union movement that took place in the late sixties – when Jack Jones assumed the Leadership of the Transport and General Workers' Union and Hugh Scanlon the Presidency of the AUEW. These changes at the top were reflected lower down the trade union structures too. For the first time the Labour right could no longer rely on an automatic majority in the 'block voting' at Labour Party Conferences.

Following these significant changes in the unions, Wilson could no longer be viewed as a 'left of centre' leader captured within a 'right of centre' movement. He became a freer spirit with more room to manoeuvre between the more equal factions. He made use of this freedom; he showed no inclination to stem the left advance within the party apparatus; indeed he welcomed it, as it made his own position that much more secure – he was no longer open to threats to his Leadership from a pre-eminent right.

Further, Labour's surprising loss of the 1970 election, followed by four years in opposition, also strengthened his hand. The left advanced within the party organization during these years. They made no real gains in the Parliamentary Party, which if anything was more to the right than in the 1966-70 period. However, the kind of issues which Edward Heath presented to British politics in these years strengthened the Labour left's hand in all sections of the Labour Party. The Industrial Relations Act, the compulsory prices and incomes policies leading to outright confrontation with the miners, and Britain's entry into the Common Market all conspired to give the left weapons in the political battle within the Labour movement. How these issues were ultimately resolved is of less importance than that they were used, quite skilfully, by the senior left leaders to advance their objective position in the only institution they care about.

Labour's opposition years propelled the party ever leftwards. For the first time since 1945 the Labour left gained control of the NEC. A new kind of NEC was born: one which could abolish the proscribed list, and, in relative secrecy, open up contacts with East European Communist parties. This new political alignment within the Labour movement also expressed itself at constituency level in the selection of candidates. When Labour returned to office in February 1974 the Tribune Group had grown in numbers and was to further improve its position in the October election of 1974. The Parliamentary left had become a serious force in the PLP. Although still short of a majority in the PLP the Tribune Group and their supporters in the Government and Cabinet, could ally with the centre to assume a majority. One such poignant example occurred in 1975 on the Common Market issue when a majority of the PLP voted against the renegotiated terms of entry. The strengthened position of the left within the PLP was confirmed by the surprisingly high vote, 137 out of 313, for Michael Foot for Prime Minister in 1976. Michael Foot, it should be noted, went through a very extreme phase in the middle seventies. As a minister of the crown he attacked, in an unprecedented manner, a High Court Judge. He also declared himself in favour of a 'Socialist Republic'. These declamations, together with the general political support he offered to the extremist NEC whilst a senior member of the Cabinet, were somewhat at variance with the standard depiction of him as some kind of 'constitutional Whig'.

During his Premiership, Wilson displayed no particular anxiety about the changing complexion of his party – apart, that is, from routine verbal lashing for 'activists' in local parties, attacks which he balanced with similar invective against 'right' factions. Whilst in office he seemed more concerned with the role of Roy Jenkins and Reg Prentice, particularly Prentice. Wilson's complex about the Social Democrats reached theatrical proportions when he launched into an attack upon some of us in the Social Democratic Alliance following a newsletter the SDA published at the Labour Party Conference of 1975 complaining about Labour's increasing contacts with East European Communist parties. He called the SDA an 'anti-party group' and added, to the great confusion of delegates: 'We have seen them at it before, a coup executed a few weeks before the last February election, a coup designed not to help the Labour Party, a coup designed to make it impossible for some of us to carry on.'⁵ He was evidently referring to a letter that had been signed by Sir Reginald Goodwin, Sir Ashley Bramall, Labour candidates and Councillors in support of Reg Prentice following Prentice's 1973 speech calling upon moderates in the Party to 'stand up and be counted'.

It was only after his resignation that Wilson's fears about the changing complexion of the Party were openly expressed. He argued in 1976 that: 'Different forms of what are called neo-Trotskyites, and Marcuseism and Maoism, IS [International Socialists] and all the rest . . . some of these are represented in the House.'⁶ Yet whilst in office, Wilson was far from forthcoming about the changing political currents in the party both inside and outside Parliament. He had a thesis for dealing with the left problem. It was a two-pronged strategy. First he would attempt to absorb the Parliamentary left, the 'Bevanites' (Castle, Greenwood, Crossman, Cousins, Wigg, Shore) by offering them the sweets of office. This would temper their radicalism – which was not particularly impressive to begin with. Secondly, he would simply ignore the extra-Parliamentary left (the Annual Conference and the National Executive Committee). As long as no central political challenge was launched that would upset his government or, when in opposition from 1970 to 1974, his Leadership of the party, the left could, with his benign neglect, do as they wished with the movement. They could pass resolutions critical of the Labour government and of the party leadership in Parliament; they could improve their numbers on the National Executive Committee; they could even go as far as to allow Labour MPs to be expelled as candidates by their local parties – all of this as long as it did not affect the conduct of the government. Wilson would never meet any left-wing challenge within the movement head on until and unless his own position was threatened from the right. This was because Wilson could always count upon left support in a political crisis. But the right was relatively docile during these years as the party machinery cranked ever leftwards. On two occasions, however, things very nearly got out of hand. The first was over the Common Market dispute, but in the end a formula was found to keep the party united. The pro-Market faction within the PLP was allowed to vote against a three-line whip, the terms were to be renegotiated and a referendum called upon the securing of new terms. The second occasion concerned the growing rebellion within the leadership of the party on the part of Reg Prentice and the attempt of his local constituency party to oust him as candidate. In the end the right refused to support Prentice (as we shall see later) and Wilson was able to soldier on, until his surprising resignation.

In one sense Harold Wilson is the 'guilty man' of his political generation. The fears harboured by some of the more astute Gaitskellites, and by Gaitskell himself, about the damage a Wilson Leadership and Premiership would do to the party were fully borne out by events. No Marxist he; but his whole thesis of Leadership enabled the extreme left to build their beachhead in the party and the unions to the point where they achieved a majority. This was Wilson's gift to his successor. Callaghan inherited a pitiful hand. It was the product of the strategic incompetence of the man who led the Labour Party for thirteen years.

Callaghan

Jim Callaghan came from a different stable from Wilson's. Apart from an initial flirtation with Labour's left in 1946 over the Government's foreign policy,[7] Callaghan pursued an orthodox career on the right of the party for three decades before becoming its Leader and Prime Minister in 1976. Indeed, during the height of the visceral factional in-fighting which took place under Gaitskell's leadership he was one of Gaitskell's most dogged supporters. During the unilateralist controversy in 1960 Callaghan was the only senior figure to lend unwavering support to Gaitskell. By 1962 Callaghan had become so identified with the 'hard right' that he lost his seat on the constituency section of the NEC. Yet Callaghan was no 'intellectual'; he was not part of the more theoretical 'revisionist' group of MPs who gravitated to Frognal Gardens (Gaitskell's home). Rather he was a more traditional Labourist, rather like Ray Gunter and the trade union leaders who provided Gaitskell with his base in the trade unions and the party apparatus. And it was Callaghan's instinctive Labourism, together with (no doubt) a good dose of native opportunism, that led him to head the fight in the Cabinet, some years later, against Wilson's *In Place of Strife* trade union reform proposals.

As the seventies developed a distinct ambiguity developed within Callaghan's political character. He was very 'conservative' in his instincts (like all Labourists) and very much a 'movement man'; yet the very movement to which he was dedicated and which had given him so much was being radicalized in front of him. His natural allies in the trade union leadership of the fifties and early sixties had departed the scene and Callaghan had very little in common politically with the new leaders of the unions (Jones, Scanlon, Clive Jenkins, McGahey, Buckton, Briginshaw and so on). Also, Callaghan was obviously even less at home with the 'new left' in the Parliamentary Labour Party. For a time after his election as Leader and Prime Minister, Callaghan looked as though he might stand his ground against the Left. He certainly refused to adopt Wilson's tactic of balancing right against left. He made a tough, virtually monetarist, speech to the Party Conference of 1976; at that same Conference he made a little noticed (but in the politics of Labour rather important) intervention in the debate about party-to-party relations with Eastern bloc regimes; he was much more instinctively hostile to the NEC left majority than his predecessor had been. And it seemed, during the early part of the 1978-9 wage round as though he was finally going to risk a major confrontation with the trade union leaders. Yet at some point during the 1978-9 winter of industrial dislocation Callaghan made up his mind — his contradictions were resolved in favour of his 'movement' impulse. He shrank from a fight over wages policy and, partly in consequence, from a showdown with the NEC. Wilsonism had returned.

Of course Callaghan's position in the party and movement was a relatively weak one. First, he only became Leader by a small margin. Second he, unlike the last right-wing Leader, could not command the loyalty of the NEC or the Annual Conference. In fact his political opponents were 'dug in' in the party apparatus. Thirdly, Callaghan was a relatively old man compared with his two Labour predecessors; he did not have the inclination nor the necessary personal reserves to engage in a protracted strategic struggle with the Labour left. Furthermore, outside Parliament he had no proper base of support and lacked the energy and time that would be needed to create one. There was also little in the way of a body of intelligent, idealistic and imaginative younger intellectuals and organizers whom he could call upon for support. Callaghan was very much a stopgap Leader, presiding. And as he presided the battle for the succession went on below him in the Cabinet. As though aware of these limitations, Callaghan concentrated upon state issues and appeared to ignore the politics of Labour.

But Callaghan's 'legacy', as it was building up, was rather more destructive than this. Not only was he going to bequeath, by omission, to the nation a united Labour movement controlled by the left but he was, by commission, contributing to the collapse of political authority. As his government stumbled to its close in 1979 he seemed ever more eager, in public, to proclaim and commend his own impotence as Prime Minister and that, too, of Parliament. The message was not an unintelligent one: governments can no longer govern; Parliament has become unimportant (this was particularly noticeable in his attitude to Prime Minister's Question Time and in his proclaimed distaste for debating industrial relations matters across the floor in the so-called 'forum of the nation');[8] the nation could only be effectively governed by 'social contracts', 'concordats', deals between the administration and trade union leaders. This was a complete return to the general thesis of British internal statecraft initiated by Wilson in 1974. But the seeming (temporary?) realism of the message could not obscure its moral bankruptcy. It is one thing for a Prime Minister to actually govern according to these new rules, quite another to proclaim to the world that no other way of 'governing' is possible. Hugo Young reported that during the IMF crisis of 1976 Harold Lever went to Washington and

> he elaborated Callaghan's much-repeated alarum about the dangers to Parliamentary democracy from too stringent an onslaught on PSBR (public sector borrowing requirement) and embellished it by pointing out that harsh cuts in public spending would inevitably entail a serious cut-back in Britain's army in Germany . . . . Helmut Sonnenfeldt remembers: 'Lever was very dramatic in representing the effects of what was happening in London . . .'

Young reports William Rogers of the US State Department as saying,

> We all had the feeling it really could come apart in quite a serious way. As I saw it, it was a choice between Britain remaining in the liberal financial system of the West as opposed to a radical change of course, because we were concerned about Tony Benn precipitating a policy decision by Britain to turn its back on the IMF. I think if that had happened the whole system would have begun to come apart.

Young also reports Brent Scowcroft, of the White House National Security Council, saying of the British IMF crisis: 'It was considered by us to be the greatest single threat to the Western world.'[9] Essentially what all of this amounted to, according to Young's sources, was a Callaghan-inspired declaration to the Americans that Britain had, essentially, ceased to be a parliamentary democracy: that democratic politicians could no longer take the appropriate action to solve Britain's financial crisis without precipitating a revolutionary situation. The argument, evidently, was that *no* government could take the necessary action. This, if true, was as complete an abdication of authority as is conceivable; and was in line with Wilson's and Callaghan's general thesis that power had already passed from Parliament to another forum (a condominium of government and unions).

Again, irrespective of the merits of that case, those who proclaim it have to answer a further question: if it is proclaimed from the top that power has passed away from Parliament, why should not, as a consequence, extraparliamentarism as a way of life become entrenched? This public declaration of powerlessness is tantamount to an invitation by the Prime Minister to all organized groups to challenge the system. And, they increasingly did. Callaghan, the *In Place of Strife* manoeuvre notwithstanding, had entered office with so much promise: he departed his 1976 – 9 term as Prime Minister by a demonstration of his impotence.

The Social Democrats

Yet the full responsibility for the inadequacy of the political statecraft of the leaders of the Labour movement of the seventies cannot lie with Wilson and Callaghan. Both of them only remained in power because they had the support of the Parliamentary Labour Party. The left Parliamentary faction (as we have seen) had their own reasons for supporting them (certainly in any real crisis). Yet the Parliamentary right also acquiesced in the general strategy of the Labour leadership.

From Wilson's assumption of the Leadership in February of 1963 the Parliamentary right was never again to launch a central counterattack to recover the levers of power within Britain's premier political institution. And without such an attempt not only the Labour Party and movement but the political axis of the nation would tilt over leftwards. A heavy responsibility rested on the leaders of the Labour right during this period. That they, as a group, did not rise to the challenge affected the future course of British politics, a course still being run. Of course the 'Parliamentary right' was not united.

There were, broadly, three groupings. First, the 'loyalists'; this group, mainly trade union MPs, were inclined to support the Party leadership almost as a matter of principle. On the back benches they were a solid addition to the 'payroll' vote (the MPs in the government who, because of their position, were governed by 'collective responsibility' for Cabinet decisions). Secondly, there were the 'Jenkinsites'. This group tended, during the Wilson years, to see Roy Jenkins as a natural rallying point behind which the 'social democratic' forces could gather. During the seventies this 'Jenkinsite' faction was highly organized, extremely loyal and had very good relations with the press. As late as 1976 it could still muster 56 votes for Jenkins in his bid for the party Leadership. Yet this group was seen by the average Labour MP as rather too remote, too 'intellectual', far too concerned with Europe, too 'middle-class' and politically incestuous. Neil Kinnock had some fun at its expense at the Labour Party Conference of 1978; referring to the Leadership election campaign of 1976 he said:

. . . there was among the candidates, for instance, one Roy Jenkins — Taffy as we used to call him [laughter]. And there is a story told — it is a bit of black propaganda that was put about, but I think it illustrates the point of the leadership election very adequately — about an elderly Yorkshire Member who was sitting in the tea room, and was approached by one of Roy's acolytes — sorry, I mean supporters — and asked: 'Will you be voting for Roy Jenkins?' And the Yorkshire Member said: 'No lad, we're all Labour here' [laughter]. [10]

Thirdly, there was a small number of more robust, independent-minded men who were even more disillusioned with Wilson's leadership than were the Jenkins faction. They included Reg Prentice, Brian Walden and John MacIntosh. MacIntosh was a dedicated European: Prentice and Walden were sceptical (although they both supported the European cause in the 1975 referendum). If these men had been at the top of the Parliamentary right in the 1970s and possessed of a large following the whole history of the period may have been dramatically different.

The first two Wilson governments posed few problems for the right. They acted well within the post-war social democratic consensus which had been built up since 1945 by Labour and Tory administrations alike. Indeed, if anything, the record of 1964 – 70 was more revisionist than might have been thought possible under Wilson. Jenkins's Chancellorship at the end of the period was correctly monetarist (the kind of administration of the economy favoured by Sir Keith Joseph). Also, incredibly and unfathomably, Wilson set his mind to a major reform of trade union power by his *In Place of Strife* proposals of 1969. These proposals, including provisions for a 'conciliation pause', plans for dealing with inter-union disputes and in certain circumstances a compulsory strike ballot (an idea that had been specifically rejected a year before by the Donovan Commission), were anathema to the Party's left wing. Yet, it was the Labour right who sabotaged the White Paper. Wilson was forced into a humiliating climb-down after it became apparent that he could not carry his Parliamentary Party on the issue. Most of the trade unions were implacably opposed to the proposal and so was a sizeable proportion of the Parliamentary Party including many 'loyalist' and non-factional MPs. It would have been a very difficult exercise to bring off in this environment. Yet no attempt was made on the right of the party to rally around this unusual bout of Wilsonian daring and give leadership in the struggle. In fact, the very opposite was the case. Jim Callaghan and Tony Crosland were opposed to the enterprise from the beginning and attempted to use this uncharacteristic act of Wilson's to undermine and overthrow him. As the momentum of opposition to the proposed Act built up the rest of the right crumbled under the pressure. Indeed, there was an unedifying scene in the Cabinet meeting of 17 June after the Chief Whip had reported that in his view he could not guarantee the Bill's passage. Peter Jenkins reports a crumbling of the Cabinet, including the hard-line social democrats, before Wilson's eyes.[11] Indeed, even by that time it might have been too late to salvage the legislation. But, as the Labour right had refused to campaign on the issue we shall never know the strength it could have brought to bear in this very important battle. The loss of *In Place of Strife* was a psychological blow to the whole political system; and it left its mark on the Conservative Party. As Labour could not force through even the most sensible trade union reforms then subsequent Tory administrations were going to be defensive and timid in constructing and selling their own proposals.

The action of Labour's still dominant faction during this episode was characteristic of its general performance since Gaitskell's death. It was without a leader of real stature; it was without a central political strategy; it was divided, lacking the coherence and commitment needed to re-establish itself. Above all it would not risk splitting the party under any circumstances. It must have seen that *In Place of Strife* was a potential axe for splitting the movement. It refused to wield it.

Following the *In Place of Strife* fiasco Wilson soon recovered his position within the party. He remained the most acceptable possible Leader for the left. As the party went into opposition in 1970 he became unassailable; particularly so because as the two broad factions became more equal in power he could in consequence straddle them with greater ease. And it was during this period that the leadership of the right passed to Roy Jenkins.

Jenkins had been a successful Chancellor, and had grouped around him the middle-class highly educated 'Gaitskellites'. These MPs were culturally as well as politically more attuned to Jenkins than to the other possible contender for the leadership of the right faction, James Callaghan. Callaghan had had an unimpressive record in office during 1964-70, was considered far too reactionary by the revisionists (particularly so because of his attitude to immigration questions during his period at the Home Office) and, anyway, seemed uninterested in leading a faction.

In the early seventies Roy Jenkins embarked upon a series of speeches which appeared to challenge the authority of Wilson as party Leader. Jenkins was articulate, robust and had made fewer compromises with the left than any other senior Labour figure. It seemed for a while as though he was donning the mantle of Gaitskell. A comparison between Gaitskell and Jenkins is interesting. In cultural terms both Gaitskell and Jenkins could be tarnished, by the left, with the brush of elitism and remoteness. Neither was possessed of a regional accent − very important in the egalitarian world of the organized British working-class movement; both had 'coteries' around them. Yet, for all this, they were both politicians who were attracted to great causes − Gaitskell to NATO, Jenkins to Europe − and through these were able to build up constituencies of support outside the party apparatus. Their political horizons were both set way beyond the confines of their party: they were both potential 'splitters', and the left knew it.

However, Gaitskell's great cause was more popular amongst Labour voters than was Jenkins's Europeanism. As Jenkins emerged as the leader of Labour's right in the early seventies he brought with him the European problem. For years he had been a leading advocate of Britain's entry into the Common Market − he had opposed Gaitskell on this issue in 1962. Heath's election victory in 1970 brought the issue of Europe back into the foreground of British politics. Under Jenkins's guidance, therefore, the Labour right became identified with pro-Europeanism, a minority position within the Labour movement as a whole and, moreover, one that involved some of the most visceral cultural, psychological and social undercurrents to be felt in British politics for many years. While Jenkins was leader of the right and as long as the Common Market was the dominant issue Labour could not be captured back for the right – indeed, rather the opposite; the right's objective position within the movement as a whole was bound to be weakened.

Even so, Britain's entry into Europe assumed for the Jenkins faction the proportions of a crusade. Jenkins and his supporters were prepared to go all the way on this question, something they were, peculiarly, not willing to do on the issue of the nature of their own party at home. It was as if a calculation had been made: that the simple act of getting Britain into Europe was itself some kind of ultimate defence against the left at home in Britain. Jenkins resigned from the Shadow Cabinet on the European issue and led 69 MPs into the Conservative lobby against a three-line whip. Hence it was on the European issue that the Labour right's flag was nailed to the mast, the left faced down and real power politics employed.

None of this 'heroism' on the part of the Labour right, of course, guarantees that Labour will not unfurl the anti-European standard in future. Although in the aftermath of the referendum decision in 1975 the Labour Executive stated 'the debate on Britain's membership of the European Community is now over' it went on to announce that the referendum 'did not and could not close the debate on the Community's structure and policies'.[12] That Labour, in the eighties, will make a firm commitment to withdraw is not fanciful. Already by the time of the direct elections to the European Parliament the Labour Executive had laid down stringent conditions on its own candidates for that Parliament. One fascinating condition was that any money a Labour European MP should receive from the Parliament for research facilities should go to Transport House. Evidently, no pro-Market Labour MP in the European Parliament was going to be allowed to build up an alternative local organization based upon money from Strasbourg. As the *Financial Times* put it: 'This will prevent any move by

European MPs to build up their own research empire'[13] – for *research* read *political*.

Yet although the European rebellion of 1973 soured Roy Jenkins's relations with the Labour Party, and ensured that he could never lead it, the 'Jenkinsites' remained a force to be reckoned with. Yet Jenkins and his supporters left their rebellion at this point. No other issue could stir them so powerfully; and certainly not the gathering threat to the right's historic dominance of the party apparatus.

One of the first tests of resolve came over the challenge to the candidacy of Dick Taverne at Lincoln. For years past Taverne, one of the central figures in the Campaign for Democratic Socialism (the group which organized support for Gaitskel in 1960), had been the target of a group of left socialists within his constituency party. This group, as with most socialists, were utterly unrepresentative of the Labour voters in the constituency, a thesis that was proved beyond dispute when the Labour voters of Lincoln turned the left Labour Party out of control of the local council during a period when it seemed that a viable and lasting alternative local Labour Party was being created. Taverne's opponents seized upon the fact that he voted against a three-line whip in the Commons vote on European entry in 1973 in order to legitimize their long-standing campaign to remove him as candidate and Member of Parliament. The National Executive Committee was presented with a major problem when his local constituency party decided to drop him and sent their decision to the NEC for endorsement. In the past serious pressure would have been brought upon the constituency party to rethink; alternatively the constituency might even have been wound up. Yet, Labour's new left-wing NEC upheld the decision and seemed only concerned to make sure that the correct procedures had been gone through. They decided to take an *administrative* rather than a *political* view of their function. More interesting, though, than the NEC's role in this dispute (which was hardly surprising given its political complexion) was the attitude of the pro-Common

Market Labour right. Put simply they ditched one of their major supporters. At one point Dick Taverne was led to believe that Roy Jenkins himself would come to Lincoln during the by-election campaign in order to speak on his behalf. This, of course, would have led to a momentous split in the party as Jenkins, then the undisputed leader of the right pro-Market faction in the Parliamentary Party, would be supporting a candidate against one from his own party. Yet it was not to be. A major, and possibly historic, split in the Labour Party was averted and Taverne, although he went on to win two elections as Democratic Labour candidate, was forced out of British politics. What is also of great interest in the Taverne saga is the fact that so disillusioned with the Labour party had traditional Labour voters become that large numbers of them were prepared to vote consistently against the party of their habitual choice on an issue – European entry – that had never had much popular appeal. In fact, if the pro-European Labour right had wanted to reconstruct British politics over the European issue they probably could have done so. They could have used the European issue as the pretext, widened the debate to include the changed nature of the Labour Party, accused the left of subverting the political organization of Labour, set forth their own candidates and created a new left-of-centre party. With Jenkins as Leader, and no matter how unpopular European entry, the very least that could have been done would have been to threaten the left with this reconstruction and to save Taverne. The ditching of Taverne was the first major show of weakness, of lack of will. It was the green light for the events surrounding the end of Reg Prentice's career at Newham.

Prentice presented both left and right with a much more profound problem than Taverne. He could not be typified as being a pro-European, nor with being an extreme right-winger. He had come top of the Shadow Cabinet in the elections of 1973. His own personal rebellion against the drifting politics of Labour involved his refusal to countenance Labour's increasing habit of setting itself against the rule of law. He started a campaign on the question of constitutionalism and began to publicly spell out the actual nature of the political change that had overtaken the Labour party. This was much firmer ground on which to fight the left than the narrowness of Europe; and Prentice, as a senior front-bencher and then a Cabinet Minister, could rally wide public support behind his campaign. Yet he was the only senior figure to fully understand that the only way to properly tackle the left was to attack them *openly* and to raise the all-important question of the extremism of the left and the threat that it posed both to the Labour Party and to the nation. Yet, he too, as with Taverne, was to be seriously let down. Although he secured the support of a majority of the PLP by way of a letter written to his constituency party asking them to reconsider their decision to sack him, and although Roy Jenkins, Shirley Williams and Tom Jackson (of the Post Office Workers' Union) turned out to support him at a meeting in Newham, no further support was forthcoming. The Labour right in the Parliamentary Party was simply not prepared to risk a major organic split in the party over Reg Prentice.

As well as refusing to support Taverne and Prentice, the Labour right was wary about any serious attempt to raise the question of the changed nature of the Labour left and to campaign vigorously against it. A group of grass-roots supporters of the traditions of Labourism set up an organization called the Social Democratic Alliance in the summer of 1975 and it attracted considerable publicity for its robust condemnations of left-wing excesses. At the Annual Conference in 1975 it attacked the new departure of the NEC in arranging party-to-party exchanges with Communist regimes abroad and also raised the issue of senior Labour figures speaking at and associating themselves with Communist Party organizations. This caused consternation within the counsels of the Labour right. The chairman of the SDA, Peter Stephenson, although he had helped draft the document, resigned. So did others. The SDA had evidently gone too far. According to moderates within the PLP it was 'counterproductive' to fight the left in this way. The battle should not evidently be ideological and in the open. It should instead be carried on by hard work at local and trade union level. The anti-SDA argument from within the Labour right was that the Labour Party machine could be recaptured by patient hard work at grass-roots level alone and without the kind of public 'hyperbole' that would alert Labour voters to the deep-seated problems within the party. Wilson himself wanted the left problem dealt with in this way, as did virtually the whole of the right wing within the Parliamentary Party. Consequently another organization was established calling itself The Campaign for a Labour Victory. The leading lights behind this were William Rodgers, who had masterminded the earlier Gaitskellite CDS, Shirley Williams, John Cartwright and Ian Wrigglesworth (both important Manifesto Group MPs). It seemed as though the right was set upon a serious exercise to recapture the party in the way they had done over fifteen years before when Gaitskell was in trouble over defence. The difference between 1960 and 1976, however, was marked. Constituency parties had changed complexion, as had the trade unions. To 'fight back' would therefore be difficult, particularly if the aim was to recover control of the NEC for the moderates. The CLV made no progress at all in their campaign. In fact they lost ground. At the 1978 Annual Conference, a target date for them, not only did the NEC swing further left (with the addition of it of Denis Skinner, Neil Kinnock and Douglas Hoyle) but one of the founders of the CLV, John Cartwright, was himself thrown off by a Tribune member, Leslie Huckfield. The later decision to suspend publication of *Socialist Commentary* appeared to set the seal of failure upon this particular phase of Labour right activity. With the leaders of the right in Parliament unwilling to raise an ideological opposition to the left and unable to recover ground organizationally, the Labour Party apparatus was abandoned as the arena for left-right struggle. The Premiership of Jim Callaghan, and the increasingly beleaguered PLP, became the last hope.

The Labour right were not simply content however to allow the left to take over the party machine. They also lent themselves and their considerable political influence and electoral attraction, to legitimizing a fundamentally new national political settlement. The political and constitutional conflict between trade union power and the parliamentary state, always nascent, came to a dramatic head during the latter years of the Heath government. Whatever the merits of Heath's policies and tactics in dealing with the trade unions during those years the Conservative administration, through its majority in Parliament, did represent the duly constituted government of the country. Its Industrial Relations Act was but the implementation of proposals put before the electorate in 1970 and, according to all available polling date, remained popular; although its prices and incomes policy was not a part of its manifesto in 1970 it became law by due process and was no more nor less legitimate than the many radical departures from the mandate of both previous and successor governments. At no point between 1970 and 1974 did it stray outside the bounds of constitutional authority. Heath's government was inept, inflexible and politically unsophisticated, but that was all. It did not represent a threat to democracy itself. The threat came from sections of the Labour movement which it, with every constitutional right, attempted to withstand.

If the Labour right, in the form of the Parliamentary Leadership of the Labour Party, had sided with Heath against the attempt to undermine Parliament then the contours of the political map of Britain in the 1980s would today look very different. 'Siding with Heath', however, did not mean agreeing to support his policies. Labour had no obligations there. It could have opposed the Industrial Relations Act, opposed the prices and incomes policies, opposed the economic and social policies – but all within the framework of law. It should have insisted that the law be obeyed and then changed after a new Parliament was elected. It was the Labour right's refusal to pursue this normal constitutional course that not only undermined Heath but sabotaged the Parliamentary system itself. When the London dockers, under Communist leadership, flouted the Industrial Relations Act the Labour right, apart from Reg Prentice, was silent. It saw no obligation to defend the rule of law against the power of those who sought to flout it. When the local council at Clay Cross broke the law Labour went even further. It actively encouraged law-breaking. First, at its Annual Conference of 1973, the leadership of the Party urged acceptance of a resolution stating that: 'Upon the election of a Labour Government all penalties, financial or otherwise, should be removed retrospectively from councillors who have courageously refused to implement the Housing Finance Act, 1972.' Edward Short, the Deputy Leader of the Labour Party, supported this motion in words which came near to incitement to break the law. Of his speech, which was not condemned by any senior Labour rightist, the authoritative *New Law Journal* wrote:

A future statement on the same lines, only slightly less carefully worded, might even be construed as conspiracy to break the law, and one can only wonder at the motives of Mr. Short's colleagues on the NEC in allowing him to act as the fall guy in a very dangerous situation . . . One can only assume that Mr. Short, whether for political or personal reasons, was not in full control of his political faculties when he made that speech, for it was a disaster — a disaster that could have far-reaching consequences so far as the Labour Party, and even democracy in this country, are concerned.[14]

Secondly the incoming Labour Government preceded to act upon this motion by introducing into the House of Commons the novel act of recompensing law-breakers, by relieving them of their penalties established by a duly constituted court, for acts which were illegal. This sordid piece of legislation was manoeuvred through the House by Anthony Crosland. His actions in this matter caused him much personal anguish; yet by this time he had a settled determination to remain on the course which might have, had his untimely death not intervened, led him to the Party Leadership. He had given up on any further additions to his considerable intellectual legacy. Douglas Eden has written: 'I remember him saying in 1971 that he could make no further additions or revisions to *The Future of Socialism* or *The Conservative Enemy*: there would be no more original works.'[15]

The advice given to the Labour Cabinet about this extraordinary action (relieving law-breakers of their penalties) by the Lord Chancellor and the Attorney-General must have been interesting. The shabby reputation of Labour's law officers amongst constitutionalists derives from Labour's handling of the Clay Cross dispute.

In any clash between labour (either a trade union or a Labour-controlled local authority) and the state it is natural and legitimate for the Labour Party to take the side of the labour 'interest'. After all, this is primarily what the party is in politics to defend and further. To campaign for a change in the law, to organize voluntary contributions for those who suffer under it, to pledge repeal − all of this both preserves Labour's unique relationship with its own constituency and places this commitment within the general constitutional framework. Indeed this is the supreme task of Labour leadership; it is what differentiates Labourism from revolutionary politics. To take the opportunity of an unpopular Conservative government in order to undermine and sabotage the constitutional system itself was an act of abdication on the part of the Labour right. In order to gain power they severely weakened a political system which protects the British working class from more arbitrary forms of rule − a one-party state run by socialist bosses or an authoritarian rightism. Furthermore, they lost credibility in the party by yielding under pressure to a left wing that had previously respected though opposed them. By refusing to stand firm on the constitution at a time when the nation was undergoing severe social and political upheaval Labour's social democrats reduced and diminished themselves and the tradition they represented. The Labour right will not be able to recover.

And so was ushered in a new political settlement. Authority drained out of Parliament; and the Labour right, having helped to diminish Parliamentary sovereignty, then went on to set up a government/trade union condominium which found its expression in the 'social contract'.

The central plot in Labour's story in the 1970s is not one of some great left-wing triumph of will, ideology or tactics. The Labour left are certainly the victors; but they were handed their victory by the Labour right. Wilson, Callaghan and the social democrats adopted a strategy that was bound to fail — conciliation, compromise and party unity at all costs. The alternative strategy was never tried.

The alternative strategy was simple: Labour's leaders should have issued an ultimatum to the advancing left — '*either* we have our way and Labour is returned to its traditional social democratic principles *or* we will split the party'. Such an ultimatum would have stood every chance of being successful. The senior figures of Labour's Marxist wing were well aware of their own political unpopularity, of the gains that had been made by and through a united Labour Party, of the dangers of political isolation.

In such an atmosphere, with Labour's leaders obviously prepared to go to the brink, the Labour right could have recaptured the party apparatus. With the threat of an organic split hanging over them even Jones and Scanlon, and the Communist Party factions within their respective unions, would probably have given way. And with the Transport union and the Engineers reconstructed politically then the NEC would automatically follow suit. Such an obvious confrontation between right and left within the Labour movement would also have improved the popularity of the Labour governments.

Even if the Labour left had refused to yield the right would still have been in a commanding position. At any time after February 1974, under the leadership of a Labour Prime Minister, a new party could have been created and that new party could have gone to the country on a separate platform and with a separate organization. Labour's left-wing NEC would have been able to retain the title 'Labour Party' but the new grouping could have used the more alluring term 'Democratic Labour' to describe themselves. 'Democratic Labour' – given a lead from the very top – would have carried in their ranks all the respected and well-known Labour leaders. The public would not have seen these figures as 'renegades'; rather the (correct) impression would have been created in the public mind that the National Executive was at fault, that its extremism and intransigence had caused the split. The new 'Democratic Labour' Party would have had funds, candidates and a political organization at its disposal within days. In fact, the Liberals could have been the basis for it; or, in the event of Liberal dithering, a new political organization could have been set up overnight – from scratch. 'Democratic Labour', given proper political leadership, would have provided a rallying-point for thousands of disillusioned activists; it would have stirred into political activity many of those who during the sixties had fled from the politics of Labour and who found the dreary political machines incapable of channelling or expressing their idealism and enthusiasm.

'Democratic Labour' would have won great electoral victories. It is inconceivable that the rump (NEC) Labour Party – isolated, attacked for being under extremist control, propounding socialist polices unpopular with the voters – could have beaten 'Democratic Labour' amongst traditional Labour voters. Indeed, 'Democratic Labour' would have secured a majority of Labour votes in virtually all constituencies.

In traditionally safe Labour seats many 'Democratic Labour' MPs would have been returned. In marginal seats

'Democratic Labour' candidates might have split the left vote and let the Conservatives in — but perhaps for only one election. Yet so disillusioned was much of the traditional Conservative vote, and so unanchored was the floating vote (as we saw with the huge swings to the Liberals in 1972, 1973 and at the February 1974 general election) that 'Democratic Labour' might have won some of the marginals outright. It is not fanciful to suggest that 'Democratic Labour' — gaining a majority of traditional Labour votes, acquiring 'floating voters' and those who rarely vote, adding as well some traditional Conservative and Liberal voters — could have been returned in an election with a majority in its own right. For instance, 'Democratic Labour' might have won seats like Barking and Dagenham, Chester-le-Street and Barnsley. If the sitting MP had stood as 'Democratic Labour' victory would have been assured. If not, but with Labour's established leaders supporting a 'Democratic Labour' candidate, then the sitting MP would have been in serious trouble. 'Democratic Labour', in a general election called in such circumstances, could have won over 200 safe Labour seats and up to 100 marginals. After all, in 1931, in the circumstances of a far less impressive schism in the Labour Party than the one envisaged here, NEC Labour won only about 50 seats.

Before holding such a crisis election Labour's Parliamentary leaders could have tested the water. They could have invited one of the moderate Labour MPs who was in trouble with his left-wing caucus and under threat of de-selection, to resign and fight a by-election as 'Democratic Labour' candidate. At that by-election, in flagrant confrontation with the NEC, Labour's leaders could have publicly supported and spoken for this 'Democratic Labour' candidate. The result would have been illuminating. Dick Taverne, with no backing at all from any Labour MP or senior Labour figure (and during a period when Labour was in opposition) won a resounding by-election victory as 'Democratic Labour'. If Wilson, Callaghan, Jenkins *et al.* had publicly supported him it is doubtful whether the official (NEC) Labour candidate in

Lincoln would have held his deposit.

What was it that prevented Labour's moderate Parliamentary leaders − all of whom were aware of the gathering left-wing advance within the party apparatus, all of whom could at least glimpse the potential in 'Democratic Labour' − from so reconstructing British politics? Part of the answer lies with the old problem of 'who will bell the cat?'. None of Labour's senior Parliamentary leaders wanted to 'go it alone' into the 'Democratic Labour' option; at no time could enough of them be gathered together to form a 'bloc', so none took the initiative. It is my view that one *senior* Cabinet minister, willing to see the whole strategy through, to develop the case against the left in robust and coherent terms, and backed by a very small handful of MPs (many of whom were to lose their candidatures in any case), would have caused a stampede.

Then there is simple inertia, present in all parties at all times in all political systems. The inertia on the Labour right after 1974 was made more comfortable by the left's sensible strategy of allowing the moderates to hold office in the government whilst denying them power in the party.

Also present in the minds of many of the seventies moderates was a fixation about 'the Labour movement'. Years of service to the party induces a psychological loyalty *not* to the working people (Ray Gunter's 'people from whence I came') but rather to the byzantine structures of the Labour hierarchy − a political machine that delivers to most Labour politicians what status, wealth and power they cannot otherwise achieve. Loyalty to 'this great movement of ours' was no longer an idealistic invocation; it had degenerated over the decades into a sordid rationale for employment.

On top of these limitations imposed by careerism there was a phobia about raising the communist issue. Labour's right wing in the seventies was 'anti anti-communist', at least in public. In keeping with the times the Labour right considered anti-communism far too crude; to merely raise the issue of communism within Labour's ranks was to invite charges of McCarthyism, hysteria, unseriousness. Although communism is the over-arching challenge to this generation of British and Western democratic leaders, as Fascism was in the thirties, and although the extent of communist (Trotskyite and CPGB) infiltration into Labour was known, it was still far safer to be considered a non-communist than an anti-communist. Gaitskell's fighting speech at Stalybridge in 1952, when he raised the issue of communist infiltration into the Labour Party and so impressed the trade union leaders of the time, became but an embarrassing memory – even though the underlying situation had worsened since those years. If Labour's right were to launch any coherent and powerful counteroffensive (either within the Labour Party or by breaking out of it) it would have to use anti-Communism both as a legitimate reason for its new posture and as a very effective means of discrediting the left amongst the voters. This it was not prepared to do.

Perhaps Labour's thoroughly modern moderates simply did not possess the will, the stamina or the imagination to sustain the kind of systematic campaign needed to break out from their beleagured laager in the PLP. The social democrats of the 1970s were often depicted, some of them unfairly, as being 'wet'. A new centre party will not survive for long without a shade more robustness than that displayed in the seventies.

So the Labour right soldiered on within the party: but it justified this error on grand strategic grounds. It was suggested from the highest quarters that if the right should break out then the Labour Party would be left in the hands of the Marxists; this would unnecessarily polarize British politics and produce an extreme left-wing-dominated Parliamentary Labour Party, under Benn or worse, that would sooner or later win an election and take power. This thesis was, and is, riddled with flaws. First, by detaching the Labour right from the Labour Party there is every chance that NEC Labour will cease to exist as a Parliamentary force. Secondly, even if NEC Labour did retain a significant Parliamentary presence and even, as is most unlikely, it remains Her Majesty's major opposition party, it would find it very difficult to actually *win* elections. It would, more likely, simply take on the role of the Eurocommunist parties of southern Europe: mass parties with a significant following but unable to secure much beyond a third of the vote. The British left would have become effectively isolated.

CHAPTER 4

Socialism and the British: the Left against the Working People

The Decline of the Labour Party

As the political character of the Labour Party changes, so its hold on popular support loosens. It is an interesting irony that as trade union membership rises, support for the political left declines. Measured both in terms of votes at elections and by active party membership Labour is becoming less popular, less rooted in the industrial nation and less of a natural political expression of the working people.

In 1951 Labour received the largest vote of any political party in British history. The years 1951 to 1974 are a story of dramatic electoral deterioration. In 1951 Labour's share of the popular vote was 48.8 per cent. In February 1974 it was 37.2 per cent. In October 1974 it rose only to 39.2 per cent. By 1979 it was down to 36.9 per cent. In 1951 Labour's vote as a percentage of the total *electorate* was 39.9 per cent. In February, 1974 it was a mere 29.2 per cent. By October 1974 it had fallen further, to 28.5 per cent. By 1979 it was 28.1 per cent. What is even more intriguing is Labour's declining support, at the polls, amongst the 'working class'. Precise comparisons between the early fifties and the seventies are difficult to come by; but what is certain is that Labour's traditional mass 'working-class' support continues to shrink. Turnout at the polls in traditional Labour areas continues to fall (certainly when compared to the late forties and early fifties) as does turnout as a whole. Indeed, in the first general election of 1974 there is some evidence to suggest that, contrary to the national pattern, there was a swing *away* from Labour amongst skilled workers (C1 social class category); and that there was a lower swing to Labour amongst the unskilled manual groups than amongst the higher managerial and professional people.[1] Also, if one adds into the picture of the historically dwindling Labour vote, the votes added to it by some of the immigrant communities (particularly those of West Indian origin) then the loosening of Labour's grip upon its traditional 'working class' support becomes even more apparent. In the 1979 general election Labour's claim to be a 'workers' party' looked even more threadbare; millions of trade union members (and their families) voted Conservative or Liberal and there were savage swings to the Conservatives in traditional 'affluent worker' constituencies south of the Trent, particularly in the New Towns; 'working people and their families' were simply not responding to a party which promised 'irreversible shifts' in power and wealth in their direction.

Labour's shrinking electoral base might, of course, have shrivelled even further if Labour's Parliamentary leaders had not lent the left-wing party apparatus such respectability during the three most recent general elections. Labour's NEC was wrested from moderate control in 1973 and it would have been instructive if this newly left-dominated NEC had been able to appeal directly to the electorate, shorn, that is, of any 'social democratic' cover. The British people have never been presented with the chance to pronounce upon an overtly socialist party primarily because when elections come around Labour's socialist component (the outlandish left rhetoric as well as the socialist leaders) remains effectively hidden from view.

Yet there have been a few occasions when the interested observer has been allowed a glimpse at the real views of Labour voters. One such was during the Common Market referendum of 1975. In a sense the campaign turned not on the merits of the Common Market issue but rather upon the popularity of the various leadership groups that were supporting the opposing cases. The anti-market case, which was by no means unpopular, was nevertheless diminished by the fact that its main proponents resided on the Labour left. Even with such a populist issue behind them the Labour left could only gather about a third of the voters behind them. Another glimpse can be afforded by the result of the 1979 European election in the city of Liverpool. The Labour Party in this huge metropolitan area had become so radicalized that it could choose as its European Assembly candidate Mr Terence Harrison. Harrison was a member of the editorial board of *Militant*, the newspaper of the Trotskyite faction within the Labour Party that had been the subject of an investigation about infiltration into the party by Reg Underhill, the national agent. It seemed inconceivable that Labour's leadership – either the Parliamentary leaders or even the National Executive Committee – could endorse such an avowed revolutionary Marxist as a candidate. The Social Democratic Alliance raised the issue in public and advised Labour voters in Liverpool not to vote for such a candidate, whose views were so utterly divergent from Labour traditions. The result of the election was instructive. Labour lost this safe seat; the swing to the Conservatives was over twice the national average. Enough Labour voters, when told the facts by those within the Labour tradition, will simply not support such extremism even when it is made seemingly respectable by the 'Labour' label.

Active, voluntary support for the Labour Party is also dwindling. In fact, Labour can hardly any longer claim to be a mass movement. By the 1970s its active organization throughout the country had reached skeletal proportions; and in many areas was non-existent. Although Labour's total 'membership' figures, published annually by the party, amounted in the late seventies to over six million, these figures are fictitious. They include well over five million who are in no sense real members of the party – they are corporate members (affiliated to the party *en bloc* as it were, by virtue of their membership of a trade union). The *real* individual members are those who pay their subscriptions directly to the party. On Transport House's own figures these voluntary members have fallen from 876,275 in 1951 to 659,058 by 1976. This 1976 figure, however, is also fictitious. Labour's General Secretary, Ron Hayward, has admitted as much: 'We still have fictitious membership figures . . . you know it and I know it. Many parties are content to confine their membership in a small clique and make little or no attempt to enrol new blood.[2] Labour leaders have known the reason for the 'fictitious' nature of Labour's published voluntary membership for some time; it is that constituency Labour parties affiliate to the national party on the basis of a minimum of 1000 members – whether they actually have that number or not, and many of them do not.

In a recent penetrating commentary in *Political Quarterly* on the decline of Labour Party membership, Colin Martin and Dick Martin attempted to cut through the fog and arrive at a true picture. They quoted a Gallup poll survey of 1977 as estimating that Labour's true membership was 'at best' 445,000. They also reported on other surveys which had placed the figure even lower: one, in 1975, at 250,000, another, in 1976, at 300,000.[3]

Yet even these figures are an overestimate of *active* party membership. Many people join the Labour Party 'on paper'; that is, they simply pay their subscription but take no part whatsoever in party affairs. Many of these 'paper members' are utterly uninterested in politics, some may not even vote Labour at election times. An active type can get family, friends and acquaintances to join the party, as a personal favour, and even pay the subscriptions himself. The idea here is to build up the 'paper' membership of a ward or branch so that, by virtue of this high membership, the ward or branch becomes qualified to send more delegates to the local constituency General Management Committee where most of the important political decisions of the constituency are decided. This 'paper' membership of a ward, through diligent work by a few activists, can in some cases be as high as 300; yet the activists who actually turn up to the ward meetings could be as few as ten. And it is from amongst numbers as small, or often smaller, than this that ward delegations are selected and General Management Committees composed. At selections for Parliamentary Candidates, often in safe Labour seats, a ward meeting of ten or under is not unusual. In a 'working-class' area in which a polytechnic or university or college of education is located, a small group of students can dominate a local ward, or wards, and quite rapidly build up a majority of delegates.

Then there is the fiction of 'Labour Club membership'. In many constituencies membership of the Labour Party is a condition of membership of a Labour Club. Consequently, hundreds of working people who want to drink and relax in the club have, formally at least, to join the Labour Party. Many are in fact anti-Labour (certainly anti-socialist), more have vague Labour sympathies; few wish to take part in Labour Party activity, particularly when it takes the form of radical *agitprop* carried on by small coteries of young enthusiasts. Yet their numbers 'on paper' count in determining party membership and delegate strength.

What, then, is Labour's real active membership? Surveys are basically inadequate because they can never properly measure 'activity'. From my own experience as a candidate in both urban and rural constituencies it would seem that a good though unsystematic test of active membership — that is, committed party workers involved in the week-to-week or month-to-month management of the party's affairs — can be derived from the numbers attending General Management Committee meetings held every month. It is extremely rare for an active party member not to be able to attend a GMC in one guise or another: as a branch delegate, or Co-op delegate, or socialist society (Fabian) delegate, or trade union delegate — a way is usually found. Consequently a liberal estimate of active Labour Party membership would be one that *doubled* the numbers on the General Management Committee of a local constituency party and then applied that measurement throughout the country. On this basis Labour's real activist membership cannot be much more than 100,000 persons. This is a measure of the genuine local activity generated by the 'mass party of the working class'; and describes the full extent to which a skeleton organization can pose as a mass political party.

In some areas of the country Labour Party membership ('paper' or active) amounts to a scandal. There are some Labour Members of Parliament who 'are sitting on majorities propped up by party memberships as low as 100'.[4] Some very senior Labour figures represent constituencies where the Labour party, in any real sense, hardly exists at all – where party membership can be measured on the fingers of a few hands. It has been estimated that about only one in thirty Labour voters actually belong to the Labour Party; and that Labour is 'among the smallest of the Western European socialist parties on the basis of numbers of members per 100 voters'.[5]

The rapid decline in the number of Labour agents is a symptom of the more general collapse of the Labour party at local and grass-roots level. Labour's Annual Conference report for 1977 announced that: 'There has been a further fall in the number of full-time agents, the number now standing at 86.'[6] This is out of a total of 635 constituencies, and many of these full-time agents are not to be found in inner-city 'working-class' seats (East Anglia, for instance, has a disproportionate number). At the end of the decade of the fifties Labour could boast 225 full-time agents.[7] Furthermore, Labour is increasingly unable to sustain its dwindling band of agents out of local funds; a National Agency Service, deeply resented by many of the older party members who remember times when local activity sustained their local organization, has been set up to make funds from the centre (trade union money essentially) available. In 1977, 26 out of the 86 full-time agents were employed by this National Agency Service run from Transport House.

Labour Party membership is not only very small and active membership miniscule, but it is also changing its social composition. Put crudely, the voluntary side of the party is becoming increasingly middle-class and 'professional'. Hindess has argued that we have witnessed over the last decades a general 'working-class' estrangement from politics but that this general pattern is particularly, and poignantly, relevant to the Labour Party. He suggests that in the 1950s ward Labour parties 'in the middle-class areas were smaller, and often non-existent' whereas 'in the working-class areas ward parties were generally larger, or at least more active.' He suggests that today's (1971) picture is rather different: in the Labour party at city level 'it is clear that all categories of manual workers are under-represented, the skilled workers least of all, while the professional [classes] are the most over-represented.'[8]

For anyone who knows the Labour party, Hindess's thesis has the ring of truth about it; indeed the flight of labour (particularly skilled manual labour) from Labour has continued, and probably at an accelerated pace, since Hindess first reported this trend in the early seventies. A Labour candidate recently described to me the social composition of a selection conference in a safe Labour area: 'The room was full of "intellectuals"; it was as if no one in the Labour party worked with their hands anymore; schoolteachers, local government people, civil servants, union organizers and officials, clerical people, lecturers, the local newspaper reporter, students.' When my own local Labour Party management committee met to consider my expulsion from the party (after twenty years of membership) the committee room was virtually devoid of manual workers. The decision about my membership was taken by about thirty people, many of whom had been members of the party for a matter of months. There are two points about these impressionistic but not atypical reports. First, Labour, at local level, is increasingly governed by a cadre of activists with few roots in industrial England but possessed of an outlandish mock-proletarian political rhetoric. Secondly, they accurately depict the loss of interest in the voluntary work of the party by manual workers, public and private, and their families. In fact, about the only source of continuing contact that the new 'public-sector, middle-class' Labour party (at local, voluntary level) has with its much vaunted 'working-class' constituency is through contacts with local trade union officials and shop stewards.

The relatively affluent skilled or semi-skilled manual worker (and their families) have fled from the politics of Labour. The desert which is Labour party organization in traditional Labour areas is the terrain onto which has marched the 'new class'; and Labour's 'new class' is socialist.

Socialism against the working people

There is a kind of circular process at work on the left. Labour declines from a mass party of the working people into a vanguard activist group of 'professional, middle-class' cadres; this social transformation has crucial ideological implications in that varying forms of 'socialism' become entrenched; as 'socialism' extends so the party's active support is further eroded. The root cause of Labour's decline remains the popular resistance to socialism at all levels of British society, and not least (and, perhaps most keenly) amongst traditional Labour voters.

We must, however, be clear what is meant by 'socialism' in this context. Modern British socialism – the socialism of the Labour Party apparatus and that of the British left intelligentsia both inside and outside the Labour Party – has two broad currents. The first is that held by some of the bosses of the Labour movement at the centre of affairs in London. This is a kind of modernized and more acceptable

East European fifties socialism ('Stalinism with a human face', or 'TUC socialism' or 'NEC socialism'). This current has little in the way of theory to sustain it; indeed it is largely uninterested in philosophy, political thought or speculation. Its primary concern is to secure institutions, agreed between state, party and unions, which will entrench the power of the Labour movement *apparat* over society and the working people. At the domestic level it is wholly at home with the world of planning agreements, nationalization, boards of control — in other words, big corporation socialism. At another level it sees Britain as eventually becoming an appendage of a Soviet-dominated Europe. Labour's NEC, should such a geopolitical speculation be vindicated by events, would be an appropriate body to administer a 'Finlandized' Britain.

The second current consists of a motley assortment of heavy progressivism drawn vulgarly from a misunderstanding of the wider liberal tradition but dressed up in pseudo-Marxist terminology and 'working-class' culturalism. This is the governing bunch of ideas and reflexes which is to be found in the newly-radicalized constituency Labour parties and amongst some, younger, trade unionists, particularly in the shop steward movement. To fully illustrate what this amounts to in political practice and propaganda it is worth quoting, at length, from the statement of aims of the *Socialist Campaign for a Labour Victory*, a *Labour Party* group that has the support of some NEC members, Parliamentary candidates and local government figures (particularly influential in this organization is Ted Knight, the Leader of the Labour-controlled Lambeth Council and a 1979 Parliamentary Labour Candidate):

> *Make the bosses pay, not the working class! Millions for hospitals, not a penny for 'defence'! Nationalise the banks and financial institutions without compensation. End the interest burden on council housing and other public services . . .

*Scrap all immigration controls. Race is not a problem; racism is . . . Purge racists from positions in the labour movement . . .

*The capitalist police are an enemy of the working class. Support all demands to weaken them as the bosses' striking force: dissolution of special squads (SPG, Special Branch, MI5 etc) . . .

*Free abortion and contraception on demand. Women's equal right to work, and full equality for women.

*The Irish people − as a whole − should have the right to determine their future. Get the British troops out now . . . Political status for Irish republican prisoners as a matter of principle . . . The strength of our labour movement lies in the rank and file. Our perspective must be working class action to raze the capitalist system down to its foundations, and to put a working class socialist system in its place . . .[9]

Such is not just crude propaganda. It is genuinely believed and felt by many in the 'grass-roots' of the Labour Party.

The 'NEC socialism' held at the centre and this loose, chaotic socialism of the 'grass-roots' represent the 'dynamic' ideology within Britain's left-wing party. This amalgam amounts to a total degeneration of *any* kind of traditional socialism. It obviously owes nothing to the social democratic tradition; nor to the Christian Socialist tradition; nor indeed to what little indigenous British Marxist tradition there was. Lesek Kolakowski, who witnessed the degeneration of socialism within his native Poland, has argued, with a force that can easily apply to modern British socialism: 'At present, Marxism neither interprets the world nor changes it: it is merely a repertoire of slogans serving to organize various interests, most of them completely remote from those with which Marxism originally identified itself.'[10] The various interests which modern British socialism seeks to organize and entrench are the central trade union barons on the one hand

and the 'new class' in the constituencies on the other. Any deals that can be made along the way with corporate and financial or state power are quite acceptable.

This degeneration of socialism in Britain can help to explain why the modern British socialist mentality holds so little appeal beyond the ranks of the left activists. It simply has no popular roots; and in particular has no authentic relationship with the working people for whom it so loudly proclaims a special role. Indeed, nothing is more contrived and disingenuous than the use made by modern British socialists of the 'working class'. The term 'use' here has relevance because the relationship between socialists of most kinds and the 'working class' is essentially instrumental: the 'working class' is perceived as an instrument, as a mechanism, for political change. The 'worker' is a means to a political end. The *condition* of the working people is a constant concern, their *opinions* much less so. The 'working class' has to be 'persuaded', 'educated', 'made to see', riven of 'false consciousness'. The abstract future, for the socialist, supersedes as a concern the real present and the opinions of the real people who inhabit that real present. Of course, this attitude to the working people has a long socialist pedigree. The Fabian Society, in its 1896 report, was brutally frank:

The Fabian Society has no romantic illustions as to the freedom of the proletariat from these narrow ideals. Like every other socialist society, it can only *educate* the people in socialism by making them conversant with the conclusions of the most enlightened members of all classes.[11]

The Fabians were at least an intelligent elite. Today's nascent socialist elite is narrow, bitter and unlearned.

This attitude of socialists to the working people may help to explain, in part, why socialism in Britain has, outside the 'new class', hardly any support to speak of at all. The Labour party has held on to its mass support because it has hidden, at election times, its socialist component. Even the general membership of the Labour Party, certainly that part of it that is 'working-class, is hardly socialist in any real sense of the term. Tom Forester's study of the political attitudes of the Brighton Kemp Town Labour Party membership is very revealing on this point. Most 'working-class' members of the party gave as their primary reason for joining: 'to further the interests of the working class' and this was interpreted in senses that had hardly any relationship to socialism at all. Forester writes that: 'The *working-class* respondents were concerned primarily with the central issue of working-class living standards',[12] much less so with abolishing capitalism, 'building socialism', imposing Clause 4 and so on. If this was the response of Labour party *members* in the declining Labour Party of the seventies, how much less socialist in their impulses must the rest of traditional Labour voters be, let alone the mass of the working people?

If those working people who either support or vote for Labour are hardly socialist in their attitudes, what of those working people who do not vote at all? Are they, as some new left theorists would have it, alienated from the system awaiting the arrival of a socialist party to which they can flock? Hardly, it would seem. Hindess has argued that there are two kinds of 'working-class' political apathy. First, there is the 'apathy of those who are reasonably content with things as they are'; second, there is the apathy of what he terms the 'politically isolated, of many of those in the more working-class areas of Britain's towns and cities. Here there is at best a grudging acceptance of the present system, not because the system is particularly good, but rather because there appears to be no real alternative.'[13] Hindess does not argue that this 'politically isolated' worker is in any sense attracted to socialism. Indeed, in the system which the modern British socialist wishes to construct the 'politically isolated' would probably feel more isolated and alienated; and there would be more of them. In sum, the working people of Britain − certainly if they vote Conservative or Liberal, probably if they vote Labour, sometimes even as Labour Party members − find socialism profoundly unattractive.

At the very heart of the matter of socialism's present unpopularity is the assault which the modern British socialist
mentality makes upon the past, and the identity which derives
from a sense of continuity between past and present; that
identity which gives a person meaning. Hugh Thomas, in
discussing the British problem, has lamented that: 'Our present behaviour forms so marked a contrast with our national
character in the past (and still admired abroad) as in itself to
create a crisis of national personality.'[14] The modern British
socialist needs this crisis in national personality in order to
succeed. Consequently, and because of its very nature,
modern British socialism seeks to destroy the past. Yet it is
the widespread resistance to this destruction that accounts for
socialism's lack of appeal to the British – that continuing,
almost stubborn, national trait that may yet save us from the
new elite.

In political terms the British past contains two crucial
traditions which have left their imprint; two impulses that run
widely throughout present society. First, there is a keen sense
of freedom, or liberty; second, a continuing longing for community out of which the only true freedom can spring. This
sense of liberty on the one hand and longing for community
on the other is a strange, seemingly contradictory, amalgam.
Yet this contradiction is what Britain is all about as it stands
astride the excessive, unanchored individualism of the
American 'new world' on the one hand and the community-
based traditionalism of what is left of the 'old world' on the
other. The balance between these two impulses shifts from
time to time and the conflict between them will go on. But
this does not matter here. The fact is that the modern British
socialist class sets itself against *both* and derives from *neither*.

First, the continuing sense of freedom. If the British ex·
perience stands for anything at all that is at all unique then it
must be the evolution of freedom and the traditional liberal
way of life. Many on the right, particularly more traditional,
paternalistic conservatives (who understandably fear the consequences of much of the excessive freedom of modern life)

should ponder the point, as they too readily exalt national traditions over abstract concepts (like freedom), that notions of freedom are indeed part of our national tradition – we cannot will them away even if tempted to. It is British philosophy that pioneered such concerns – Hobbes, Locke, Mill. In institutional and political terms Britain, uniquely, developed the Parliamentary system of government, the associated freedoms and civil rights, and the rule of law. In economics the national tradition has made a singular contribution both to the practice and theory of the free market system, to free trade, and later to the pluralistic mixed economy. As change took place so such change was adapted, relatively successfully, to this evolving, underlying structure.

It is important to realize that the dominant impulses within the emerging politics of Labour in the nineteenth and twentieth centuries were largely bereft of a vindictive need to expunge the freedoms enjoyed by the top classes in Victorian Britain; rather, the urge was to gain for the working people the kinds of freedom (and affluence) that liberal, democratic development had secured for other classes. The rhetoric of the early politics of Labour was couched in terms of Britain's more general history of freedom – the 'rights' of labour, 'freedom and dignity of labour' and the like. The leaders of the early Labour movement were inspired by the British liberal tradition, not opposed to it; they saw themselves as standing in the traditions of the Chartists, some even of Cromwell and Hampden. Even the collectivist side of Labour, the trade unions with their emphasis upon solidarity and collective bargaining, usually only believed in such collective action not as a good in itself but as a means to secure for its people some individualist aim, some place in the liberal sun. Collectivism was a tactic or a technique, not an end. Even Labour's primary intellectuals – that is, those thinkers whose lives were bound up with the Labour Party, not with ultra-left sects — have owed much more to the historic liberal tradition than they would often admit to. It is for these reasons that socialism – meaning anything more than simple justice and the extension to everyone of the rights of 'free-born Englishmen' − seems so discordant in the politics of Labour; and why modern British socialist and communist (Marxist, Leninist) thinking is such an obvious breach with the national traditions of the past politics of Labour. In short, the British liberal tradition and impulse rubbed of on the workers. Barnett makes the point that not only was liberalism 'triumphant' in the *political* world of the early twentieth century, but that 'liberal principles equally dominated public opinion at large'.[15]

There is no reason to believe that this sense of freedom has particularly diminished amongst the wider public even though society and economy have become more organized and bureaucratic. It carries on in its new environment. In fact, a great popular desire for economic freedom is all around. The spirit of entrepreneurship has not yet been kicked out of the British; there is a continuing public esteem for the small businessman; the British still *want* reductions in taxation (both national and local); owner-occupation of homes is still valued, particularly amongst those who rent, both in the public and private sector. Even the increasing incidence of strikes (which reached a troublesome head in the 1978-9 wage round) can be seen as an assertion of individual impulses. Workers throughout the country 'put their families' first − ahead of the claims of the wider community. Large numbers of ordinary people were simply not content to accept a 5 per cent norm handed down by a failed bureaucratic class or, often, a higher figure set for them by agreements between government and trade union bureaucracies. The leaders of the national community had failed to control inflation; strikes were but the product of workers attempting to protect themselves in the only way they knew how in an environment of political failure. Although strikes are often used by socialists for their own political ends (as a means of weakening the liberal-democratic state and society in preparation for the transformation to socialism) such a *political* objective among the strikers themselves was virtually absent. The con-

tinuing impulse to economic freedom can take strange twists.
Ian Gilmour has argued:

Had the entrepreneurial spirit, the Protestant work ethic and other
fuels of capitalism remained a more powerful force in Britain since
1945, this country would not have fallen, economically, so far
behind its neighbours. Those virtues can and must to some extent
be revived.[16]

The question remains whether they can be revived. There obviously comes a point – a certain level of state spending
and/or ownership, a certain level of numbers employed in the
public sector, a level or rigidity and bureaucracy in private
sector management – when such a revivification becomes
impossible (without, that is, catastrophic social upheaval).
And Ian Gilmour has also warned against the mistake 'of
thinking that everybody is willing to reform himself by self-
denial into a capitalist overnight'.[17] Yet the popular culture
of Britain retains an individuality in the face of seemingly impossible odds. In an environment in which the balance has
tilted far too much towards the state, the time has come for
the elites of the country, which have always found this undercurrent of vitality somewhat suspect, to stand aside. Of
course, the one elite that has no intention of doing so is the
socialist class within the Labour Party.

The sense of liberty in the British tradition has a moral
dimension – not simply an economic one. Orwell suggested,
in 1941, that:

The liberty of the individual is still believed in, almost as in the
nineteenth century. But this has nothing to do with economic liberty, the right to exploit others for profit. It is the liberty to have a
home of your own, to do what you like in your spare time, to
choose your own amusements instead of having them chosen for
you from above.[18]

Here we see, in the language of the essayist, an attempt to
describe (and approve) a *moral* commitment to freedom (or

liberty or privacy) that is devoid of any economic underpinning. Indeed, Orwell's attack upon 'profit' is part of a moral attack upon 'capitalism' that was so much a feature of traditional socialist thinking: the notion that human freedom is diminished, not enhanced, by private profits, 'labour as a commodity' and so on. And the force of this moral argument has certainly gained more momentum as consumerism has grown space. This is a point often ignored by classical economic liberals and is the ground on which the traditional left walk with most assuredness. Brian Crozier has written, of the excesses of modern consumerism, that: 'Herbert Marcuse and others who criticised the absurdities of this state of affairs were not necessarily wrong because they happened to be Marxists. It was possible to be right about the diagnosis and wrong about the remedies proposed.'[19] Even so, the modern British socialist class has tended to abandon this moral critique in favour of a senseless and absurd class theory about capitalism. Also, the powerful theory of 'alienation', of 'homelessness in the world' has simply not been developed by the British left beyond a crude propaganda point against 'capitalism'. The modern British socialist seems unable to display how 'alienation' will be overcome 'under socialism' either practically or theoretically or how the moral order 'under socialism' will be any better than that now in operation. The likelihood is that it will be much worse.

So the search for a truly *moral* basis for freedom will no doubt continue. But until it is found it is decidedly preferable to stick with what we have − freedom set, in part, in the context of economic pluralism, indeed guaranteed, in part, by it. John Lloyd has asked: 'Is capitalism the only true guarantor of freedom? Or, at least, *some* capitalism the guarantor of *some* freedom?'[20] The answer must be a decided 'yes', and most certainly to the second question.

All the evidence also points to a continuing belief on the part of the general public in free institutions: in parliaments, free trade unions, a free press and the like. Notwithstanding the failures of leadership elites and Britain's continued unrepresentativeness at political level (a point developed in the final chapter), the impression remains of a people desperately trying, against great odds, to retain their democratic institutions. There is certainly an increasing distaste for politicians, a falling turnout at elections; yet even amidst all the despair the British somehow retain a robust distrust of fanaticism — the kind of fanaticism which if unleashed could destroy what is left of constitutional government. The fact that the National Front and the avowedly Marxist parties do so badly at elections illustrates a surprisingly deep resource in the public for retaining democratic procedures, a commitment not wholly shared by the elites, who all too often are ready to abandon these procedures (particularly Parliamentary sovereignty) in favour of bureaucratic fixing by corporate groups.

So embedded in the political culture are Britain's liberal democratic traditions, so profoundly are they still felt throughout all sections of society, that even the great social and industrial dislocation of the seventies (which so battered Parliamentary authority, the rule of law and liberal constitutionalism) have not succeeded, yet at least, in removing from Parliament its political legitimacy. Reduced though it is in stature, weakened in power and unattractive though many of its inhabitants may be, Parliament has somehow, someway survived — at least as the great liberal symbol of our national aspirations. Even if Britain has changed, few of us want to believe that Parliament no longer counts. This sentiment is, of itself, very important. It represents a determination that the liberal democratic tradition shall not die in Britain: that the liberal past can accommodate the modern society and economy.

The residual power of Britain's premier liberal institution has even caused the modern socialist left to pause for thought. In the contemporary political environment no faction-seeking power can afford to set itself against Parliament too overtly. Even the Communist Party of Great Britain commits itself to the 'Parliamentary road to socialism' and argues that under 'socialist democracy' 'Parliament would be the sovereign body in the land, exercising its powers as the elected representatives of the people without restrictions imposed by the Common Market or by the actions of the big monopolies and financial monopolies';[21] and then, interestingly, 'There would be full democratic control of the Cabinet by the parliamentary majority.'[22] This echoes an objective proclaimed by leading members of the Tribune group. As Maurice Cornforth, a leading communist theoretician, has written:

The point is not to get rid of representative assemblies and rule without them, but to turn them into effective instruments of popular domestic control . . . wherein the political representatives of working people carry out the business of *control* in the interests of and under the instructions of members of the organizations that sent them there.[23]

Of course 'the organizations that sent them there' will have to be the *party* (and Cornforth could hardly have been referring to the Communist Party which has no seats and no likelihood of any). This key notion of party control of Members of Parliament is one that is extremely popular amongst the socialist class within the Labour Party, and recent constitutional developments within the Labour Party have accelerated its arrival. The strategy is to work for the socialist transformation of society by ensuring that parliamentary groups are no longer independent of the party apparatus. The party apparatus will control the parliamentary majority and through its hold over the parliamentary majority it will also control the government of the country.

Modern British socialists have attempted to monopolize concern for 'the community'. The constant refrain is for the need to restore 'community values' in the face of 'capitalism' which, it is argued, ineluctably destroys them. Two recent examples of such thinking, both in high polemical style, are of great interest. First, a powerful intervention in the debate on law and order at the Labour Party Conference of 1978 by Bob Marshall Andrews (of Richmond Labour Party):

. . .in this generation since the war we have destroyed their communities, we have blighted their environment, both in terms of scale and size, we have thrown them into an educational experiment, a magnificent educational experiment, and then taken away the funds that were necessary to make it a success. And those who get through that social assault course are told at the end of it . . . You are not necessary. You are not wanted . . . I will tell you the cause of crime in this country . . . It is the lack of values endemic in a capitalist society . . . You have got to have a new set of values. Those are socialist values . . .[24]

Secondly, Jeremy Seabrook (the author of *What Went Wrong?*, a disturbing account of, in his own words, 'the pain and resentment which remains in working-class communities') has described his own feelings about contemporary 'working-class' community life:

You can almost feel a growing cynicism about people, the growing power of commodities. Here, as everywhere else, working people try to make sense of these changes . . . the talk is decreasingly of neighbours, comrades, kinfolk: the responses to human beings tend to be to scroungers, idlers, spongers, vandals . . . muggers . . . and material things evoke the loving responses formerly accorded to human relationships — a beautiful bedroom suite, a lovely kitchen range, a holiday of a lifetime, the dream house.[25]

Running through these commentaries, and others (though usually less eloquent) is a single, underlying, unifying theme. It is that working people are essentially the victims of a system, and that on *that* account their actual views and responses have no independent validity or merit. Policy makers and elites should therefore, rather as with the paternalists of an earlier era, cease treating working people as individuals with valid views and opinions but, instead, as helpless victims of 'the system'. The modern British socialist seems more alarmed at working people worrying about muggers than about muggers themselves. This inability to 'side' with working people, to identify with them, to be 'of' them as well as 'for' them, is constantly exhibited in new left writings. Modern British socialists decry what is mockingly referred to as 'respectability' amongst certain 'working-class' families. These are the workers who will not accept the class analysis assigned to them, whose Christian non-conformity, private property consciousness, thrift, identity with nation and its symbolisms (or whatever) lead them to become 'respectable' and into becoming voting fodder for Labourism and the Tories. This inability to properly identify with working people, notwithstanding all the powerful rhetoric of concern, comes through clearly in Seabrook's implicit attack upon the materialism of the life of working people. There seems little understanding of the point that it is not 'the system' that induces such materialism; rather it is the natural enjoyment of material things, an enjoyment made more profound because of the poverty that had gone before or the lower living standards that to millions of working people are always a fearsome possibility. Nor is there an appreciation of the fact that the 'system' is in part, at least, a *product* of these 'working-class' people's desires. Modern British socialists seem to find it inconceivable that modern society might not have been imposed upon the workers — that, with all its excesses, it might be the result of earlier democratization. We see, again, even through some of the most moving accounts of working-class life, that nascent socialist elitism rearing its head.

None of this is an attempt to diminish the reality of the 'destroyed communities' of 'working-class' Britain; nor to argue that certain aspects of modernity and late industrialism (though not in a unique sense 'capitalism') have not placed great stress upon human values — incidentally in *all* communities, not just those of the working people. Rather, it is to question the validity of the modern British socialist critique of 'the assault on community'. Indeed, it is to go further. It is to suggest that, at bottom, the modern British socialist has very little concern for community, except as a tactical contraption to throw against 'capitalism' in a political battle.

First, let us ask the question: who, or what, is responsible for much of the uprootedness of British 'working-class' life? The answer 'capitalism' or 'the capitalists' is simply not good enough. Industrialism certainly herded together in cities, in squalor and poverty (by today's standards), the early 'working class' of the late eighteenth and the nineteenth centuries. Yet, out of these same industrial communities, the products of 'early capitalism', sprang the comradeship, kinship and sense of community that, it is now lamented, has disappeared. As late as the 1960s (certainly in the 1950s) many of the traditional 'working-class' communities of Britain were not unpleasant places to live in. They combined the warmth and meaning derived from localism and familiarity with increasing material standards. After over a century of rapid 'capitalist' growth, organic 'working-class' communities were developing; the existing council estates (now the older estates) were well kept; people had pride, a sense of belonging, a sense of 'respectability' – that much mocked working-class characteristic. Indeed, in the areas where traditional working-class communities still exist these standards and characteristics still prevail, not least of all in the 'working-class' communities in the villages of Britain. In short, 'capitalism', certainly as it had developed into the 1950s, had not only created these communities but, having created them, had not destroyed them either. As it developed it had simply added affluence. What dislocation had occurred had been piecemeal and easily digestible.

It was during the 1950s, and since, that the massive uprooting of the working people of Britain took place. The working people of London, Birmingham, Liverpool, Manchester, Bradford, Newcastle – most of the major cities – have suffered a dislocation that has transformed the sociological landscape of post-war Britain and is a cause of much suffering and true 'alienation'. Whole working-class communities have been destroyed and removed, with their erstwhile inhabitants distributed amongst new estates often far from the old city centres. The New Towns, the overspill developments and the high-rise blocks of flats (either in, or on the outskirts of, the major cities) are now the distressing environmental lot of those who inhabited the working-class communities of inner urban Britain in the fifties.

Apart from the ghastly architecture of these new Fabian ghettos, life within them can be empty and often fearful. Two, not atypical, examples will suffice. The 'overspill' estate for the East End of London in Witham, Essex, where I was Labour candidate in the 1970 election, is constructed like an army barracks and is ill-served by transport and shops. The newly-arrived working people from London are cut off, socially, culturally and physically, from the village people of Witham and are not made to feel particularly welcome (except, that is, in the local Labour Club). Many of the newly arrived families sorely missed their erstwhile community life, which although less materially well off was in other senses richer and possessed of greater meaning. Attempted suicides were not uncommon. Another such 'overspill' development is the Greenstead Estate in Colchester. This depressing environment — again the architecture is appalling, the services few — is regularly vandalized by gangs of youths. Richard Hoggart has argued that: 'These estates are improving but many of them look inorganic and are inorganic; they have no natural centres and their layout does not encourage centres of social life — "a graveyard with lights", said a teenager of the main street in one such brick and concrete estate.'[26] Things have got much, much worse since Hoggart wrote those words in the late sixties.

It was primarily a socialist (Fabian) idea to remove the urban working class, uproot them and thereby inadvertently cause so much suffering and anxiety; it was part of what Marshall Andrews depicted as a 'great educational experiment'. It was the Fabian-influenced London County Council that set the pattern for New Town and 'overspill' (or expanded town) development, a socialist 'experiment' which subsequent Labour LCCs and GLCs continued to look upon with affection and pride; and it was an 'experiment' the fundamental assumptions of which were only questioned during the Labour administration of 1973-7 at County Hall. Of course, Fabians were not ignorant of the severe stresses which their own planning mentality had created amongst the British working people. The Labour bureaucracy (which the Fabian tradition has now atrophied into) has given this problem considerable attention. The Labour Party's Annual Report for 1967 stated that: 'The social problems which may arise for new communities were made for the improvement of the 'social and recreational' facilities of the new dispossessed.[27] In most Labour Party socialist thinking, 'community' can be simply re-established by a declaratory policy objective issued from Smith Square; there appears to be little appreciation of the spontaneous nature of community development. The uprooted working people would continue to be organized by 'social and recreational' facilities.

If the planning bureaucracy, heavily influenced by Fabian planning mentalities, was partly responsible for the uprooting, then the later new left reaction to the problem carried the debate into greater levels of confusion. A thesis emerged that the planners were but responding to 'capitalist development', were but its unwitting accomplices. Of course, in a limited sense, the planners were indeed responding to social and industrial change; but the main impetus behind the new and 'overspill' towns lay in the imagination of the planner, not in industrial need and change. There were no throbbing centres of industry waiting for exploited workers to arrive before Basildon or Crawley or Kirby or Milton Keynes or Harlow or the overspills were constructed in the mind and then on the map. The 'graveyards with lights' were primarily the responsibility of an intellectual design by elites (who wanted the cities relieved of overcrowding); but the whole exercise was too brutal, too ruthless and too swift, the kind of brutality and ruthlessness that is invariably the unwitting end-product of a planning mentality. Of course, the motive behind many of the tower block developments was economic; but it would have been 'economic' under socialism too.

To lay the emptiness, uprootedness and the 'pain and resentment' of British working people's lives today at the feet, solely, of 'capitalism' is sloppy. They are the result of factors and developments far more profound than the simple question of any particular form of economic organization. These factors, yet dimly perceived, are certainly not wholly or primarily related to whether or not the factors of production are held in private or in public. If the socialism of the governing groups in the Labour Party — bureaucratic, statist, an organized society beyond the wildest imaginings of the early Fabians — was to come to pass, no solution would be found to the 'alienation', 'soullessness', *anomie* of the council estates. Consumerism would not disappear; it would take the form of 'people's stores' and in place of advertising there would be socialist action posters.

Yet, amidst all this confusion one thing stands out: the inorganic nature of the modern British socialist conception of community — communities do not grow, developing freely over time, as did the old communities of working-class Britain; rather they can, somehow, be created. This was the assumption of the Fabian planning mentality and it is carried into further stages of imposition by the modern socialist class. What, for instance, are these new 'socialist values' that are going to replace the 'lack of values endemic in capitalist society'? How exactly are communities going to be *reconstructed* so that these 'values' establish themselves? And how can any sense of local community reassert itself in the face of the highly centralized bureaucratic forms of organization which the modern socialist class actually propose at the level of policy (even though the rhetoric is imbued with localism and co-operatives)?

Finally, there appears no conception that a new set of values (or, more probably, 'old values' reinvogorated and reinterpreted) may come from the people themselves, struggling in their everyday existence, making do without traditional ties, learning to live in the world. As Ben Wattenberg said of the Americans during the turmoil of the sixties, and amidst constant talk of all-pervasive unhappiness and 'alienation': 'Problems abound. But these folks can cope . . . Don't ever sell these folk short.'[28] So, too, for the British.

The modern British socialist's concern for the integrity of working-class community life is further discredited by the general attitude of the socialist to the daunting question of race and immigration. Again the modern British socialist appears as an outsider looking in, sharing in few of the problems but constantly ready to impose a solution. This vantage-point is understandable amongst the better-off, progressive elites; less so amongst socialists who claim an authentic relationship with the working class. The British left sets its face like flint against seriously thinking about this problem. Yet it is in the context of the dislocation of traditional working-class community life over the last twenty-five years that the intractable problems of race relations and immigration should be set. For on top of all the other aspects of change, so rapid and relentless, has come — for the working people — the searing adjustment to the arrival of new cultures and races.

In a sense the whole debate about the total numbers of Third World immigrants in Britain is not the issue: the real problem is that new immigrants have settled in large numbers in concentrated form in the working-class areas of the major cities. By and large, as with other things, it has been the working people *alone* who have had to deal with this particular, and traumatic, form of change. Their reaction to this mammoth social and cultural upheaval in the inner city areas is typically described by the left intelligentsia as 'racist'. The Anti-Nazi League, under the directing hand of the Socialist Workers' Party, proclaims that it is in business to combat 'racism' — some even use the term 'working-class racism'. The impression is created that an incipient 'racism', never properly defined, is just below the surface amongst working people and that, unless action is taken, it will mushroom into a major political force. This underlying assumption that the working people are potential 'racists' will allow no evidence – for instance the paucity of support for the National Front – to shake it. Indeed, this depressing judgement by sections of the left of the potential political character of the class in which they place such hope for the future of socialism is a feature of the schizophrenia on the left about the working class more generally. Furthermore, it is ironic that those whose 'view of man' is supposedly so optimistic should, when it comes to evaluating the potential of their own indigenous working people, become so despairingly, contemptuously, pessimistic.

In fact, pseudo-scientific theories about superiority and inferiority are wholly absent in the working people's reaction to immigration and race relations. The reality is very different from the manufactured myth. Certainly working-class hostility to Third World immigration is a fact of British life. But hostility is not 'racism'. And the unfriendliness that exists has little to do with notions of the worth of the immigrants; it has much more to do with the fact that their arrival has unsettled and disturbed traditional community life. A sense of community, if it means anything, must mean the identity that derives from a settled and relatively predictable environment. Substantial Third World immigration into traditional working-class areas of the inner city cannot but upset that settled and predictable environment. It represents substantial change. Rather as with the changeover to decimalization, *anything* unfamiliar, and Third World immigration is certainly unfamiliar, is resented and leads to an underlying, often bitter, grumbling. The socialist generation is selective about change: it is acceptable, evidently, to attack the changes brought to working-class life by industrialism, commercialism, the 'growing power of commodities' – such change, incidentally, is relatively favoured by real working people – but unacceptable to react against changes of a profound cultural kind. And not only is such a reaction unacceptable; it is vilified as evidence of crypto-fascism.

It remains a poignant commentary upon the relationship of the modern British socialist to the reality of working people's lives that the only politicians who have seen fit to raise the issue of immigration in any sense which is congruent to the feelings of the British working people are located on the centre and right of national politics. The Labour left (and socialists more generally) simply cannot speak the language of the people on this issue.

Instead, it has been left to others to raise this intractable problem in public, to articulate the majority opinion. On the Labour side, Bob Mellish, Tony Crosland and Jim Callaghan have all ventured into this difficult, though profoundly important area. Mellish, an articulate and folksy Labourist, raised the issue directly at the Labour Party Conference as early as 1965. He provoked the left in the Conference by saying:

Go to Victoria Station . . . and see hundreds of these people coming from the West Indies – no home, no jobs, some of them without friends, and nothing to be done for them. Stop being humbugs. Let us face the fact that we have a job to do with one million of our people here now.[29]

Mellish was concerned primarily about housing. He never quite recovered politically from that speech, was always suspected on the left of 'racism'; such direct talk, echoing the genuine fears of working people in an over-crowded island, was unacceptable to the socialist generation. Tony Crosland, in an article in the *Observer*, in 1973, set the immigration question in its community context:

Large sections of our working people have real grievances which they believe will be intensified by continued immigration . . . . And people of an older generation, who have spent their lives in a close-knit working-class community, inevitably feel bitter when they find the local pub or cinema or corner shop taken over by a different community with an unfamiliar culture . . . . To condemn such feelings as racialist is libellous and impertinent. They reflect a genuine sense of insecurity, and anxiety for a traditional way of life.[30]

Such a reasonable and uninflammatory defence of working people's attitudes towards immigration was nevertheless met by a chorus of abuse from his Labour Party colleagues, most typically on the left (although some from the 'liberal' right). Those of us who urged upon him the need to continue articulating the working people's views on a whole range of issues – for fear that Labour was losing its roots amongst its own supporters – were met in typical Crosland jestful style: referring to the ordeal he underwent following his remarks on immigration he referred to 'having gone through Passchendaele and the Somme'. Jim Callaghan, whilst Home Secretary in the late sixties, also came in for considerable criticism because of his attitude to the Kenyan Asian problem in 1968. Mellish, Crosland and Callaghan were in no sense 'racists' – they were simply keenly aware of the mood of the British working people and were not content to dismiss it as 'vulgar' or 'unhealthy'. On the Conservative side, Enoch Powell's very special relationship with the working people (and large numbers of Labour voters) – a relationship which, arguably, put the Conservatives in in 1970 and out in 1974 – derives almost exclusively from a widespread feeling that he was the only politician willing to articulate popular opinion on the subject. His specific recommendations for policy were of far less importance than the sense he engendered that someone 'up there' was in touch, that the political class was not wholly set against national sentiment. Mrs Thatcher also gained considerable working-class support for herself and her party when she raised the issue in March 1978.

In a sense the fierce, visceral reception given to those politicians – Mellish, Crosland, Callaghan, Powell, Thatcher – who periodically raise the issue in public debate is more important than the issue itself. It displays a deep distrust of fellow-countrymen of the kind that inevitably both induces and displays an authoritarian mentality. This authoritarianism takes two forms. One is direct and overt. The National Union of Students attempted to impose a ban on 'racists' (a term used so liberally as to exclude many, quite liberal, Conservatives from speaking at universities). The other is even more insidious. By the use of the term 'racist' to depict the feelings of the working people on the issue of immigration an attempt is made to censor genuine grievances by unfair extremist labels and frightening parallels with the European past. And this brutal propagandizing is unleashed upon millions of people who fought for their country in the war against fascism – and often *by* those who did not. Of course, to label the National Front as 'racist' and Nazi is both fair and correct. To extend such a label beyond an insignificant section of the white working class is absurd.

The impertinence of socialists towards the working people is breathtaking: a generation of working people who entered the war against the Germans partly at least because of their liberal traditions ('for freedom') is assailed for its 'illiberality' (indeed its incipient 'racism') by those who reject the liberal philosophy and the liberal-democratic state and by those who argue that the political culture of the British is far too suffused with 'bourgeois' liberal values. By and large the use of 'racist' labelling by the left is tactical, not principled. First, it is a method of coalition-building. By launching campaigns 'against racism' other non-socialist groups can be tempted into alliances with the extreme left. The most successful left parties at this manoeuvre are the Communist Party and the Socialist Workers' Party. Secondly, socialists fear that too public a discussion of the immigration problem – in any other terms, that is, than round condemnations of 'racism endemic in a capitalist society' — will lower 'class-consciousness' by a substitution for it of 'ethnic consciousness'. Robert Nisbet has written: 'Ethnicity is, along with family, locality and religion, among the most ancient and powerful bonds of mankind. Only the political illusion could have

caused us to forget this fact. We are relearning it today.'[31]
Nisbett wrote these words in an attempt to explain the increasing awareness of 'ethnicity' amongst the various 'unmeltable' groups in the United States. Whether a wave of British ethnicity (or Scottish, Welsh, English ethnicity) is likely is highly doubtful; although a serious backlash against the too rapid and brutal cutting away of traditional homogenous communities cannot be excluded. The objective of a racially harmonious society (tolerant, free, unneurotic about the subject) cannot be aided by the suzerainty over public comment that some left groups attempt to achieve by labelling any manifestation of public opinion on this subject as 'racist'.

Nor is the modern British socialist particularly able to identify with the profound desire on the part of ordinary people and their families to live in peaceful, law-abiding communities. The growth in crime, and the increasingly ugly vandalism which disfigures much of the physical environment of working-class Britain, is now at least acceptable as a topic for discussion. In 1978 even the Labour Party Conference debated the issue. A resolution was put down by Liverpool West Derby CLP which argued that: 'This conference resolves that bold and resolute action is now urgently needed to combat the menace of vandalism, wanton destruction and needless violence.'[32] It was seconded by Jack Smart (the leader of the Labour group on the Association of Municipal Authorities) who argued that:

Law and Order, and the concern with it, is not the property of just one party. It has to be the concern of everyone. The rise in crime is not simply within the experience of the rich. They do not have to live in vandalized communities. They do not have to drive the trains which have missiles thrown into the cabs. They do not have to take charge of the buses and deal with the rowdies.[33]

Smart was echoing the views of Labour voters − for once, as he spoke, the authentic voice of millions of Labour voters

was forcing its way into a Labour Conference. Yet the proponents of this motion, all Labour men of long standing,
who were articulating (in Seabrook's words) 'the feeling of
pain and resentment . . . in working-class communities', were
then subjected to a constant stream of abuse from younger
members of the Conference: 'I wondered where on earth this
motion had come from, and what place this motion had at a
conference of the Labour Party . . . some of the sentiments in
it would be more appropriate to the National Front than to
the Labour Party'; 'I . . . urge you . . . to reject this appalling
motion [applause]. This is a wonderful motion for Rhodes
Boyson and William Whitelaw.'

Then, too, there is the sense of belonging to a *national* community. Here again the impulses of the modern British
socialist run directly counter to those held widely amongst the
working people.

Britain is still a nation. It has national institutions which,
though severely battered and possessed of less authority than
hitherto, are still intact. Moreover, the British inhabit a society which can still draw upon both national memories of
achievement and a sense of continuity, important resources in
times of crisis and stress. The working people of Britain still
consider themselves part of the nation, indeed perhaps more
so than do many better-off, less rooted classes. 'Nationalism'
is altogether too academic a word to describe the continuing
sense of nationhood felt by large numbers of working people;
much better is patriotism. This involves a feeling of belonging, a pride in national success and an anger at national
failure. This kind of patriotism has nothing to do with a longing for national aggrandizement, which in any event is a
peculiarly inappropriate desire given Britain's power and
standing in the world. Modern British socialists typically
describe this kind of popular sentiment as 'chauvinism'.

That the working peole still feel this sense of nation, no
doubt more weakly than before, is often easy to illustrate.
The Silver Jubilee of 1977 is an interesting example. In many

working-class districts of the country quite spontaneous celebrations sprang up. Of course this kind of festival could simply be dismissed as an excuse for a party; but if this is the case then the events which are selected for this excuse are instructive. May Day is not selected; rather it is the celebration of monarchy as an important symbol of nationhood that is chosen.

This continuing sense of nation presents the extreme left with an acute problem. On the one hand the nation state is perceived as the main instrument for the transformation to socialism. Nationalization, the extension of the role of the *National* Enterprise Board, *national* planning agreements, greater public spending by the *nation* state, the use of institutions of the *nation* to control the multinational companies, and the rhetoric of nationalism as set against the influence of 'foreign' and British capital and the EEC – all of this is part of the appeal and programme of the socialist generation. Yet, at a fundamental level, socialists are opposed to the nation. It is unthematic theoretically. Socialism's fundamental category of change is class, not nation. National defences should be cut and socialists feel uncomfortable with national symbols such as the flag or the monarchy. In short, British identity is not to be encouraged, except in a very limited and specifically economic sense – as a means of emphasizing the nation state as a planning unit to weaken 'capital' or as a means of getting Britain out of the Common Market.

In a sense the developing anti-EEC posture of the Labour left is their only hold upon popular imagination and appeal; and the potential for further accretions of popular support behind anti-Common Market rhetoric (even behind a policy for withdrawal) should not be discounted. Britain's centre-right establishment have consistently underestimated the potentially momentous consequences for internal British politics of their seeming abandonment of the patriotic cause. The over-feverish commitment of the establishment to the European cause, and to the institutions of Europe (particularly the Commission), has played into the hands of the Labour left.

Even so, the developing anti-Common Market posture of British socialists is not founded upon any genuine or authentic notion of patriotism or upon the concept of national *political* or cultural sovereignty. Rather, it is based upon a narrow economic thesis — that the transformation from 'capitalism' to 'socialism' can best be achieved by disentangling the British state from the 'multinational'-dominated EEC. Here, again, the socialist, because of narrow economism, is unable to express the cultural and political roots of the discontent of the British with the developing institutions of the European Community.

That modern British socialism should be so profoundly unpopular, so set against British instincts and values, is no accident. Modern British socialism is a lineal descendant of the earlier upper English intellectual socialist revolt against the masses. Most of the inheritance of the Webbs and the early Fabians is still present. Certainly the social snobbery and condescension has gone: no longer is the British socialist world riddled with patronizing references to the workers or suffused by class-conscious do-gooding. Today's socialist does not 'discover' the working class in quite the same way as did the guilty left-wingers at the turn of the century — there is no 'slumming' or 'East Ending' as it was then known. Also, there is no modern equivalent of Beatrice Webb's remark about Britain's involvement in the Boer War as an 'underbred business'; the opposition to the Vietnam war was purely ideological.

But if the snobbery has gone the authoritarianism has not. The desperate search started by the first Fabians for a 'hypertrophied sense of order' continues in the modern Marxist. Colin Welch, in surveying the early socialists, suggests that 'Nowhere here can we find any genuine respect for democracy';[34] and by this he presumably means not only political democracy (constitutionalism, parliamentary government) but also a proper respect (largely absent amongst Tories, Liberals and modern socialists alike) for the values, views and worth of the working people of Britain. Turn-of-the-century socialists were reacting as part of a class on the *defensive* against the emancipation of the workers that liberal capitalism was − untidily, unevenly − ensuring. Today's socialist acts as a class on the *attack*, an elite in classic Pareto style; and as Pareto suggested the triumph of the proletariat will not mark the conclusion of class struggle but rather the replacement of one elite by another, an elite that will claim to speak in the name of the workers but in reality will rule over them.

It all amounts to the same exercise: the attempt by a class or elite to impose socialist order upon supposed 'chaos', to plan and direct other peoples' lives and thoughts, to keep people in their place. This exercise is best accomplished by collectivist doctrines that, in Hilaire Belloc's famous phrase, 'proposes to put land and capital into the hands of the political officers of the community'[35] and leaves the masses propertyless and powerless. This is why the collectivist and statist doctrines of Fabian socialism and Marxism appealed so much to the English upper class leftists, much more so than the less controllable and less ordered notions of distributivism, guild socialism and the various forms of co-operative ownership. It also explains why the Soviet experiment (where the workers were suitably controlled) was so much more alluring than the American one (where the 'huddled masses' were hardly controlled at all).

Radicals and Labourists like Hardie, Bevin and Watson tended, intuitively at least, to realize the incipient elitism lurking in the heart of socialism. Today's workers' leaders (like the ex-miner, Denis Skinner, or the ex-joiner, Eric Heffer) as they rail (often with justification) against 'the establishment' do so in the name of a doctrine which was constructed to keep the working people in their place. It is a pitiful irony that today's champions of labour should so emphatically set their sights against 'capitalism' which, warts and all and suitably reformed, is about the only real friend the working people have ever had. As these leaders of working people turn away from Radicalism and Labourism and embrace socialism they invite a mocking laugh from some Hampstead grave.

Although modern British socialism (as it has developed over the last twenty years or so within the Labour Party and amongst the ultra-left groups) has few roots in the popular political culture, and a yawning gulf exists between socialist impulses and those of the British people, this does not mean that socialism has no future. Working people will continue to vote Labour in large numbers, particularly if Labour continues to hide its socialist component from public gaze (admittedly more difficult by the year) and other parties remain unalluring and unpopular. Also, large numbers of working people (for wholly understandable reasons) will continue to side with the socialist elite on specific issues as they arise — particularly welfare issues and Britain's attitude to the Common Market. Socialism has expanded in the past despite working-class preferences; and can continue to do so in the future for reasons wholly unrelated to those preferences, not least because of socialism's encampment within the ranks of our elites. However, to be successfully established in Britain, a fully socialist system will have to be *imposed*.

Such an imposition can only be carried through by a powerful state bureacracy, one that destroys the British people's link with their past, with their historically accumulated sense of freedom, community and patriotism. And one essential condition for such an imposition will be the destruction of those natural organizations which mediate between the state and the people. Local communites are one such crucial intermediate institution, and the uprooting of many of these traditional communities is seemingly an early and random warning. Family life is another great mediator between state and people; the churches yet another. Trade unions also represent the potential for such mediation. The great British paradox here is that trade unions are increasingly controlled by those who seek a society in which free trade unions are no longer wanted or needed.

The attempt to rob the British of their memories will be difficult to achieve. But the defeat of such an attempt can only be assured by the arrival of a politics that will articulate the British past, without guilt, without fear, and marshal it against those who would destroy it.

CHAPTER 5

The Future of British Politics

The consequences of Labour's recent transformation reach well beyond the narrow confines of left politics and ideology. Labour's tragedy has potentially momentous implications for national political life. It *removes* from the scene a potential instrument which could have secured that most elusive of British political requirements − a party rooted in the industrial people of Britain that can nevertheless transcend its class background and appeal more widely; a party that is radical but not socialist (except in rhetoric, perhaps, to please its intellectuals); a party of 'the left' that is also patriotic, drawing on the best traditions of its country as it seeks change and reform for the future; a party that, much contrary to the contemporary cultural and intellectual mood, has soul and vision, can enthuse and inspire without breaking into fanaticism. In sum, a popular party with popular leaders that can manoeuvre Britain, by the creation of a national concordance, through the stressful and turbulent times to come.

This, the possibility that was Labour, is now lost. The end-product of the decades of Marxist advance and social democratic careerism is Labour's 36.9 per cent of the popular vote in the 1979 election, its lowest since 1935. The Conservatives seem unable to do much better. Apart from the, probably transient, support they received from the skilled, affluent working class of Southern and Midlands

174

England in 1979, they have made over the decades no serious inroads into the constituencies Labour has deserted. They only obtained 43.9 per cent of the total vote in their recent election victory; the social base from which they draw their leaders is still far too narrow; the electorate is still excessively and frighteningly volatile. The real story of the sixties and seventies is that huge and, for the post-war years, unprecedented vote that has gone to third parties. The Conservatives (for reasons I will deal with later) may be a mass party but they do not possess, nor look like acquiring, mass, sustained popular support.

The transformation of Labour and the weaknesses of the Tories – their inability, in short, to mobilize broad support for more than a short period – has daunting implications for the future of the democratic order in Britain. Put starkly, neither party leadership seems able to meet the challenge posed by the increasing ' ungovernability' endemic in British social and industrial life. We have a genuine crisis of the whole political class – its seeming inability to say anything or do anything about social breakdown.

Michel Crozier has written, in the course of a general survey of the governability of European democracies that:

The case of Britain has become the most dramatic example of this malaise, not because it is the worst example but because Britain, which has escaped all the vagaries of continental politics, had always been considered everywhere as the mother and model of democratic processes. Its contemporary problems seem to announce the collapse of these democratic processes or at least their incapacity to answer the challenge of modern times.[1]

Since Crozier wrote those words, partly the product of the great social dislocations of the Heath era, group conflict has intensified. The strikes of the winter of 1978/79 were but the most vivid expression of an underlying industrial and social balkanization bordering on anarchy. The authority of the state, and the political system generally, has been so eroded that individuals no longer feel any overriding loyalty to the national community it is supposed to represent which can supersede particular needs and ambitions. Hence, individuals now use the force of their particular groups and associations to threaten and punish the community in order to further their, usually material, ends.

Industrial working people are usually singled out as unique culprits, abnormal in their selfishness. This selective censure is reinforced by the strikes, now at regular intervals, that cripple ambulance services, fire services, electricity supplies, transport and the like. Yet the problem is much wider than this. Civil servants at the highest level threaten strikes; and throughout the 'higher' reaches of society (in the professions, corporate managements, amongst Parliamentarians in search of a pay rise) the same particular material assertiveness is evident. From 'top' to 'bottom' of the social scale a scramble is on to assert group claims and interests with little regard to the consequences for the wider community. Indeed, it is more than arguable that those at the higher reaches of British society set the tone for the whole, and that the lack of a sense of limitation at the summit infects those on the foothills. When workers are barked at to 'get back to work' by social superiors whose motives and actions are essentially the same, it reduces the credibility of the injunction.

The general problem remains that associations and groups have increasingly ceased to assert their traditional function of intermediaries between the individual and the state, a crucial aspect of a free society. They have instead, and I am talking here primarily *though not exclusively* of trade unions, become the mechanisms whereby individuals can pulverize the national community, undermine and threaten the state itself.

The 'ungovernability' of modern Britain is most obvious at the industrial level where it impinges immediately upon material needs. Yet it is unmasked too, at the political level, in the separatist movements which have received a setback in the election of 1979 but cannot be counted out, [2] and at the social level in Peregrine Worsthorne's cauterizing catalogue of the worries of ordinary people in contemporary Britain: 'crime, violence, disorder in the schools, promiscuity, idleness, pornography, football hooliganism, vandalism and urban terrorism'. [3]

The developing ungovernability of Britain is normally laid wholly at the door of simple economic inadequacy. The argument runs that the fifties and sixties produced rising economic expectations and that when these material expectations could not be fulfilled, politics and society took the strain. Britain, inevitably, became a near-perfect model for this general thesis, a prototype for much that it is assumed will follow in the West more generally. Britain is uniquely at immediate risk because its economy (for a whole host of accumulated reasons) is uniquely unable to deliver. Irrespective of the very English complacency induced by the 'great national withstanding' of the tremors of 1973/4/5, a complacency enhanced on the right by the election of a Conservative government in 1979, there is much point to this view.

On the surface it certainly appears that the more economically successful nations of the West (West Germany, France, the United States) are also the more stable and 'governable' – certainly as compared with Britain and Italy. In West Germany and the United States there is an apparent ability to bind broad masses of people in the 'system', producing a stable consensus that limits extremism, separatism and the emergence of the kind of socialism that would transform them. Even France, which suffers from both a long history of revolutionary upheaval and (since 1920) from an incipiently powerful revolutionary mass party appears – as we enter the eighties – to be more politically, industrially and socially stable than evolutionary old Britain. To dismiss relative economic performance as an, at least partial, explanation for these national disparities is fanciful.

The legitimacy of the regimes of the economically successful may not endure − either because their economic success may not endure or because of other fundamental problems − but that a large measure of their present legitimacy is derived from an equilibrium between economic expectations and economic delivery seems difficult to disprove.

Hence, it is reasonable for those who worry about the governability of Britain, and the safety of its ancient democracy, to look for economic solutions. If Britain's travails are even in part caused by economic failure then perhaps some remedies may lie in alternative economic systems that can produce the elusive growth. This may be the impulse that accounts for the recent respectability of neo-liberal economics. Social democratic welfare Keynesianism has patently been unable to engineer economic growth commensurate with the gargantuan material appetites unleashed in post-war society. The apparently determined schema of Britain's incoming Conservative government in 1979 was to attempt a bold experiment − to revive the British economy by a more classically liberal approach, to withstand initial social dislocation (how was not clear), and thereby to get the growth needed to satisfy expectations and thereby, in turn, secure the democratic future.

A return to politics

Yet is the 'ungovernability' of Britain, the fracturing of its social cohesion and the threat this poses to the democratic order, ultimately about poor economic performance? Even if Britain was to succeed economically, can the legitimacy of our democratic order rest for long upon such slender foundations, such narrow, and narrowing, considerations? Is not the real crisis a political one, to do with more profound inadequacies? − to do, for instance, with a severe crisis of *political* authority? Robert Nisbet has written that: 'I believe the single most remarkable fact of the present time in the West is neither technological nor economic, but political: the waning of the historic political community, the widening sense of the obsolescence of politics as a civilized pursuit, even as a habit of mind.'[4] Nisbet goes on to argue that by the term 'political community' he does not mean simply the state but 'the whole fabric of rights, liberties, participations, and protections' which have been built up by the political community as it succeeded the Church as the main focus of man's hopes and aspirations. He points, by way of an example of the historic strength of the political community, to the willingness of men to make sacrifices when necessary in the name of political patriotism. Nisbet in 1975 was making, in some respects, the same point as that argued by Walter Lippman over twenty years ago — that modern democracies had lost their way because they had lost their concern with 'public philosophy', a philosophy of civility, the idea that the political community should transcend individual, sectional and particular interests: in other words that the notion of the public good should pervade our lives. Brian Crozier, at the end of his powerful work *A Theory of Conflict*, takes up this notion: 'We shall not reverse the trend towards self-destruction until political leaders learn afresh the need, in their own enlightened self-interest, for a public philosophy.'[5]

We can see the 'obsolescence of politics as a civilized pursuit, even as a habit of mind' operating at various levels in modern Britain. There is a turning away from politics by both elites and ordinary people. The field of politics, both action and commentary, is increasingly deserted by anyone with a pretence to intellectuality, anyone concerned with 'truth and eternal values'. There is no intellectual, and little social, status to be gained by the life of politics (by being a political philosopher, commentator or actor). Much more fruitful, for instance, is the life of literary criticism or art or history. Politics is considered dull and routine compared to the glitter of literature or art, no matter how precious, pretentious and artificial the criticism. For many Western intellectuals art is the most elevating form of consumption in which the number of performances attended, or the variety of artists discussed, become matters of social standing. The growing sense of 'the obsolescence of politics as a civilized pursuit' was most forcefully displayed in the aftermath of the revelation in 1979 that Anthony Blunt, a senior figure in the art establishment, had been a traitor to his country. The 'art above politics' culture reached its apotheosis in the surprisingly large number of eminent people who excused such treason or felt it mitigated by the traitor's contribution to art history. Alternatively, many of our better intellectuals are immersed in the past; our newspapers and periodicals are inundated with endless political controversies from history, revisionism upon revisionism, almost as though there was a fastidious agreement that the political present is too unsavoury and undignified for such subtle and sensitive minds.

As well as an intellectual distaste for politics there is also a conscious and proselytizing rejection of it. There is a tendency amongst those who value freedom, who are worried about socialism (particularly libertarians) to suggest that it is concern with politics that has itself weakened the democratic society. Arianna Stassinopoulos ends her recent fascinating work *The Other Revolution* with the bold prediction that 'democracies will be saved only if men turn away from political solutions and return to themselves.'[6] Such a rejection of the life of politics and the political community is often part of a broader movement back to individual spiritual salvation. But it can also take the form of a retreat into dangerous superstition, as the recent growth of pseudo-religious cultism can testify.

Also, the 'obsolescence of politics' can be glimpsed in the contemporary failure to properly acknowledge the primacy of political claims over economic ones – even at such an ultimate level as national and Western security. For decades the *political* argument against Western trade with the Soviet Union has been subordinate to the *economic* pressures which have enabled the Soviet Union, through massive Western transfers of food and technology,[7] to divert resources to military might. The recent respectability accruing to classical liberal economists often serves to give extra legitimacy to this attack upon politics. William Roepke, one of the intellectual fathers of the West German economic miracle, and himself a humane classical liberal, is reported as telling a nice story against the anti-political nature of extreme economic liberalism:

Roepke . . . remembered Von Mises saying that if only the principles of free trade have been followed from the beginning, World War II might never have happened. I don't recall Roepke's exact reply to this, but he was, in effect, struck dumb. And he remarked to me that it was incredible that anyone with a fair knowledge of German or of European history could reduce the German question – the darkest and most sombre question of the age, with myriad roots reaching back hundreds of years – to a mere set of economic arrangements. For Roepke, this kind of economic determinism, though employed in the defence of capitalism, is just as fallacious as the Marxian version of economic determinism . . .[8]

Amongst the general public the rejection of politics is most clearly reflected in the collapse of popular esteem for public life. The growing disenchantment with public authority is evident in a pervasive cynicism about politicians. There has always been a generalized distrust amongst the public for politicians but some amongst them have stood out, have been held in awe and respect, have been able to command attention, even loyalty. Today none do, and as these responses to democratic politicians drain way so too do they in like measure from the democratic state. The traditional literary or aesthetic critique of democratic politicians – that they were timid, compromising, tame, unheroic – was not so total and widespread a view until fairly recently. Today, politicians in democracy are shrivelled in size; they become no larger than life, very ordinary. The skills they are seen exhibiting are not particularly special, those necessary in any large modern corporate organization – managerial efficiency, a nose for avoiding conflict, an acceptable mediocrity, a certain *fainéant* smoothness and a public language that must not inspire. In the late sixties Henry Fairlie adumbrated two categories of parliamentary politician, the 'Ordinary Member' and 'the Extraordinary Member'.[9] He warned us against great men. In a lordly aside he argued that 'We should be careful not to jettison him [the 'ordinary member'] for whatever impertinent replacement the London School of Economics or the University of Sheffield may offer us.[10] Yet he also recognized that in democratic politics there was a role for 'extraordinary' men, particularly on the front benches.

The problem is that such 'extraordinariness' is now very thin on the ground. The politician who can stir emotions, take risks, raise the public consciousness – the man of 'pertinacious intriguing, prickly sensitiveness, irritable genius, self-deceiving rectitude' – is nowadays considered by his 'peers' as something other than a politician. Such has been the fate of Enoch Powell. Hugh Thomas, in lamenting the demise of the national hero in our contemporary life, recently asked: 'Can we see Nelson in our mind's eye in the age of the telex?'[11] The problem certainly is this; but it is also that we cannot see with our physical eye, even in the age of television, anyone who approaches the contemporary hero that Churchill, Lloyd George and to a lesser (and more narrowly party-political) extent, Gaitskell and Macmillan were. Can we honestly say of anyone in Parliament today, as John Maidston said of his boss Oliver Cromwell, 'A larger soul that seldom dwelt in a house of clay'?[12]

Politicians are also widely perceived as, in the standard colloquialism, being 'in it for themselves', as no longer possessed of any causes greater than themselves. Nisbet referred to a time when 'political government . . . *signified* some degree of austerity in life, commitment to the public weal, of a willingness to forgo most of life's luxuries in the name of service'.[13] Today's politicians appear far too concerned with personal rewards, particularly money and security, to retain public confidence. Such confidence ebbs away amidst the genuine public outrage which greets politicians every time they raise their salaries. This public response is often unfair, as British parliamentarians are not very well paid, but the screaming from the back benches (broadcast on the radio) at the government minister who was attempting to limit a recent MP's pay award was both unedifying and unseemly. Also, politics has become a career like any other − involving shrewd calculations about salary, pension and the like. This does not help to set the politician above or apart from the rest of the community.

The concerns of the career tend to supersede the cause. What greater and nobler cause for a Member of Parliament can there be than the sovereignty of Parliament itself? Yet, when this cause is abandoned by MPs so facilely, as it was during the struggles between Parliament and the labour movement during the Heath government, public cynicism can only grow. The high scepticism that argues that none of this is of any account because politicians have always been thus, misses two points. First, that whether or not this is true at least in the past there was pretence and hypocrisy. Today, politicians, in the world of the mass investigative media, can no longer be protected. Secondly, that in a period when the democratic order is at stake democrats cannot afford the luxury and comfort of putting all our inadequacies at the door of the timeless weaknesses of 'the human condition'.

Of course, popular disenchantment with public life goes far wider than the standard suspicion of politicians. Fewer and fewer public institutions retain any respect. To Parliament (particularly since broadcasting) must be added the courts (particularly since their obvious malleability in the face of political pressure − again in the mid-seventies), the churches, the political parties, local and central government − all are diminished and less legitimate.

A standard explanation for this pronounced loosening of the authority of government and public life is that it results from the increased reach and power of the state and the public sector. Authority diminishes as power extends. This, however, is only a partial answer. For the kind of suspicious contempt felt widely for 'public authorities' is also, in great measure, felt for other large and powerful institutions whether public or private. Hostility to and suspicion about politicians and public institutions has spread also to other elites: to the professions (particularly lawyers but also accountants and doctors), to businessmen (particularly corporate leaders), to trade union leaders and officials. Journalists, by all accounts, are held in the lowest esteem of all.

The crisis in public authority, in the authority and attractiveness of politics, has causes more profound than the recent expansion in the public sector of the economy. Part of the problem lies in some of the features of modernity that have overtaken us with a speed that leaves us impotent and breathless. Excessive individualism, an individualism previously tempered by social deference or by christianity or by, say, political patriotism, in a serious problem. For without such a tempering, individualism can descend into mere egotism, increasing self-centredness and indulgence and all the ugliness of the modern 'cultivation of sensibilities'. Modern British Conservatives, who quite understandably have reacted passionately against the recent growth of state power, should be chastened by Edmund Burke's aphorism that 'Men are qualified for civil liberty in exact proportion to their disposition to put moral chains upon their own appetites'. The loosening of these 'chains' are evident everywhere in modern Britain. All the classical English philosophers, whose works our modern intellectual libertarians lean upon, have warned of the limits of individual assertiveness and placed freedom in the context of notions of public good. The reaction of many of those Russian dissidents who have either escaped or been exiled to the West (men and women who have proven by their very lives their personal commitment to freedom) to the excesses of Western individualism should be a salutory lesson. The breaking down of communities and community feeling, both local and national, has proceeded too fast, leading to a rootlessness and alienation which undermines political authority.

A further problem, perhaps the most intractable of all, is the increasing domination of life by the mass media, made possible by the great advances in technology. By their very nature the mass media, no matter the intent of their *apparat*, diminish public authority. Politicians become but part of an endless parade of images that cross the screen – only an aspect of a panorama that includes pop stars, comics and other entertainers, journalists and commentators. This deficiency for the political class is not put right by the quality of the specifically political mass media (television and radio programmes specifically devoted to politics). Again by its inherent character, media coverage of politics and public life is trivial, fatuous and partial. It cannot be otherwise. The seeming inability of the political class to withstand its deadly embrace only adds to the problem. Politicians seem only too ready to be embraced by the media. We have not yet worked out a mechanism which can preserve political authority and dignity in its presence. De Gaulle understood the problem rather better than most democratic politicians: his most effective national broadcast, at the height of a great national crisis, was delivered *on purpose* over the radio only, the television being forced to carry his voice over a still picture of the Elysée Palace. He knew how to keep his distance.

We must add to the unconscious and inherent destruction of public authority by the media a more recent and certainly conscious attempt on the part of some of its cadres to diminish public officials. Part of the motive for this is the noble one of exposing wrongdoing and hypocrisy in high places. Yet this political satire industry, which started during Macmillan's government, has become so powerful that no area of public life is beyond ridicule. A new anti-political clerisy has emerged led by a self-indulgent group of parliamentary sketch-writers that, in pointing up the pomposity and humbug of parliamentary politicians, diminishes and helps to destroy not only the political class but the legitimacy of political life itself.

The increasing bureaucratization of politics is another cause of the loss of the authority of democratic politicians. Public life, as it becomes more bureaucratic, loses its appeal and allure. The function of the politician changes and is seen to change. He becomes a manager and manipulator, and even these skills are increasingly ineffective as the apparatuses in which they work become larger and more byzantine and as, equally insidiously, the culture of the *apparat*, what Max Weber termed 'the supreme mastery of the bureaucratic way of life', becomes more pervasive. The politician, even if inclined, is decreasingly able to deal in the world of political ideas or to become the interface between ideas and action. In government it will take an extraordinary minister, the kind not usually thrown up by the parliamentary process, to dominate his departmental officialdom. Increasingly it is the civil service that becomes the broker between the various interests, foreign and domestic, that need to be reconciled. British politicians are seemingly unable to introduce into the system at the very top of the civil service structure their own trusted political advisers. The notion that an incoming government should make political appointments at Permanent Secretary level is anathema. In opposition or on the back benches the politician is limited by the powerful party machines: by the whips, whose control in the Conservative Party over patronage and position is inordinate, and by local party caucuses, increasingly unrepresentative, who in the Labour Party are an ever-present threat to the independence of an MP and a serious buffer between him and his electors.

As public life, and within it the life of politics, becomes increasingly discredited there emerges a tendency, at all levels in society, to relapse into private life, to see only a private morality. Loyalty to family and friends becomes sufficient, all that really matters. E. M. Forster dignified this notion with his perverse aphorism that if he had to choose between betraying his friend and betraying his country he hoped that he would have the courage to betray his country. The outside world, the public world including government, is viewed as hostile, unfriendly, treacherous and not worth the effort. Furthermore, the very possibility of a public morality (of 'good government') is denied; and attempts to create it considered incipiently totalitarian.

There is a central problem with this view. Put simply, it assumes that the health of the public sphere does not matter, that individual, family, private life can be insulated from public, that public corruption does not become private corruption. The indivisibility of the public and private spheres has most recently been best proclaimed by the late Goronwy Rees, who lived through those shadowy times in the thirties when tortured and pampered souls used Forster's ingenious precept to justify their treason (and who escaped from it all with honour and integrity intact). Rees argued: 'Forster's antithesis was a false one. One's country was not some abstract conception which it might be relatively easy to sacrifice for the sake of an individual; it was itself made up of a dense network of individual and social relationships in which loyalty to one particular person formed only a single strand.'[14] Furthermore, the defence of a free and good society which depends exclusively upon *private* morality leaves a crucial field to the totalitarians and it is the very nature of totalitarians to invade the private world. In short, the defence of freedom needs a political, public, dimension if it is to survive. To turn away from the political community would be fatal for democrats. No matter the unsavoury nature of public life and the terrifying forces of aspects of modernity that propel so many people back into private contemplations and enjoyments, we need a return to politics, not an abdication from it.

A national consensus

Only by an appropriate public philosophy can the democratic
order in Britain be secured for the future. But, more than this
too: we need a relevant public philosophy in order to avert
the kind of social and industrial breakdown which we witness
ever more clearly every winter. Such a 'public philosophy', I
will argue, needs to assert a modern and relevant conception
of nationhood and democracy; and I will deal with these
imperatives in turn and suggest that our present political
parties and system cannot provide the institutional form for
their expression.

A renewed sense of nation amongst the British can provide
our society with the unity it so patently presently lacks.
'National unity' is usually dismissed as a meaningless cliché
out of the mouths of moderate men 'with much to be
moderate about': but a new, modern and relevant patriotism,
and a politics that articulates it, can provide us with a sense of
national cohesion. An assertion of the importance of the
common national community can provide us with a *politics*
that can transcend individual, group and class interests which
are almost always pitched in economic terms. A politics that
can tap the reality of residual patriotism is reaching for the
only public or political instinct that remains that can unite us.
It will be difficult to unite the peoples of these islands by any
other appeal; and international public policy or philosophy
will have little meaning, an ideological posture will divide.

National cohesion is an imperative not only for our
increasingly balkanized and conflict-ridden domestic society,
but also to secure Britain's interests in a world that is
becoming increasingly hostile and fragmented. The stability
of the post-war, 'cold war', world is now at risk. The
infirmity of the United States following the Vietnam tragedy
has brought into being a wholly new 'correlation' of world
forces. The Soviet Union is now the pre-eminent military and
political power in Europe and, notwithstanding the high
cynicism of some Western European elites about the

'conservative', indeed 'decadent', nature of the Soviet ruling class, this new international fact must pose a serious threat to Britain's security, independence and freedom. Third World hostility to the West appears as an endless seam to be worked, and the raw materials upon which we depend are no longer secure in terms of price or supply. Furthermore, the erstwhile comforting unity of the West is fracturing. Serious rivalries between the United States, Japan and Western Europe – and within Western Europe – are emerging about trade, oil and defence. The various Western national interests look more divergent today than at any time since the late 1940s. Mary Kaldor, in a recent fascinating book, *The Disintegrating West*, has speculated about an 'environment . . . about oil and dollars and food and conflicts in the Third World – through which Atlantic conflict will evolve'.[15]

A renewed sense of nationhood, of modern patriotism, need not spill over into bellicose chauvinism or 'Little Englandism'. It need breach no alliances. Indeed a renewed sense of our own commonality and identity will only serve to make us more urgently aware of those alliances – particularly the NATO connection – upon which our security depends. It will also help to provide us with a keener sense of our national interest and destroy the lingering myths about Britain and the world that so dominate the higher reaches of our national life. (For instance, British membership of the Commonwealth no longer serves any useful British national interest. The Commonwealth was created solely as a means of adjusting our society, particularly its elites, to the end of Empire. That adjustment should now be deemed to have taken place. We should end the farce of a 'special' relationship with countries whose real interests are linked to the Third World rather than to the West, and who, incidentally, do not even accept the monarch as head of state. We should substitute instead friendly bilateral relations. The unity of the West in the face of the serious threat from the Soviet Union and the burgeoning cartels of the Third World elites should remain our primary concern.)

The problem at the heart of British politics is that neither of our present parties can properly articulate, in an authentic manner, a genuinely 'national' appeal. As I argued in Chapter 1, and at the beginning of this chapter, the Labour Party under Gaitskell's leadership may have been on the verge of developing into a genuine national democratic movement which could have unified Britain in a way that our political parties, as they have developed since the early sixties, can now no longer do. Essentially, Labour was emerging into that elusive but commanding position – neither Marxist nor Tory, able to synthesize the major opposing interests in the nation. It could command the support of the broad mass of working people (including the institutions of organized labour) because of its historic links with the trade unions, its obvious concern for the poor, its 'social conservatism' on a whole range of issues that are still ignored in metropolitan political life. At the same time this mass popular appeal, backed by what was then a genuinely mass political party with a large organization, was able to embrace the liberal political traditions of the nation – constitutional government, political freedoms, the rule of law, and to a lesser extent the liberal economics of the past – through its resolute commitment to the mixed economy. In this sense it was drawing on a wide national consensus that united classes by merging the more collectivist traditions of the working people with the individualistic traditions of the middle. None of this was particularly carefully thought out; it was just happening. Britain was developing a patriotic movement.

Then it all went wrong. Labour today, as at presently constituted, is unable to provide such an appeal. It will, never again, be able to be a popular, unifying force. First, it is decaying as an organization. It can no longer claim to be a mass political party. Its individual membership has dropped alarmingly.[16] The Labour Party today is but simply the political arm of the trade union bureaucracies; and these bureaucracies, comprising very small numbers of officials, run both the TUC and the Labour Party Conference, one for industrial purposes, the other for political. In the constituencies the flight of the working men and women from Labour means that very small groups can dominate.

As well as being very small in numbers, Labour is also increasingly internally divided with no single locus of power. Each identifiable Labour Party group – the career social democratic parliamentarians, the left parliamentarians, the trade union career bureaucrats, the assorted Marxists and Marxist-Leninists in the constituencies – appears increasingly to see the Labour Party in instrumental terms. Labour is to be *used*, either as a career or for some obscure ideological end. Hardly anyone who joins the party or works within it does so any longer as part of a commitment to a cause greater than their own individual interest. There is no unifying vision, nor even a unifying instinct; comradeship is a sham.

On the conventional political level both traditional Labour Party factions, the 'left' and 'right', are no longer able to make a political appeal that can unite the nation. The 'left' continues to flirt, and more, with doctrines that are perceived as alien and dangerous. Apart from the orthodox Marxists there is also embedded within the left a fellow-travelling element that will never be able to break completely from a pro-Soviet position. This kind of politics will continue to alienate the vast majority of Labour's traditional industrial support and stands absolutely no chance of attracting anyone else. Even if the 'left' could overcome its pro-Sovietism it will still be lumbered with its class analysis and rhetoric which will for ever reduce it to a faction unable to make a national appeal. Labour's 'left' faction will, of course, begin to deepen and make more pronounced an anti-Common Market position; but even here, where it will be on apparently solid patriotic territory, it will not sound authentic, nor indeed *be* authentic. The Labour left's resistance to British membership of the Common Market will not spring from a sense of national tradition and culture but rather from an outdated class analysis, essentially 'internationalist' in character.

The Labour 'right' faction will also find it hard to make a national appeal. Although it undoubtedly possesses more popular appeal than Labour's 'left' faction amongst Labour voters this popular appeal is the product of its history, not of its present. Labour voters remember its past; they think of it as more patriotic, more conservative, more moderate, more in keeping with the national tenor. Yet this, of course, is a misconception. Labour's thoroughly modern moderates are no such thing. Modern 'social democracy' has lost both its intellectual ferment and its social roots. The Labour right used to be a powerful amalgam of quite formidable intellectuals and more formidable working-class Labourist politicians. Today, neither exist. The middle-class social democrats seem incapable of putting up much of a defence against the assaults made upon their intellectual inheritance by both Labour's 'left' faction and by the resurgent neo-liberalism of the British right.

But Labour's 'right' faction has lost something even more precious than intellectual smartness. It has lost that Labourist leadership — most typically represented in the post-war years, by Ernest Bevin — that connected it to its social roots in the urban working class. Modern middle-class social democrats simply cannot speak the language of Labour working people. In fact they hardly know them. They possess hardly any of the real conservative instincts of Labour supporters. They are far too viscerally committed to social liberalism, indeed to permissivism; they have forfeited any patriotic appeal because of their over-eager need to get in on the new Common Market career structure. It is hardly surprising that the modern Labour 'right' has been unable to withstand the charge made against them that they are fundamentally out of touch. A strange twist in Labour's recent story is that this charge has been made by the Labour left. David Marquand reports that the middle-class 'social democrats' had to withstand a 'strange, inward-looking proletarianism, which became increasingly prevalent in the parliamentary party and in the party headquarters in the late '60s and '70s'.[17] That the social democratic careerists were out of touch with mainstream opinion was fair enough; but for that charge to come from the *left* was strangely ironic – for Labour's 'left' faction is even more remote. The fact is that *both* Labour factions are now incapable of sustaining a popular appeal, albeit for different reasons.

In the short run the Conservatives are the obvious beneficiaries of Labour's inability to provide a national, unifying, politics. The Conservative Party remains a mass organization and is the electoral repository for anti-socialism. In a period when Labour is in secular decline the Conservatives, simply by virtue of their position as the alternative major party, will seem to be invincible. Yet there is little evidence that as Labour declines the Conservatives can move into the vacuum in anything other than a transitory sense. For instance, even though the Conservatives achieved a remarkable swing to them, by previous standards, in the 1979 election, they still only managed to attain under 44 per cent of the popular vote. The Conservatives secured, particularly in the Midlands and the South of England, large numbers of skilled working-class votes (this was particularly evident in the 'New Town' and 'overspill' seats – the Basildons, Harlows, Stevenages) but it must remain a very open question whether the Conservatives will be able to hold on to these new electoral recruits for more than one or two elections. The new 'working-class Tory' is only Conservative in an instrumental sense — in 1979, because of the Conservative promise to cut taxes, and, of course, Labour's record of actually cutting living standards. There is nothing more lasting or profound that is attracting these workers to the Conservative cause. If the Conservatives fail to 'deliver' then these new recruits will leave in as big a drove as they entered.

Furthermore, the fluctuations in two-party government over the last two decades has tended to obscure the central point about the British public's reaction to the two decades of acute national decline and failure. Essentially what has happened is that both major parties have declined and third parties have gained. The fact that these third parties, particularly the Liberals, are often widely perceived as both frivolous and divided, only reinforces the argument that suggests a weakening hold by Labour and Tory on the public mind. A simple statistical point underscores the secular inability of the Tories to gain from Labour's decline. The average Conservative percentage of the popular vote in the most recent three general elections is only 39.3. Their previous average in three elections (1964, 1966 and 1970) was 42.9. This represents a decline of 3.6 per cent. Labour's decline on the same basis is 7.3 per cent. Both parties have lost. During this period third parties raised their votes by 10.9 per cent.

Why have the Conservatives been unable to capitalize upon the failure of Labour? Why is there no 'natural governing party' in Britain, only alternating failures? Part of the answer must lie in the raw fact that the Conservatives, like Labour, always seem to fail to deliver the economic fruits which they promise so regularly at election times. This, of course, is a generic problem for any party in a democratic system. First, it seemingly feels obliged to pitch its own appeal, to test itself, in an economic context. This cannot succeed in modern Britain. Yet, and this is the important point, the Conservatives seem unable to 'soak up' this loss by a more sustained long-term popular appeal based upon firmer ground. At first sight this seems strange. After all, the British people are socially very conservative and the Conservative Party has been able to bind large numbers of people to them by this 'conservatism' irrespective of their economic performance; yet, over these same years, the party has become less conservative in the sense we are using it; and this process must have taken its toll on deep underlying support. For instance, the party of nation and patriotism is now seen as the primary political pressure group for a Eurocratic future. On social cum moral questions the Conservatives have not been able to distance themselves from the too rapid progressivism and permissivism of Labour; the

Conservatives, during the Walker tenure at the Department of Environment, tore up the traditional and familiar local counties of Britain in order to replace them by bureaucratically determined new regions and 'localities'; the Conservatives made no objections to the deeply resented decimalization surgery. The party of patriotism, 'respectability', community and tradition had turned into something else. It was competing with Labour in too many areas, and, like Labour, it was failing in most of them.

Apart from this flight from traditionalism (or whatever) the Conservative Party has simply been unable to become popular. This has to do more with its *personnel* than with anything else. The key to British politics lies in that magical combination of 'Labour men and conservative measures'. The Tories can provide neither. It will take a major upheaval within the Conservative Party to transform it into a genuine 'national' party that can reach out to the British people and secure their emotional commitment, the kind of support needed to sustain it through the awesome years that are coming. Put simply, its leaders at all levels are far too removed in social terms from the nation they seek to represent and need to mobilize; as such they become sitting targets for their opponents.

This raises the whole question of the Conservatives and 'class' which is the key to their social unacceptability and the primary source of so much of the instinctive hostility to them. The Conservatives will never be able to make a genuinely national, broad appeal whilst they are associated in the public mind with privilege, and furthermore with privilege that is neither earned nor the product of success. Conservative leadership is, by and large, drawn from a very narrow social and educational background. Ian Gilmour has argued that 'the Conservative Party is even more unrepresentative socially than most other democratic parliamentary parties, though this is partly explained by the tying of the trade union movement to the Labour Party.'[18] Conservatives retain a stubborn inability to attract into their leadership ranks any but a handful of people from urban and suburban working-class or lower middle-class Britain; and those whom they do attract are either isolated (like the occasional Conservative political leader) or very effectively contained (like some of the populists on the back benches). Essentially, Conservative leadership is, quite correctly, associated with the public schools and Oxbridge and the social problems they bring to British life: over 90 per cent of the 1963 Conservative Cabinet came from a public school background, though it was down to 67 per cent by 1970.[19]

As for the public schools it is not the type of education that is the problem, nor is it really that such an education can be bought. Rather it is the associated cultural paraphernalia that so separates the public schoolboy (at least until recently) from the rest of British society, turns him almost into a creature from another planet. The peculiar accents, the social incestuousness and awkwardness, the consciousness of privilege or guilt about it or both — all set the public schoolboy apart. John Rae, in his usual insightful manner, has argued that the British public schools have undergone a revolution in recent years. He seemingly accepts Lindsay Anderson's portrayal (in the film *If*) of the traditional public schools of the past as 'hollow and fatuous institutions clinging without conviction to outworn codes of behaviour, where sadism and homosexuality flourished behind a facade of team spirit and hypocritical religion'. Yet 'the beating of boys by boys and the often crippling segregation from the opposite sex' are cited by Rae as traditions that are now 'under attack'.[20] But the attack is rather late in the day and will not work its way through our elite life for many years to come. To the outsider, and to the foreigner, British elite life seems often to be some kind of private feud between vying factions of public school boys grown old and powerful: between schools themselves and between those who hated their schools (and often turned socialist to seek vengeance) and those who accepted them. British political life has been the playground for these feuds and the rest of Britain has had to live with their consequences.

In any event the traditional public schools have produced a caste that 'stands out a mile' from the average British worker. Perhaps there was nothing particularly wrong with this when these schools were the breeding-ground for a remote elite which was to run our Empire, and when they could, at least, claim the saving grace of success. Today, however, all that is left to run is a declining and conflict-ridden society, and when that country is no longer prepared to tolerate overmuch upper-class silliness and snobbery the product of this kind of background is precluded from commanding the necessary support. In fact he can only create further conflict and division.

Of course, the Conservative Party have recently chosen leaders whose background does not spring out of this narrow public-school life — grammar-school products who received public-school 'polish' (second-hand) at Oxford or Cambridge. As Stephen Toulmin has argued, 'the clothes and voices of the upper classes are not hard to copy. Enough working-class boys have made it into Oxbridge Fellowships, from the late 1940s on, for that to become quite clear'.[21] Yet there is a tragedy in all this. In the process of becoming 'upwardly mobile', 'becoming Tory', they have had to adopt most of the mannerisms and culture of their 'betters' to the point where, to the rest of the community, they become indistinguishable. In an article on Lord Dacre's recent appointment as Master of Peterhouse College, Cambridge, Ian Bradley reported in *The Times* (30 December 1979): 'An ex-Fellow of Peterhouse who has now moved on to considerable academic eminence elsewhere warns that the new Master "will find his old-fashioned High Toryism confronted with a lot of lower middle-class social climbers who are trying to look like High Tories".' Britain must remain one of the few places in the industrialized world which can still produce such magnificent social tragicomedy.

And ideas and life-styles picked up at Oxbridge or public school or both filter through into British management, an 'institution' virtually indistinguishable in the public mind from the Conservative Party. Anthony Sampson has written that

British industry, given half a chance, always tended to settle down into the comfortable style of the country house . . . . While German industry took on the characteristics of a Prussian regiment the British preferred the more relaxed and class-conscious tradition of Upstairs Downstairs, with some accretions from Oxbridge high tables. As more Oxbridge graduates went into industry they brought with them a hankering for claret and butlers: they converted business meetings into seminars and management papers into theses, and arranged conferences at their old universities.[22]

Professor Toulmin has a nice, relevant passage on the problem from which a quotation at length is justified:

Are the attitudes of English management really so distinctive? If so, then the stereotypic roles of Norman/Saxon confrontation are deeply embedded in the tastes and work habits of the managerial class in Britain – and of their families, remembering all those disparaging generalizations about 'Labour' and 'the workers' that I have heard over the years from the mouths of Tory ladies – quite as much as they evidently are in those shop-floor workers who reject 'management' itself as a symbol of overlordship. A number of recent items . . . come back to my mind: reports about British factories set up, or taken over, by firms from other countries, in which Worker-Management relations are said to be excellent . . . the managers are reported as saying, 'British workers are just fine'. But then, as you read on, it becomes clear that the chief factor in transforming the situation has been the conduct of the managers themselves. They have come to work as early as anyone else. They have taken their coats off and rolled up their sleeves. They have no special executive dining rooms or WCs. They have mucked in with everyone else. In a word, they have *not* acted like the 'Normans' they were naturally expected to be, and the workforce has responded accordingly. Will the whole of British industry have to be taken over and managed by Europeans, Americans and Japanese before the long-standing cycle of stalemate and hostility between labour and management can be broken?[23]

Is it here, in this continuing sense of 'overlordship', that is to be found the key to the sheer *enmity* felt on the shop floor to much of British management? Toulmin reports the view of an old Texan of German ancestry and language: 'It is understandable, he says, that shop-floor workers should *envy* these managers who make more money, live in better neighbourhoods, and drive more expensive cars than they do; and this kind of envy can be found in Germany as much as anywhere else. But the sheer *enmity* towards the managerial class that he too has found among British factor workers is unlike anything he has ever met with in Germany.'

In a sense the great argument about social mobility in Britain is irrelevant in the face of this more profound *sense* of class as a source of enmity and division operating throughout British society. It may indeed be the case, as Sir Keith Joseph has argued (drawing upon studies by John Goldthorpe), that 47 per cent of men in higher professional, administrative and managerial occupations come from either manual or lower-level non-manual backgrounds. [24] Professor Dahrendorf is no doubt correct when he suggests that 'there is not one index of social stratification by which Britain differs significantly from other developed countries'. [25] Professor Peter Bauer, in his powerfully argued essay *Class on the Brain: the Cost of a British Obsession*, [26] has also suggested that British society is much more open and mobile than egalitarians acknowledge; yet he concedes that Britain, notwithstanding such mobility, is a nation in which acute perceptions of class retain their hold. Surely herein lies a point: mobility indices hardly matter overmuch if those 'mobile' people from the working and lower middle classes assume, upon 'making it', all the social and cultural characteristics of 'gentlefolk manqué' in what is still a nation of 'labourers'. These statistics certainly disprove the crude Marxist analysis of class in Britain, but that is about all they do.

Whilst the Conservative Party continues to be associated in the public mind with the public school/Oxbridge/managerial/professional conglomeration of elites, so long will the mainstream of opinion retain its deep suspicion of Tory motives. Do they really have the interests of the whole nation at heart? Is the constant talk about pride in country really authentic? Also, is the newly acquired economic liberalism a real commitment to establish a prosperous, mobile, independent society? Put starkly, is the Conservative Party only interested, at bottom, in preserving the property, income, wealth and status of 'Tory people', of 'keeping the muhjiks off the lawn'; and are all the policies, adopted philosophies and political rhetoric but a means to these ends? That these suspicions are held — and held widely — is testimony to the fundamental weakness of the Conservative Party as it confronts the daunting problems of the eighties and tries to build a popular consensus for its policies.

The Conservative Party, no doubt often unfairly, will continue to be adversely affected by the eclipse of the 'Establishment', as scandal after scandal weakens what residue remains, in Britain's increasingly undeferential society, of respect for traditional social authority. Whether an 'Establishment' actually exists or not is beside the point; it is widely believed that enough well-connected people with what used to be called 'social standing' no longer live lives that are exemplary and indeed use their positions quite ruthlessly to protect themselves when they get into trouble. Gone is Dr Arnold's notion of 'A thorough English gentleman – Christian, manly and enlightened . . . a finer sentiment of human nature than any other country . . . could furnish'.[27] Malcolm Muggeridge has suggested that the English may have embarked 'upon the last stages of the long-drawn-out obsequies of the upper classes. Never again, we may be sure, shall we hear any serious suggestion that so-and-so, being a gentleman, may be relied on to tell the truth, be loyal to his country and behave with sexual propriety.'[28] It was the Blunt affair, so perfectly capturing what so many had felt for so long about so few, that unleashed such splendid hyperbole from Muggeridge; but its underlying thesis is now a settled aspect of national sentiment, and is not good news for the Conservative Party. Jo Grimond could write of the Blunt exposure: 'Mrs Thatcher, given the limits imposed by British hypocrisy, behaved with sense and courage', but 'If the Tories really want to prove that they are now the party for the common people, they must not be seen as the protectors of the Top people.'[29]

The Conservatives, notwithstanding this social narrowness, have occasionally thrown up leaders who transcended class and who could make a broader, more national appeal. Even so Tory governing circles have always been intensely suspicious of such characters – of their popular support, constant searchings for realignments and general unpredictability – lacking in Tory team spirit. Joseph Chamberlain, who brought his whole faction over into the Conservative Party and injected new life into the inert body of turn-of-the-century Toryism, was never properly accepted. Nor was F. E. Smith. Nor was David Lloyd George, who was probably available to lead the Tories after 1916. Oswald Mosley, long before he went fascist, found the Tories too limiting. Winston Churchill only got the leadership through war. In the post-war period Ian Macleod was somehow somewhat suspect; Enoch Powell left to find a new political home. It is current conventional wisdom that had Powell not advised the electors to vote Labour in 1974, had he stayed around as a Conservative or an Independent Conservative for Wolverhampton South West, then he would have succeeded to the Tory leadership upon the demise of Heath. This argument underrates the suspicion of Powell amongst Conservative leaders, not because of his views on immigration but because of his popularity with Labour voters.

A large enough British consensus may indeed be induced to support a Conservative-backed incursion into trade union power (particularly into the power of the left bureaucracies in the Labour movement) and into the overweening state sector. But it will not do so for very long if the reason for such an incursion turns out to be not the reassertion of the national community over 'over-mighty subjects' (trade union or state bureaucrats) but rather the restoration of the privileges of the modern conglomeration of elites that support the Tories. A return to a land fit for property-speculators, professional restrictive practices, corporate excesses and public school social hegemony will simply not be tolerated. Nor will a Conservative Party that cannot make an appeal to over-riding common interests of community and nation, that cannot break that stubborn 'group solidarity' that Dahrendorf sees in Britain as over-riding 'all other loyalties and motives'.[30]

Britain needs a political leadership that is not associated with historic class antagonisms – 'men and women who have broken free from the established patterns and restrictions of the backgrounds from which they came. Mostly they are people for whom their work comes first and social attitudes a poor second. They are much more common on the Continent and in America than they are here. Britain must breed more of them more quickly.'[31] Such a political leadership — one drawn from an indeterminate social class – will start with a powerful advantage: it will not, instantly and instinctively, set whole sections of the population against it. Recent educational reforms have set this possibility back. The dismantling of the grammar schools, pursued with such zeal by the Labour elite and broadly acquiesced in by the Conservatives, has destroyed a valuable institution for the creation of such a class. In Gerald Frost's words: 'Despite the periodic bouts of moral frenzy during which the egalitarians rant . . . about class injustice and exploitation, they themselves have been busily kicking away the ladders up which resourceful working-class people were once able to climb.[32] We are now left with a rigid two-sidedly antagonistic secondary educational system which the much maligned 1944 Education Act had attempted to break: public schools flourish; the bulk of the rest of the secondary school community go to Comprehensives where, no matter how valiantly some educationalists strive against it, social resentment will aggregate. It is a fascinating commentary on the subtle, almost incomprehensible, workings of the British social and political elites that all the egalitarian obsessiveness of the fifties and sixties ended up with the demise of the grammar schools and not with the abolition of the public schools. Even Anthony Crosland, himself a keen advocate of Comprehensive education, nevertheless could argue that: 'I have never been able to understand why socialists have been so obsessed with the question of the grammar schools and so indifferent to the much more glaring injustice of the independent schools.'[33] Both Labour and Conservative political elites who allowed this to happen will rue the day in terms of future social cohesion.

A popular politics

It can hardly be surprising that our modern political class find it so difficult to make a national appeal whilst, at the same time, they possess such a pronounced distaste for democratic politics. At the very heart of the British problem is the resistance to democracy on the part of its leaders. This is not to argue that Britain is not a 'democracy' — its representative government, free speech, concern for liberties set it apart from most of the nations of the modern world as a civilized place in which to live. Yet, this said, and it cannot be said too loudly in the context of the enveloping despotisms all around it (in the East, in the Third World and in the British Commonwealth), there still remains in British political culture too great a suspicion of 'the people'. De Tocqueville observed that 'the sovereignty of the people' was the fundamental principle of most of the British colonies in America. Decades after full enfranchisement it still cannot be said of Britain, as he could say of British America:

The principle of the sovereignty of the people is neither barren nor concealed, as it is with some other nations; it is recognized by the customs and proclaimed by the laws; it spreads freely, and arrives without impediment at its most remote consequences. If there is a country in the world where the doctrine of the sovereignty of the people can be fairly appreciated . . . and where its dangers and advantages may be judged, that country is assuredly America.[34]

This eulogy of British America may sound somewhat discordant in the face of the continuing European intellectual suspicion of 'the age of the masses' (a suspicion which reaches its most coherent form in better modern European socialism). Modern critics of 'mass democracy' – drawing upon the challenges embodied in the warnings of Burckhardt, Kierkegaard, Spengler and other oft-neglected prophets – can seemingly only rail against modern society and man. One cannot help thinking that much of the criticism of mass democracy is really a criticism of democracy itself; that attacks upon 'mass society', 'mass democracy' and the like are but an acceptable means of attacking majority rule, universal suffrage and the like. But until our contemporary 'philosophers' can come up with some understandable and *practical* alternatives – and alternatives that do not relapse into tyranny or worse – mere political mortals have no option but to plough on, placing their trust in their fellow human beings. In any event it would be strange indeed if such a powerful and profoundly attractive notion as democracy can be stopped dead in its tracks. De Tocqueville asked: 'Would it be wise to imagine that a social movement the causes of which lie so far back can be checked by the efforts of one generation? Can it be believed that the democracy which has overthrown the feudal system and vanquished kings will retreat before tradesmen and capitalists? Will it stop now that it is grown to strong and its adversaries so weak?'.[35] Yet in Britain it must remain debatable whether even now, after centuries of formal democratic development, we have fully overthrown the feudal heritage. Tawney's 'sentimental aroma of the aristocratic legend' can still be inhaled in most areas of British commercial, industrial, managerial and administrative life. Governing people still see expertise as ungentlemanly, technical ability as less valuable than classicism, business − even for businessmen − as a sideline.

We can see the distaste for the 'sovereignty of the people' operating at all levels in British politics and society: in the stranglehold of the party machines over popular politics; in the inability of Parliament to properly enquire into the byzantine and secretive corridors of Whitehall; in the unrepresentative nature of trade union oligarchies; in the 'remoteness' of management from workforce; in the seeming ease with which minorites can entrench themselves.

This is a point that has been pursued over the years by Ronald Butt. Recently he has argued that:

Parliamentary democracy is going wrong not because it is democratic but because it is not democratic enough; because it is too often used as a facade behind which devoted campaigners of minority interests can bring the sort of society they approve of into existence without any real reference to the people. Old loyalties, old patriotism, and old nationhood have been cut up and a 'new society' that is both alienated and in danger of fragmentation has been bribed by consumer goods, punished by curbs and controls, and deprived of responsibility. [36]

Butt further suggests that 'the "liberal establishment" has relied on the apathy of the electorate to enable it to reshape to an approved model − only to find that its control of events is now disintegrating.' [37]

I agree with Butt. The need is to extend and deepen the democratic system, to attempt to translate the abundant rhetoric about 'democracy' into reality, to draw upon our democratic heritage rather more fully than our modern elites have been prepared, up until now, to do.

What Britain urgently needs is a heavy dose of intelligent and hard-hitting populism; a populist twist to an old democratic culture that would give our present system that touch more popular authority and power. Anthony Crosland seemed to sense the need for this. He put it in Labour Party terms:

The need for a populist streak in our thinking becomes greater as the social composition of the Parliamentary Labour Party changes and college graduates (and often lecturers) increasingly outnumber trade union MPs. The temptation becomes even stronger to seek the esteem of the liberal audience of columnists and television commentators, college graduates also, with essentially middle-class values, who since childhood have seldom ventured out of the introverted world of central London into the rougher provincial world where most Labour voters live.[38]

Crosland recounted a story about his period at the Ministry of Education when five times as many Labour MPs attended a debate about overseas students' fees as about primary schools. He added: 'This cannot be right.' Crosland was a curious blend of liberal-socialist and populist. He was, in many respects, the central architect of the post-war thinking of the 'liberal establishment' but nevertheless tended to sense its flaws and deficiencies. This was part of his egalitarian distaste for central London fashion; but, more profoundly, the product of a serious democratic urge within his political personality. His constant references to the political opinions of his constituents in Grimsby, and his measurement of political action by reference to their views and instincts, was not a pose.

From a more conservative perspective George Gale has made very much the same point as Crosland. He has argued that: 'The Conservative Party needs to lose its fear of the people. It needs to stop viewing popular opinion with distaste. There is nothing the matter with populism as such: indeed it goes well with the elitism which Conservatism addresses but which the Conservative Party is also shy about.'[39] Both Crosland and Gale, from differing contemporary political standpoints, echo that historic popular radicalism that has all but drained out of our present politics.

We have to go back to Disraeli and Joseph Chamberlain to see it properly articulated on the right. Disraeli's powerful statement that 'In the great struggle between popular principles and liberal opinions, which is the characteristic of our age, I hope ever to be found on the side of the people, and the Institutions of England . . . . Liberal opinions are very convenient opinions for the rich and powerful' is as valid today but rarely proclaimed. It would somehow seem dissonant for a Conservative to flirt so overtly with 'the masses'. This kind of populist position was essentially the ground which Labour filled for a while before it deserted it as it embraced socialism. Labour could have become the true expression of British urban populism, a real left-of-centre working-class party. Peter Wiles has argued that

urban populism is characteristic of Britain. Richard Hoggart [*The Uses of Literacy*] presents us with the whole syndrome; Moral Force Chartism and the general society of nineteenth-century Birmingham were also fairly pure examples. Physical Force Chartism was populism urbanised . . . . The Labour Party [note that it is not called socialist] counted among its origins trends that can only be called urban populism. These trends are now winning out over the state socialism contributed by the Webbs, who were profoundly anti-populist. The Lloyd Georges, father and daughter, fit so ill into the British party system because they are singularly pure populists.[40]

Wiles wrote these words in the late sixties; but even as they were being printed Labour was changing. It was the Webbs who were 'winning out'. Labour had become socialist; it had ceased to be popular, to be rooted in its working-class constituency.

Let us, at this point, be clear about what is meant by a populist politics for modern Britain. Many attempts have been made to get to grips with 'Populism' and most of them have come to the unsurprising conclusion that it cannot amount in any strict sense to a coherent system of political thought or philosophy, an ideology or whatever. Rather, it remains an *approach* to politics, 'a syndrome not a doctrine', 'an emphasis, a dimension of political culture in general'.[41] None of this is a mark against Populism; it simply adds up to the point that Populism resides firmly within the democratic tradition as a sub-branch, so to speak, of democratic politics more generally. Essentially it represents an affinity for the *majoritarian* pole of the spectrum within democratic politics which has such majoritarianism at one end and minoritarianism at the other. Although conscious of the need to protect minorities, an intelligent populist approach would place less emphasis upon these than upon the rights, liberties, interests and security of the majority – that is, when they clash.

The populist aspect of the democratic heritage is that which draws its inspiration from 'trusting the people' and to representing their views, preferences and instincts. It yields before De Tocqueville's 'moral power of the majority'. It demands of politicians that they echo, *in broad terms*, the underlying political culture of their nation; that they respond both to popular traditions and to spontaneous changes within the political culture rather than attempt to impose an elite-derived system of values upon it; that, in effect, they do not, profoundly and at bottom, distrust, suspect (and secretly loathe) their own people. Incidentally, I have never fully understood upon what possible basis (excellence, exemplary personal conduct, greater courage or whatever?) the *modern* British political elite can make a superior claim to judgement than the majority of their fellow citizens.

None of this need preclude political leadership. A political leader in a democracy must preserve the freedom to persuade the majority when they are wrong and to decide as between popular aims when they contradict each other – as they often do. Yet, populist politics would tend to see the role of a political elite as that springing from the popular political culture, not set against it (no matter how dab-handedly) as is so often the case in Britain. It would elevate those politicians who could best give voice to popular sentiments (and frame all the various policies and programmes broadly in tune with these sentiments) rather than the other way around. Indeed, it would *define* political leadership in terms of its success in uniting leaders and led, politicians and people, elites and masses. It would, to adopt Cowling's arresting phrase, help in 'manufacturing a spiritual glue that would bind down the elite and force it to use a language that would bind it to everyone else'.[42]

Such a majoritarianism is not anti-elitist in any permanent sense. The populist imperative does not urge that elites should cease to exist. This kind of utopian fantasizing is largely the product, these days, of 'new left' posturing about 'workers' control' and the like. Rather, the point is that political elites should be properly representative (both in instinct, policy and indeed, within sensible limits, in ways of living too) of the people as a whole. Much will depend upon what the political elite is like, what it is up to, how it comports itself. Professor Lazer of the City College of the City University of New York, who has worked extensively on British Populism, argues that:

Populism is a movement based upon the belief that the majority opinion of the people is checked by an elitist minority. The basic working definition reveals that its followers are majoritarian but with a negative, critical emphasis. They feel that, despite their numbers, the political system has been unresponsive to their needs and demands, which have hardly been articulated, much less aggregated. Their frustration has diluted and corroded their faith in democracy, their belief in parliamentary institutions, and their respect for political parties.[43]

Professor Lazer is here describing a general phenomenon; his words however can also serve as a pretty valid description of modern Britain. In any event, the problem is not the *fact* of an elite but rather its nature. An elitist minority does not, by the sheer fact of its existence, ineluctably set itself against popular opinion: that it has tended to in Britain, and that Britain is so closed and incestuous at the top, is a source of danger to the democratic liberal order.

A populist politics, demanding a political class more sensitive to the majority, presents democrats with a formidable problem. Populism's majoritarian flavour gives rise to concern about how, in a properly constituted democratic system, to best protect minority rights. This is a genuinely difficult question − and the marshalling of a new political consensus, the real majority, must set its face like flint against the erosion of civil liberties or persecution (after all, it is in order to protect the liberal, democratic order that the mobilization of a new populism is needed). Yet, one point seems certain: the rights and health of minorities can only be guaranteed by a stable, secure, relatively homogenous social environment in which the majority do not feel edgy, in which the majority feel properly represented by their leaders and institutions. That the modern British majority do feel increasingly insecure and unsettled should be a source of concern for minority groups.

Furthermore, the majority must not feel that minorities are becoming over-assertive and overweening or that they have some special hold on the governing elite which majorities cannot attain. This was, essentially, Crosland's point about middle-class pressure groups. It applies equally today to immigrant groups (particularly to their articulate leaders), to 'gay liberation' organizations, to political extremists and other minority interests which are seen to threaten the identity and traditions of the general community. A sense of limitation is needed by some of these minority groups, a sense often present in the minorities themselves though not in their leaders and proselytizers. Also, to depict the majority (non-immigrants, non-'gay liberationists' and so on) as nascent thugs who wish to oppress these minorities − a depiction readily expounded both by minority leaders themselves and by many in the governing political elite − will not help minority causes. Nor, more importantly, is it accurate. Even a cursory glance at what opinion poll data is available about majority British attitudes to minorities displays, on the part of the general public, a healthy balance. There remains a resolute opposition to persecution and a general predilection to 'live and let live'. Few wish to intrude upon minorities, expel them or even force them to conform. But, at the same time, there is an apparent determination to protect existing ways of living. The majority remains passive; it only becomes active (or actively hostile) when attacked. C. S. Lewis put it rather well, in a way that is apposite here, in the course of an essay on patriotism: 'Of course patriotism of this kind is not in the least aggressive. It only asks to be left alone. It becomes militant only to protect what it loves. In any mind that has a pennyworth of imagination it produces a good attitude to foreigners.'[44] As with 'patriotism' so with populist politics. As with 'foreigners' so with minorities.

The major argument for a populist approach to politics in modern Britain remains the need to reinvigorate the democratic and liberal system against its enemies. There is no better antidote to extremism than to open up British politics to the people. Communism and fascism advance in Britain through elites and activists: they do not spring out of the popular political culture. Consider the extent to which extreme socialism in Britain has advanced simply by virtue of its hold upon powerful elite groups (both social and political): if Britain's trade unions had been democratized or the Labour Party had instituted primaries for the selection of candidates then Marxism would be wholly absent from British political life – it would have been restricted to the universities and polytechnics. Furthermore, instead of leaving the field of rhetoric about 'the people', 'the workers', the 'masses' to the left intelligentsia, democrats should challenge the extreme left on their own ground. 'The workers' should be taken up as a cause; this may be difficult for the Conservative party to do but if this kind of politics is articulated in a sustained and serious manner then the whole socialist edifice will crumble – or, at least, that part of it that *claims* to be democratic.

A populist approach to politics would also bring into focus what is still, for most of Britain's democratic politicians, that most blurred of images – Britain's 'real majority'. British political discourse is contorted, not to say exhausted, by debates about 'the centre', 'the middle ground', 'the common ground', the 'mainstream'. There is obviously a notion about that there exists some hidden national constituency, some popular consensus that goes undetected and unexpressed. It remains the great failure of the domestic political statecraft of our generation of politicians that no single party has been able to identify, let alone express it. Separate parties can express parts of it, some (as with Labour after the war or the Conservatives after 1959 or Labour again in 1964) can seemingly be on the verge of marshalling it – but it always slips away. Consequently the British have to face their great political agony without a single locus of organization, leaders and ideas which both embraces a large majority of them and to which they can rally – as the Americans did to their Democratic Party in the thirties and the French to the Gaullists in the sixties. The British swing back and forth with accelerating volatility between competing failures; neither major party can sustain a strategy for rejuvenation, there can be no continuity.

The reason for this failure is simple: the search for 'the middle ground' is all too often but a probe to find areas of agreement between party politicians at Westminster. Hence, the kind of 'consensus' that is conceived is a London politician's 'middle ground', usually located somewhere between the Tory left and the career social democrats on the Labour right. This politician's 'middle ground' is then conveniently transposed on to the nation as a whole and claimed as the authentic voice of Britain. This claim is one-dimensional.

Let us construct in the mind's eye a party in Britain that would express the character of the 'real majority'. What precisely would such a party look like?

First, it would obviously be concerned to attain economic prosperity. Most of the survey and polling data suggests that politicians are right to assume that general elections are determined by the popular perception of a government's record in the economic field.[45] Yet the economism of the popular constituency pushes it in a mild 'left of centre' direction: there is a widespread belief in some form of 'just' distribution of material goods and services; a generalized predilection in favour of 'equality' of material rewards, the result both of the intellectual ascendancy of the notion of equality and of the vast increase of information about 'how others live', is deeply embedded. The Right in Britain, notwithstanding the popularity of tax cuts and proposals for selling council houses (extending property to the propertyless), is still widely seen as only interested in the comforts of the middle and upper-middle classes. Only when the right is thought to be able to improve the standards of most of the people does a popular constituency rally to it on anything more than a temporary basis. This was the case during the fifties when Labour, quite unfairly, was seen in terms of *general* impoverishment and the Tories in terms of *general* affluence. The British non-Marxist left, with its emphasis upon 'fairness', 'equality of sacrifice', the 'just wage' and with its image as being 'on the side' of the workers, will win most economic battles: not because of their superior grasp on economic reality but because of the allure of egalitarian invocations in an age of economic stringency. In the very unlikely event of a British economic miracle emerging from a neo-liberal economic strategy then a consensus might form behind a more classical free-market system. Otherwise the real majority will continue to support an unbalanced mixed economy — with relatively high levels of public spending — for the foreseeable future. The Conservatives have been sensible not to set themselves against it too dramatically. Our imaginary party would be 'left of centre' on economics; it is here that the Westminster consensus most nearly approximates to the national consensus.

Yet there is considerable evidence that the popular constituency is not as besotted with economism as many political leaders would appear to believe. Yet this is a hypothesis that has rarely been tested. The reason is simple: British party political debate takes place within very narrow parameters – a feature of political life that our imaginary party would rectify. Rarely are non-economic concerns thrust to the forefront of debate; our national media provide an endless diet of economic options and experts. When non-economic issues do appear, party leaderships usually contrive to agree, broadly, upon them, thereby removing them from sustained debate and precluding the popular constituency from being able to pronounce upon them in a sensible way.

The apparent triumph of economism notwithstanding, there is a whole world of more profound concerns still present in Britain's popular constituency. It is strange that our politicians have become so dominated by economics, particularly as the challenge for the rest of this century will be to maintain the unity of the nation, our democracy and our identity within the framework of only marginal economic satisfactions. Our imaginary new party would not make this mistake. It would tilt the argument in our political life towards the non-material: the kind of society, the kind of people we are and wish to be. We could talk less about economic projections and more about nationhood, local community, social identity, peace and order, morality (both private and public) and constitutionality. These concerns are usually dubbed by the left intelligentsia as 'traditional', 'socially conservative' or even as 'reactionary' – thereby attempting to devalue them by ridicule. Yet, in the face of all this the British have not yet been unanchored from their social and cultural and moral moorings.

For instance, notwithstanding the assault upon identity

there is wide popular support for a mild and sensible assertion of nationhood, an urge for a modern, relevant, unraucous patriotism. The public still sees the need for defending the nation and seems quite aware of the threat posed by the Soviet Union. There is continuing public esteem for the military: we do not see our men in uniform as 'enemies' of a particular class. As with the national community so with local communities. There has been a massive popular reaction against Whitehall-instigated assaults upon local community pride. The new regional bureaucratic bodies — for health, water and local government — are bitterly resented.

A party of the popular constituency would reflect in its policies and rhetoric the still powerful desire for social peace and public order. It would recognize that the gap between the public's view of crime and punishment and that of the elites is not born of a distinction between the ugly and brutal on the one hand and the tolerant and civilized on the other. Rather, it would recognize that ordinary people have to live in an environment which is increasingly vandalized, where their peace and tranquillity are more likely to be threatened than in West London and that consequently they possess a keener sense of survival and self-defence. In policy terms it would support a general toughening in sentencing policy and a strengthening of the police force. As the popular constituency retains, in the face of considerable official attitudes to the contrary, an *overwhelming* and *settled* support for capital punishment for terrorist murder,[46] a party of the people can hardly ignore it. It would argue that a renewed emphasis upon social discipline is not a threat to a free society; rather it is a prerequisite for its survival.

On moral questions a populist party would assert as valuable the Christian precepts. This, in itself, would be something of a change. On sexual matters it would, quite properly and reasonably, reflect the hypocrisy of the general public. It would not interfere in the private sphere (in 'self-regarding' actions) by the enforcement of some puritanical moral code. Yet, at the same time, it would take a strict position on *public* displays of obscenity, pornography and other manifestations of deviancy. Furthermore, it would reflect public anxiety about the *proselytizing* on behalf of deviancy that is becoming an increasing feature of our society. It should, ideally, be led by those who reflect, in their personal lives, the standards which the general public wish to see, if not to practise, as the moral guidelines for living. Austerity, probity, financial rectitude and a normal family life are no bad attributes for political leadership. Not only do these qualities free the political leader from the threat of blackmail but they also free him from the ridicule and satire, let alone the innuendo, that can so easily diminish authority.

A populist party would be constitutionalist. It would uphold the institutions of the country, the Parliament, courts and local authorities. It would be vigilant in defending the rule of law particularly against groups which seek to place themselves above it or against interests that collide with it. All the evidence suggests that there is widespread support for the assertion of the 'common interest' over and against factional or group interests. From this instinct derives the popular notion that 'trade unions are too powerful' or that 'big business is too powerful'. Our imaginary party would articulate these general (as opposed to particular) interests rather in the way that old-fashioned radicals (and the old left) claimed to stand for the generality of the community against the oligarchies of wealth and power.

The foreign policy of the party of the real majority would be less 'internationalist' than that of the political elites, but only in the sense that it would possess a keener awareness of British national interest. It would be much more sceptical about the benefits derived from membership of the EEC; it would not fully understand the proclaimed 'special' nature of Britain's relations with most of the present Commonwealth regimes; it would consider the United Nations to be, in the words of Senator Moynihan, a 'Theatre of the Absurd', dominated by regimes that put the West in the dock but too often deny to their own people the standards by which they judge the West. It would support NATO and high defence spending because most ordinary people can see a threat when it is presented to them. The political leadership of a party of the real majority would fashion policies within this broad framework. It would be more realistic about Britain's strategic interests, less sentimental and guilt-ridden.

Finally, and crucially, the general ideological posture of the imaginary party would be *anti*-socialist. This would distinguish it rather markedly from the present elite consensus, which is *non*-socialist. The party of the real majority would exude in abundance the traditional 'moderation' and anti-extremism of the British people. Yet such 'moderation' should not be equated with sogginess or 'wetness' or indeed with a general befuddled, well-meaning progressivism. Rather the much proclaimed 'moderation' of the majority of British people is better understood in the context of profound national historical impulses which resist abstract ideology. Bertrand Russell suggested that 'The British are distinguished among the nations of modern Europe, on the one hand by the excellence of their philosophers and on the other hand by their contempt for philosophy. In both respects they show their wisdom.'[47] The major 'philosophy' of the age – 'socialism' – falls within this general rule, not least too because of its continued, and somewhat unfair, depiction as being alien. The full extent of Britain's popular resistance to socialism is rarely displayed. The paltry votes received by overt and extremist 'socialist' parties should provide a clue; but because 'socialism' and Labour have become so intertwined there is a temptation to assume that half of the British electorate is 'socialist' – this even though Labour receives most of its votes because it is *Labour* rather than *socialist*.

There have been two occasions, however, when the left alone, as it were, faced the British electorate — removed from under the respectable umbrella provided by Labourist leaders. First there was 1931, when MacDonald appealed to the electorate as a National Labour Prime Minister in coalition with the Conservatives and Liberals. Labour was depicted by a Labour politician as putting its ideology ahead of the nation. It was reduced to a parliamentary rump. The slaughter would have been even greater had the remaining Labour Party also lost Attlee, Morrison and Bevin and been more overtly socialist. The anti-socialist impulses of Britain's real majority were more dramatically and precisely on display in 1975 during the Common Market referendum. The towering pro-Market majority had little to do with popular enthusiasm for the European venture and much to do with the fact that its main opponents were Tony Benn, Michael Foot, the National Executive Committee of the Labour Party and the TUC. Even more revealing would be the result of a general election in which the socialist left in the Labour Party presented themselves as a separate, fully socialist, party to the electorate. Such obvious and stubborn resistance to socialism within the popular constituency raises the intriguing question of the precise size of the Conservative vote at elections which accrues to them simply by virtue of their being seen as the only major 'anti-socialist' party on offer.

So our imaginary party of the real majoirty would be 'left of centre' (though not as left as the present Labour Party) on economic questions, and 'right of centre' (more so than the present Conservative Party) on social, moral, international issues and in ideological posture. Such is the 'common ground', the mainstream, of British politics. If such a ground were to be seized it would skew British politics away from the liberal socialism that infuses its elites and set it on a more truly democratic path.

Two points need to be made about this real majority. First, it seems possessed of a greater measure of *realism* than that of the governing elites. It would not break the back of British society by experimenting with extreme forms of socialism or classical liberalism; it has a keener, more realistic sense of the need to preserve social identity, moral values and the national interest. Secondly, an infusion of 'the moral power of the majority' into British political life would induce a greater *balance* at the helm. Of course a populist political framework for action would be philosophically confused and contradictory – but so is non-populist politics. It would be subject, too, to substantial policy changes, as popular (and often fickle) public mood alters – but probably less regularly and abruptly than intellectual mood. Popular politics – slower to move, drawing with more sustenance from tradition than fashion, less obsessed with ideology – would act as a check upon the febrile, sheltered and often rather neurotic world of Central London politics. Above all it would limit the incipient totalitarian instinct omnipresent in the world of elites and bureaucracies. The opening up of Britain to its people may appear discordantly optimistic in a pessimistic age or 'vulgar' to 'sophisticated' taste; but for all that it may be all that stands between us and the end of our free society.

A democratic Britain

Here is a riddle for our times:[48]

How can it be that a skilled workman in the West Midlands can vote for a middle-class polytechnic lecturer standing in the Labour interest who shares hardly any of these working man's views? Also: how can it be that if the same skilled workman should decide to vote for the middle-class accountant standing in the Conservative or Liberal interest, so large a proportion of his views would still go unrepresented?

The real majority – if it is to save Britain from its elites, and by turn from the modern unrepresentative socialism embedded in them – will need to be expressed more forcefully than at present. This will need institutional and constitutional reform. Our present institutions, a party-machine-controlled Parliament, undemocratic trade unions, the slippery 'concordats' between the CBI, the TUC and the government that lurk behind every crisis and emerge as the putative saviour — close the system tight rather than open it up.

The 'lion in the path' of any radical constitutional reform in Britain is Parliament itself. Virtually any serious constitutional change, of which many are proposed, involve, ineluctably, a derogation of authority from Parliament and an incursion into its constitutional and theoretical 'sovereignty'. Liberal democrats are therefore very circumspect in suggesting constitutional reforms – even a Bill of Rights – that would undermine the traditional notion of the 'sovereignty of Parliament'.

Yet British parliamentary government is not what it used to be. No longer will a rigid adherence to 'parliamentary sovereignty' preclude revolutionary change and the usurpation of traditional freedoms by an extremist elite. Some observers, most notably Lord Hailsham, have already glimpsed how Parliament could be used by a party, with a majority secured by only 35 per cent of the vote, to impose an 'elective dictatorship'. It needs little imagination to predict how a left-controlled Labour Party with a Parliamentary majority would act. It would seek to exert party control over the legislature by weakening the independence of the Parliamentary Labour Party and the Cabinet and strengthening that of the National Executive Committee. Labour MPs would simply become the mechanism for transmitting the orders of the NEC to government, and any independent-minded Labour MP would be threatened by the de-selection procedure. 'Movement' and government would become as one. The democracy of the ballot-box would be replaced by the democracy of the committed, the activists and the left ideologues. A vote at a Labour Party meeting or at a trade union branch late at night would carry far more value than a vote at the polls. The locus of national political life would shift from Parliament to the 'movement'; elections to the National Executive Committee would become the supreme 'democratic' national event, the barometer of British politics.

Hence, an assertion of the 'sovereignty of Parliament' as some ultimate democratic defence mechanism will not work. Maurice Cornforth speaks for most modern British Marxists when he argues that: 'The object of socialist revolution is not to destroy the democratic achievements of the preceding bourgeois revolution but, on the contrary, to make use of them . . . . Hence the policy of socialists must always be – and this is what Marxism quite unambiguously advises — to make use of the controlling functions of representative assemblies where they already exist . . .'[49]

Even in the absence of a left Labour majority in the legislature 'parliamentary sovereignty' can be used to entrench, organize and legitimize aggregations of power which threaten the pluralism of British society. In the mid-seventies I wrote a book lamenting the demise of Parliamentary authority, its inability to withstand the pressures placed upon it by organized interest groups, particularly the trade unions who broke Parliamentary laws because they disagreed with them. Democratic authority had seemingly been usurped by unrepresentative elites and the rule of law abandoned. Yet these traumas of the mid-seventies were resolved, following the defeat of the Heath government, by a dangerous condominium of interests. A 'Social Contract' was born through which selected highly bureaucratized groups – a party bureaucracy in the House of Commons with a bare majority, a trade union bureaucracy, the civil service bureaucracy and some business bureaucracies – publicly and unashamedly arrogated to and allocated amongst themselves the right to determine national policy across a wide field (only excluding defence and foreign policy matters). The government of Britain was virtually handed over to non-Parliamentary bodies, particularly to the trade union leaders, but 'legitimately' through the mechanism of a temporary Parliamentary majority. The 'Social Contracts' of the late seventies should remain a warning of how a party bureaucracy which possesses a majority in the House of Commons can with ease usher in a corporate condominium that discounts the paramount authority of the ballot-box and aggregates interests rather than separating them. This threat to a liberal democratic society is a temptation which will present itself to all party bureaucracies particularly in times of social upheaval.

The legalistic notion of the 'sovereignty of Parliament' can no longer serve as an ultimate guarantor of a liberal democratic society; for under its guise both revolutionary socialism and 'corporatism' can be introduced. Yet, a wholesale rewriting or restructuring of the British constitution – with properly defined separation of powers and entrenched rights on the American model – is, for the present, too ambitious. The problems of who will write it and how it will be introduced are too formidable and the introduction of a new constitution will represent too stark a break with the evolutionary system the British prefer. A small number of crucial constitutional reforms, which do not represent a total rejection of the notion of 'parliamentary sovereignty', can protect and enhance liberal democratic society as effectively as any wholesale overhaul.

Parliament, despite its battering over the recent decade, will retain some hold on the popular imagination. It will remain our central, democratic, legitimate political institution, looked to as the ultimate reconciler of interests. But it badly needs a blood transfusion from the popular constituency, the much despised 'masses', both to aid it in its battle with other institutions and to properly articulate the views of the people. Two urgent reforms are necessary. First, and by far the most crucial, is the institution of a *primary* system for Britain.

Primaries would allow voters themselves to have a say in the nomination of party candidates for elections. This mechanism would allow Labour, Conservative and Liberal voters, the electors themselves, to override the local caucuses. Candidates selected by this method would be more properly representative; it would open up the parties to public opinion, test the strength of the various factions within the parties and break the stranglehold of the central party machines. Within the Labour Party, for instance, it would settle, once and for all, the interminable debate about the Labour Leadership and the working class. Tribune candidates could stand against Manifesto candidates, and the Labour voter could decide. Furthermore, the prospect of having to face a primary election every Parliament would concentrate the MP's mind wonderfully: his eye would be upon his electors, not upon his local caucus. This process would force the MP to assume the role of a representative of the electors, not a delegate of the party. At a stroke, so to speak, the MP would be free from the pressure of the whips, the party oligarchies, and the intertwined bureaucratic pressures from the big organizations that manipulate the central party organizations. At the minimum it would allow the MP some manoeuvrability as between the organizational pressures and the electors. At the maximum it would produce that outspoken, untimid representative that we have seen in Britain decreasingly as this century has progressed. And all the time the primary system would be allowing the changing opinions of the population to work their way through the parliamentary system to the point where the parties would not only become more representative of their habitual voters but would also reflect popular opinion in their choice of Party Leaders (and Prime Ministers). The skilled workman in the West Midlands might even get an MP more in tune with his outlook; and that MP might help elect a Prime Minister with some popular political instincts.

There is a major technical problem that will need to be overcome before primaries can be introduced. At the moment British voters simply register as 'electors'. For a voter to take part in a particular party primary he would have to register as that party's supporter, as they do in the United States. Voters could register as Conservative, Labour, Liberal or whatever if they wished to take part in the primaries; if not, they could simply register, as they do now, as 'electors'. To introduce primaries into Britain would need a simple legislative amendment to the Representation of the

People Act. The political parties should not be forced to implement the primary mechanism placed at their disposal; but those that take it up would produce more representative candidates, gain publicity for themselves and be more likely to enhance their chances in the subsequent general or by-election.

Secondly, the popular constituency could more effectively speak and be mobilized by the judicious use of referenda. This suggested reform falls into a wholly different category from the primary. Whereas the primary aids the *indirect* representative process, the referenda would represent an infusion of *direct* democracy into the British system. Of course referendum results could remain purely advisory but Parliament would be in deep trouble if the result was overthrown or ignored. In any event the referendum is now an aspect of our evolving constitution: it has been used in Northern Ireland and twice on the British mainland – in 1975, and in Scotland and Wales in 1979.

There are many kinds of problem associated with this constitutional reform. What questions should be asked? Who should ask them? Many others. For the moment it is probably best to leave the decision about referenda to Parliament itself, which effectively means the government; and to restrict its use to special occasions when Parliament needs, because of a challenge to it, some added extra democratic legitimacy. If Parliament proposes a course of action that outside groups seek to oppose by means other than persuasion, then a referendum will aid the parliamentarians in their struggle. Indeed, it will do more; it will act, assuming the result is favourable to the parliamentary cause, as a constraint upon those parliamentarians who would wish to abandon their responsibilities in the face of extra-parliamentary pressure. Yet, there are some powerful reasons for attempting to place the referendum instrument beyond the total and exclusive control of politicians. A future government-controlled Parliament, Lord Hailsham's 'elective dictatorship', could use this weapon not as a means of preserving the democratic order but rather to further some tyrannical political end – history is replete with examples. Consequently the notion of the *popular initiative* should be entertained. This would enable a plebiscite to be held on any question attracting over a certain number of signatures. Both the petition and the signatures could be scrutinized by the courts.

Both primaries and referenda serve a single goal: they would make the political elite more responsive to the popular constituency. The other major institutional reform, widely canvassed, is electoral reform, whereby Britain's 'first past the post' system is replaced by some form of proportional representation. Electoral reform will certainly isolate extremism at the ballot-box and in Parliament but it will not deal with the problem of political elites and their tendency to make deals with the leaderships of the non-political bureaucracies. Electoral reform will simply create three party machines instead of two; without *primaries* the party hierarchies will continue to go unchecked by popular opinion.

Of course, no serious institutional change will be countenanced by the present regime of the parties at Westminster. For the foreseeable future the popular constituency will remain frustrated and unrepresented.

A Democratic Party?

Many of those who have thought strategically about British politics, men both of action and commentary, have been fascinated, not to say riveted, by the politics of that inadequately defined point on the spectrum – the 'left of centre'. Since the war what happened in the 'left of centre' mattered: it had become the centre of political gravity.

The reasons for this are not difficult to fathom. The war tilted the whole Western political axis to the left; parties of the right became defensive about their traditional impulses (nationalism primarily) and their more recent 'commitment' to liberal economics is flirtatious, not a rejection of the Western social democratic welfare consensus. The 'left', albeit of a mild variety, was the wave of the future. As for Britain, the same broad rules applied but with its own unique class twist. Britain is a 'proletarian' nation and to be 'left' was to be 'on their side' (little more); and the Conservatives, for all their resourcefulness, could never quite 'make base' with this heartland. Yet, at the same time, Britain's powerful liberal tradition made socialism (of any variety other than the most revisionist kind) profoundly unacceptable. Hence 'left of centre'.

In thinking about the 'left of centre' the possibility has always been glimpsed that a party could be created which would meet 'that most elusive of British needs: a party of reform with mass support amongst working people, but a party steeped in the political traditions of the country (patriotic, democratic) that was nevertheless not encumbered by the cultural and class problems presented to the British people by the Conservatives'. This was the exercise Gaitskell was obviously (perhaps too obviously) attempting in 1960 and 1961. So, in a different way, was Taverne in Lincoln in the early seventies. The failure of these enterprises eventually drove Reg Prentice into collision with the changing Labour Party and then into the Conservatives. It can help explain George Brown's resignation from the Labour Party after a lifetime's commitment. It can also help explain the unprecedented number of former Labour Cabinet Ministers who, despairing of the Labour Party, urged the electors to vote Conservative in the 1979 election; and it also explains the thousands of Labour supporters (ex-mayors, councillors, party officials) who have left the Labour party or been expelled since the fall of Labour in 1970.

The possibilities inherent in a genuine left of centre party for Britain have been seen too by those without Labour backgrounds. It has been a constant theme of Jo Grimond, the formal Liberal Party leader, who has always seen himself as a man of the left. Recently he has suggested that: 'The new left – I know Left is an imprecise and misleading word, but what other is there to describe the progressive, populist democratic side of politics? – must assert the democrat against the bureaucrat, must fight for those who start life from too low a level and must battle for the free, welfare society.'[50] George Gale, who spends a goodly portion of his time actually listening to what ordinary working people have to say, has suggested that: 'A central social democratic alliance, purged of its . . . extremists, would exert a powerful attraction for the British electorate, particularly if such an alliance were to be joined by disgruntled Conservatives . . .'[51]

It is a central thesis of this book that Labour was, indeed, such a party or as near an approximation to it as was conceivable or attainable. Yet Labour's transformation – its developing narrow socialism together with its electoral and organizational decline – has created a vacuum potentially as large as that created after 1918 when a divided Liberal Party yielded up to Labour the prize of 'second party of state'. By 1924 it was all over; Labour, notwithstanding the catastrophe of 1931, manoeuvred itself into a position whereby it inherited the bulk of working-class support. How the vacuum of the early eighties is to be filled may determine the course of British politics for decades to come.

Yet, in a sense, the 'prizes' are much greater in the eighties than in the inter-war years. Then there was both a solid Conservative vote and a solid anti-Conservative vote (which Labour eventually picked up). Today the electorate is far more volatile (as the regular wild swings between the two main parties and the large third-party votes indicate). The vast unanchored popular constituency that exists today not only beckons a 'new' party but one that, led intelligently and sensitively, can sweep the others off the board. Yet it will take an act of political imagination not seen in Britain for many a year to bring it about.

There are four possibilities. By far the most unlikely is that one of the present major parties will transform itself into the party of the real majority, will break out from its electoral (class- and interest-based) laager on to higher ground. For Labour to do this exercise would entail the complete victory of the moderates in the Parliamentary Labour party over the socialist left in the party organization: in other words a return to the political profile of the fifties when the Labour right controlled every locus of power – the Parliamentary Party, the National Executive, the Annual Conference, the trade unions. This is unimaginable. For the Conservatives to do it must entail a complete reconstruction of the party, primarily a traumatic widening of the social base from which it draws its leadership class. The necessary national appeal and popular policies would follow. It should not be forgotten that the only occasions in which the 'Conservatives' have attained more than 50 per cent of the popular vote this century was when they wrapped around themselves the 'national' label and had some representatives of labour at the highest tables. Mrs Thatcher's radical instincts could, conceivably, refashion the Conservatives in such a way, although the pressures against genuine democratization of the Tory Party are formidable. The British have in Mrs Thatcher a very unusual Prime Minister. One senses that she genuinely cares about the nation's decline and is untouched by the defeatism and cynicism which suffuses British intellectual and political life. Yet her native radicalism, optimism and populism may not be able to rekindle any flames of hope and vision amongst the dying embers of the Tory establishment.

Secondly, there is the possibility of a realignment, of a new party emerging from a combination of parts of old ones. The prerequisite for such a realignment, however, is the much heralded, though never dawning, organic split in the Labour Party. It is still not utterly impossible that in the eighties the collision of values and politics between the majority of Labour voters and trade unionists on the one hand and the socialist generation on the other may seep up through the bureaucracies of the Labour movement to the point where it splits asunder. The break-up of the Labour Party will only occur from within the trade unions — the Parliamentary Labour moderates are not capable of sustaining such a profound change in the political landscape on their own, without resources or organization. Yet, among the unions a 'Force Ouvrière' is still struggling to be born. In dramatic circumstances the moderates in the trade unions could take whole unions, or parts of unions, out of the TUC in order to form a rival, less socialist, TUC. This 'new TUC' could then sustain its own political party — presumably the Labour moderates, who could link up with the Liberals. Alternatively, the rebel unions could act as the American unions do: with no formal institutional links to any party but using their political weight to ensure, as best they can, that the political system represents their members. The fact that the AFL-CIO, the American TUC, refused to support the McGovern Democratic candidacy for President in 1972 — because its leaders believed that his political and social position was utterly unrepresentative of Democratic trade unionists — is an intriguing potential parallel with British left politics.

Of course the Labour left will attempt to 'head off' any schism; it threatens its whole strategic position, one built up over many decades. The Labour left in the early eighties is poised to control all the Labour Party organs — including for the first time the PLP — and this historic accretion of power will not easily be put at risk. In this sense 1931 is a major historical memory. Michael Foot, for one, has stated that his actions are dominated by the need to 'prevent such a catastrophe from happening again'.[52] Eric Heffer has also made very much the same point and has argued that all the Labour left need do is to wait in order to inherit the whole Labour Party *intact*.[53] The possibility of another 1931 — or worse — is the explanation of the Labour left's refusal to push their socialism within the Labour Party too far and too fast. It is the explanation of their trimming, their acceptance of high levels of unemployment under post-war Labour

230 The Future of British Politics

governments, of their refusal to break up the Labour Party over Britain's entry into the Common Market, and of their acceptance of wage restraint. These tactical surrenders are the welcome price to be paid for keeping Labour together; and each internal Labour Party battle is fought on ground futher to the left than the previous one. The aim is not simply to control a more left-wing Labour Party but to inherit Labour's traditional standing amongst Labour voters. In such a way the socialist generation can retain and improve its power within the British political system. The preferred scenario is set: with the Labour Party and movement intact but increasingly under left control, most Labour voters will continue to support it; with a 'vicious, reactionary' Conservative government to attack, Labour will unveil its 'alternative strategy', provide it with a 'human face' (primarily by electing a respectable left-of-centre leader) and be in a position after a few years to win a majority in Parliament.

The Labour left are not going to put this golden opportunity at risk by pushing the Labour right so hard that they are forced into thinking about realignment. Unless events move out of control a realignment on the left will only come out of an act of uncharacteristic will on the part of the Labour moderates.

Such a realignment, the 'regrouping of the radical centre' as it is often called, must be able to bite deep into Labour's traditional 'working-class' vote (as well as attracting to it Conservative voters, floating voters and those who rarely vote at all). It will need to develop a broad classless appeal and be possessed of a sense of the future. It can do neither if it simply becomes a mechanism for ousted parliamentarians seeking a way back to political fortune, whose political instincts are rooted in the shallow progressivism of the sixties and whose one residual political commitment is to Europe. Such a party would quickly become but a pale imitation of the Conservatives and would leave the radical, popular field to the socialist left.

The third possibility is that the Liberal Party will, on its own, be able to move into the vacuum. Given the volatility of the British electorate it is not impossible, even within the present electoral system, for this inchoate and eccentric third party to assume the proportions of a major political force. One condition precedent for a sustained Liberal revival in the eighties is an unpopular Labour Party, one which would allow the Liberals to attract to them what I will describe, with all its inexactitude, as the 'working-class right' (that area increasingly deserted by Labour). The Liberals, during the decade of the seventies, advanced more at the expense of Labour than of the Conservatives, as Patrick Humphrey pointed out in a recent article which urged the Liberals to think strategically – to shape their appeal towards supplanting Labour, not the Conservatives.[54] Of course to properly develop this strategy the Liberals will have to become more populist. As Laurence Grinling has observed in the columns of *Liberal News* 'If they [the Liberals] are still engaged in genteel discussion of wet resolutions when the moment comes, someone else will rise to the occasion (as someone else already has in Scotland): and we shall have no one to blame but ourselves.'[55]

Fourthly, the vacuum in British politics could be filled from a wholly unpredictable source. A new Democratic Party for Britain, shunning the extremes and aligned firmly to the popular constituency, could take off more quickly than many suspect. The failure of earlier very small parties – of Desmond Donnelly's rather forlorn Democratic Party and Dick Taverne's potentially more formidable Democratic Labour Party – is no guide to the coming, more unanchored, unsettled and unpredictable political world of the eighties. Once a breakthrough is made then more established political factions will tend to coalesce around a radical new force.

The emergence of a new political force in British politics – whether created by the transformation of one of the major parties, a realignment, the Liberals, or from outside the political elite – will break the cycle of alternating failures. The alternative is as depressing as it is predictable: a period of social upheaval under a Conservative government ending, either in the middle or at the end of the 1980s, with the election (*because nothing else is an offer*) of Britain's first seriously socialist administration. The tragedy of Labour will then have become the tragedy of Britain.

NOTES

Introduction: The Importance of Labour

1 Maurice Cowling, *The Impact of Labour*, 1971, p.1.
2 Anthony Crosland, The Future of Socialism, 1956, p.14.
3 Paul Johnson, *The Offshore Islanders*, p.396.
4 The Sunday Telegraph, 11 Feb 1979. Economic Opinion by
  Patrick Hutber.

Chapter 1: What Labour Was

1 Ben Pimlott, *Labour and the Left in the 1930s*, 1977, p.5.
2 *Labour's Programme, 1976*, 1976, p.9.
3 *Encounter*, May 1977, p.22.
4 'Labour's Aims' (statement by Labour NEC, March 1960),
  Labour Party Annual Conference Report [hereinafter
  LPACR] *1960*, p.13.
5 'Industry and Society' (statement by Labour NEC) *LPACR
  1957*, p.49.
6 *Labour's Programme, 1976*, pp.28-9.
7 ibid, p.27 (italics mine).
8 *LPACR 1976*, p.380.
9 *Labour's Programme, 1976*, p.22.
10 ibid, p.23 (italics mine).
11 'Industry and Society', p.49.
12 *LPACR 1960*, p.13.
13 Labour's Programme, 1976, p.121.

14 ibid, p.10.
15 ibid, p.122.
16 ibid, p.119.
17 See Roy Godson and Stephen Haseler, *'Eurocommunism': Implications for East and West*, 1978, ch.3.
18 *Labour's Programme*, 1976, p.9.
19 Ralph Miliband, *Parliamentary Socialism*, 2nd ed. 1972, p.13.
20 Tom Nairn, *The Left Against Europe*, 1972, p.49.
21 Tom Forester, *The Labour Party and the Working Class*, 1976.
22 Ross McKibbin, *The Evolution of the Labour Party, 1910-1924*, 1975, p.xiv.
23 Quoted in Forester, p.34.
24 Walter Kendall, *The Revolutionary Movement in Britain, 1900-21*, 1969, p.17.
25 Miliband, p.20.
26 Henry Pelling, *The Challenge of Socialism*, 2nd ed. 1968, p.201.
27 R. H. Tawney, 'The Choice before the Labour Party', *Political Quarterly*, July – Sep 1932, p.330 (quoted in Pimlott, p.196).
28 Miliband, p.61.
29 Kendall, p.301.
30 Pimlott, p.6.
31 Robert Skidelsky, *Oswald Mosley*, 1975. In the introduction Skidelsky sets out briefly his own political views.
32 ibid, p.13.
33 ibid. p.14.
34 Edward Carpenter, *England's Ideal*, 1906, p.41.
35 Pelling, p.161.
36 Norman and Jeanne Mackenzie, *The First Fabians*, 1977, p.31.
37 ibid, p.120. Incidentally, running through this intriguing account of the early Fabians there are references to some of their family backgrounds as 'good'.
38 ibid, p.56.
39 ibid, p.67.
40 ibid, p.46.
41 Andrew Boyle, *The Climate of Treason*, 1979, p.45.
42 George Orwell, *The English People*, 1947, pp.42-4.

43 Quoted in *Quadrant*, July 1977, p.16.
44 Samuel H. Beer, *Modern British Politics*, p.140.

Chapter 2: *What Labour Is*

1 *LPACR 1977*, p.80.
2 Paul Johnson, Britain's Own Road to Serfdom, Conservative
   Political Centre, 1978. p.6.
3 ibid.
4 ibid, p.7.
5 Irving Kristol, *Two Cheers for Capitalism*. The term 'new
   class' was first introduced into political vocabulary by
   Milovan Djilas, the Yugoslav dissident who used it to describe
   the new elite produced by communist society.
6 John Lloyd, 'Populism or Marxism', *Books and Bookmen*,
   June 1976, p.38.
7 *The Times*, 9 Dec 1972.
8 Anthony Wedgwood-Benn, *The New Politics: A Socialist
   Reconnaissance*, Fabian Tract 402, 1970.
9 Michael Foot, *Aneurin Bevan*.
10 *Guardian*, 13 Dec 1976.
11 *The Ideals of October*, Labour Party Young Socialists
   publication, 1977, p.12.
12 *The Socialist Way Forward*, Labour Party Young Socialists
   publication, 1978, p.13.
13 Parts of this report were published in *The Times*, 12 Dec
   1975.
14 *The Times*, 7 Nov 1977.
15 Interview with Giorgio Napolitano, Rome, 31 Jan 1979.
16 The Social Democratic Alliance has regularly (in Oct 1975,
   Nov 1976 and Feb 1977) given detailed examples of senior
   Labour figures who have associated themselves with
   Communist Party or Trotskyite organisations. These
   statements have received considerable publicity in national
   newspapers, and one of them was referred to the Committee
   of Privileges of the House of Commons (*Hansard*, 17 Nov
   1976, cols 1336-84, and 18 Nov 1976, cols 1580-92): no action
   was taken. These statements caused considerable controversy

in the Labour Party, though none of the facts they set out were ever challenged. By the end of the seventies, after Labour's changed political complexion had become more apparent, such exposures (although still mocked by the Labour left as 'McCarthyite') were treated in the wider political world with less incredulity.

17 There are no examples of similar behaviour by moderate MPs, who in no way share the political sympathies of extreme left organizations, to be found in the sixties and seventies.

18 Quoted in David Cante, *The Great Fear*.

19 *Morning Star*, 28 June 1977.

20 *The British Road to Socialism* (draft policy statement by the Communist Party of Great Britain), 1977.

21 *The Times*, 23 Mar 1978.

22 H. Chapman Pincher, *Inside Story*, p.26.

23 See for instance Harold Macmillan, *At the End of the Day: 1961-63*, 1973 pp.171 and 205.

24 Hugh Trevor-Roper (Lord Dacre), *Spectator*, 24 Nov 1979, p.12.

25 Robin Cook and Dan Smith, *What Future in NATO?*, Fabian Research Series 337, July 1978, p.27.

26 Quoted in *The Times*, 2 May 1978.

27 ibid.

28 *Daily Telegraph*, 7 Sep 1978.

29 ibid.

30 These remarks by Alex Kitson were broadcast over Radio Moscow and received considerable publicity in the British press.

31 *LPACR 1975*, p.23.

32 ibid.

33 *LPACR 1976*, p.193.

34 ibid.

35 *Labour Weekly*, 7 Mar 1975, reported Labour's general secretary as saying: 'I see Mr Honecker as a man of wisdom and experience very proud of the German Democratic Republic *and with every right to be proud*' (italics mine).

36 TASS statement broadcast over Radio Moscow, 2 Nov 1976.

37 Although Breznev's 25th Congress speech was a major address, Labour's NEC, who were specifically referred to by the CPSU general secretary, suffered no adverse publicity in

Britain. The Conservatives, surprisingly, left the issue alone; no 'investigative journalist' reported on its significance.

38 *Daily Telegraph*, 4 Nov 1976.

39 ibid.

40 'The Russia Complex' is the term used by Bill Jones in his work of the same title, published in 1977, to describe Labour's fascination with the Soviet experiment.

41 Jean-Pierre Dujardin, *Figaro* Magazine, 18 Nov 1978, has estimated that between 1917 and 1959 66,700,000 people died as a result of internal repression alone in the Soviet Union. Even if his carefully argued estimate is too high, the chilling enormity of Soviet repression places it amongst the great crimes of the twentieth century. It is rarely mentioned or condemned at Labour Party Conferences.

42 *Encounter*, Dec 1978, p.84.

43 Bernard-Henri Lévy, the young French 'new philosopher', quoted in a short survey of some of the political statements of this 'school' in my own article, 'The New French Polemicists', *American Spectator*, May 1978.

44 Bill Jones, *The Russia Complex*, 1977.

45 Norman and Jeanne Mackenzie, *The First Fabians*, p.407. On p.408 Beatrice Webb is reported as having written to the CP leader Palme Dutt in 1942 describing herself and Sidney Webb as 'non-party communists'.

46 ibid, p.407.

47 ibid, p.406.

48 Hugh Thomas, *John Strachey*, 1973, p.132.

49 Thomas reports that Strachey wrote to Boothby in 1941: 'You must remember that I now finally know that my world picture . . . fell to bits with the signing of the Nazi-Soviet pact' (p.206).

50 Jones, p.25.

51 *Collected Essays, Journalism and Letters of George Orwell*, vol. 1, 1970, p.373.

52 This letter was included by Orwell in an introduction to *Animal Farm*, an introduction that was rejected by publishers until it appeared in the *New York Times* in 1972. This extract is copied from *News Weekly*, 28 Nov 1979.

53 Jones, p.245.

54 Iain McLean, *Keir Hardie*, 1975, p.175.

55 For a detailed account see Alan Bullock, *The Life and Times of Ernest Bevin*, vol. 1, 1960, p.103.

56 ibid, p.134.

57 ibid, p.75.

58 Jones, p.16.

59 *Daily Telegraph*, 3 Jan 1974.

60 Denis Healey (ed.), *The Curtain Falls*, 1951, p.6.

61 Maurice Cowling (ed.), *Conservative Essays*, 1978, p.16.

62 Speech by J. Enoch Powell MP to International Society, NCB Club, 20th January, 1959.

Chapter 3: Why Did It Happen (So Quickly)

1 'TV Eye' (Thames Television current affairs programme), 9 Nov 1978.

2 *Political Quarterly*, Oct 1975, p.391.

3 ibid, p.394.

4 Both these remarks were made on 'Weekend World' (London Weekend Television) in an interview with Brian Walden, 18 Dec 1978.

5 *LPACR 1975*, p.187.

6 *The Times*, 2 Aug 1976.

7 Callaghan was one of 21 Labour MPs, some of them fellow-travellers, who signed a letter to Prime Minister Attlee in 1946 demanding 'a fundamental change in foreign policy' (*Manchester Guardian*, 16 Nov 1946).

8 Callaghan enunciated this view of Parliament as an unsuitable forum in 'Panorama' (BBC Television), 5 Mar 1979.

9 Reported by Hugo Young, 'The Callaghan Offensive', *Sunday Times*, 21 May 1978, p.34.

10 *LPACR 1978*, p.268.

11 Peter Jenkins, *The Battle of Downing Street*, 1970, provides a full account of the *In Place of Strife* controversy.

12 The Labour Party and the Common Market, NEC Statement, 26 April, 1975.

13 *Financial Times*, 13 Mar 1979, p.10.

14 *New Law Journal*, Aug 1875.

15 Letter in *Encounter*, June 1978.

Chapter 4: Socialism and the British

1 D. E. Butler and D. Kavanagh, *The British General Election of February 1974*, 1974, gave the percentage to Labour in the different income groups as follows: AB, 5; C1, −0.7; C2, 1.9; DE, 2.5. These figures are based on the National Opinion Poll post-election survey. Also, some of the results in the 'mining' constituencies in this election were interesting: there were actually swings to the Conservatives.

2 Quoted in Colin Martin and Dick Martin, *Political Quarterly*, Oct/Dec 1977, p.459.

3 ibid, pp.460-1.

4 ibid, p.462.

5 ibid.

6 *LPACR 1977*, p.5.

7 *LPACR 1960*, p.23.

8 Barry Hindess, *The Decline of Working Class Politics*, 1971, p.61.

9 *Socialist Organizer*, Mar 1979, p.2.

10 *Encounter*, Dec 1978, p.84.

11 Fabian Tract No. 70, 1896.

12 Tom Forester, *The Labour Party and the Working Class*, 1976, pp.116-17.

13 Hindess, p.145.

14 Hugh Thomas, *Spectator*, 2 Dec 1978, p.15.

15 Correlli Barnett, *The Collapse of British Power*, 1972, p.60.

16 Ian Gilmour, *Inside Right: a Study of Conservatism*, 1977, p.168.

17 ibid.

18 George Orwell, 'The Lion and the Unicorn: Socialism and the English Genius', republished in *Collected Essays . . .*, vol. 2, 1968, p.59.

19 Brian Crozier, *A Theory of Conflict*, 1974, p.231.

20 John Lloyd, 'Populism or Marxism', *Books and Bookmen*, June 1976, p.39.

21 *The British Road to Socialism* (draft policy of CPGB), 1977, sec. 1740.

22 ibid.

23 Maurice Cornforth, *The Open Philosophy and the Open Society*, 1968, p.277.

24 *LPACR 1978*, p.378.

25 Article in the *Guardian*, 28 Oct 1978.

26 Richard Hoggart, *Speaking to Each Other*: vol. 1, *About Society*, 1970, pp.48-9.

27 *LPACR 1967*, p.95.

28 Ben J. Wattenberg, *The Real America*, 1976, p.320.

29 *LPACR 1965*, p.217.

30 Originally published in the *Observer*, 21 Jan 1973; republished in *Socialism Now (and other essays)*, 1974, p.106.

31 Robert Nisbet, *The Twilight of Authority*, 1976. p.10

32 *LPACR 1978*, p.375.

33 ibid, p.376.

34 Colin Welch, 'Intellectuals Have Consequences', in *The Future that Doesn't Work: Social Democracy's Failures in Britain*, ed. R. Emmett Tyrrell, Jr, 1975, p.60.

35 Hilaire Belloc, *The Servile State*, 1913: 1977 ed., p.129.

Chapter 5: The Future of British Politics

1 M. Crozier *et al.*, *The Crisis of Democracy* (report on the governability of democracies to the Trilateral Commission), 1975, p.11.

2 The Scottish National Party returned only two MPs in the 1979 general election.

3 Peregrine Worsthorne, 'Too Much Freedom', in *Conservative Essays*, ed. M. Cowling, 1978, p.150.

4 Robert Nisbet, *The Twilight of Authority*, 1976, p.1.

5 Brian Crozier, *A Theory of Conflict*, 1974, p.237.

6 Arianna Stassinopoulos, *The Other Revolution*, 1978, p.219.

7 By far the most comprehensive study on Western technology transfers to the Soviet Union is the three-volume work by Anthony Sutton, *Western Technology and Soviet Economic Development, 1917-1965* (Vol. 1, 1968; Vol. 2, 1971; Vol. 3, 1973).

8 Patrick M. Boardman, 'William Roepke and the Third Road', *University Bookman*, autumn 1977, p.5.

9 Henry Fairlie, *The Life of Politics*, 1968, pp.11-56.

10 ibid, p.43.

11 Hugh Thomas, *History, Capitalism and Freedom*, Centre for

Policy Studies, 1979. p.7.

12 Antonia Fraser, *Cromwell*, 1973, p.809.

13 Nisbet, p.4.

14 Andrew Boyle, *The Climate of Treason*, 1979, p.384.

15 Mary Kaldor, *The Disintegrating West*, p.202.

16 See Chapter 4, pp.137-43 above.

17 David Marquand, 'Inquest on a Movement', *Encounter*, July 1979.

18 Ian Gilmour, Foreword to *Conservative Party Politics*, ed. Zig Layton-Henry, 1980, p. ix.

19 Bob Jessop, *Traditionalism, Conservatism and British Political Culture*, 1974, p.66.

20 John Rae, 'The public school revolution', *Sunday Telegraph*, 8 July 1979.

21 Stephen Toulmin, 'You Norman, The Saxon', *Encounter*, August, 1979, pp. 79-81.

22 Anthony Sampson, *Observer*, 8 July 1979, p.9.

23 *Encounter*, September, 1978, p.92.

24 Sir Keith Joseph's Gilbreth Lecture, in which he makes a case for British social mobility, was summarized in the *Guardian*, 18 July 1979.

25 Ralf Dahrendorf, 'The Class War', *Guardian*, 19 July 1979, p.16.

26 Peter Bauer, *Class on the Brain: the Cost of a British Obsession*, Centre for Policy Studies pamphlet, 1978.

27 Quoted in Correlli Barnett, *The Collapse of British Power*, 1972, p.26.

28 Malcolm Muggeridge, 'The Eclipse of the Gentleman', *Time Magazine*, 3 Dec 1979, p.33.

29 *Spectator*, 1 Dec 1979, p.17.

30 Dahrendorf, 'The Class War'.

31 Harry Whewell, 'The Class War', *Guardian*, 16 July 1979, p.8.

32 Gerald Frost, 'Britain may have classes but all their doors are open', *Daily Telegraph*, 4 Dec 1978.

33 Anthony Crosland, *The Future of Socialism*, 1956, p.191.

34 Alexis de Tocqueville, *Democracy in America*, 1835-9: 1945 ed., p.57.

35 ibid, p. ix (author's preface to 12th ed., 1848).

36 Ronald Butt, 'On Britain's decline: democratic contradictions', *Encounter*, March, 1979, p.43-7.

37 ibid, p.46.

38 Anthony Crosland, 'Labour and Populism', *Socialism Now (and other essays)*, 1974, p.100.

39 George Gale, 'The Popular Communication of a Conservative Message', in *Conservative Essays*, p.192.

40 Peter Wiles, 'Populism as an Ideology', in *Populism: Its National Characteristics*, ed. Ghita Ionescu and Ernest Gellner, 1969, p.167.

41 ibid.

42 M. Cowling, 'The Present Position', in *Conservative Essays*, p.19.

43 From a paper presented by Professor Harry Lazer to the annual meeting of the American Political Science Association, 1978.

44 C. S. Lewis, *The Four Loves*, p.27.

45 The *Gallup Political Index*, report no. 206, Sep 1977, is not untypical. In answer to the question, 'What would you say is the most urgent issue facing the country at the present time?', the result was: cost of living, prices, 41%; unemployment, 28%; strikes, labour relations, 10%; other economic problems, 6%; law and order, 4%; immigration, 3%; other, 6%.

46 The *Gallup Political Index*, report no. 201, Apr 1977, found: in favour of capital punishment for terrorist murder, 89%; for murder of police officers, 84%; for all crimes of murder, 66%.

47 Bertrand Russell, *Unpopular Essays*, 1950, p.4.

48 I have used the same expression here as Richard M. Scammon and Ben J. Wattenberg did in *The Real Majority*, 1970, where they introduced the argument that in the United States there is a marked distinction between the political and intellectual elite and the majority of Americans over a broad range of political and social issues.

49 Maurice Cornforth, *The Open Philosophy and the Open Society*, 1968, p.276.

50 Jo Grimond, *The Common Welfare*, 1979, p.33.

51 George Gale, 'The Danger in a Labour Split', Daily Express, 27 July 1979.

52 'TV Eye', 9 Nov 1978.

53 *Political Quarterly*, Oct 1975, p.391.

54 Patrick Humphrey, *Daily Telegraph*, 5 July 1979.

55 *Liberal News*, 20 Mar 1979, p.4.